Living Outside The Cubicle

The Ultimate Success Guide For The Aspiring Entrepreneur

By Darren Sugiyama

This book is dedicated to my son, Estevan. May you one day use these principles to live a fulfilling, successful and happy life.

Love, Papa

Table Of Contents

Forward: The Allegory Of The Cubicle... pg. 7
Chapter 1: Habitual Failure.. pg. 13
Chapter 2: The Ultimate Goal Setting Program................................... pg. 23
Chapter 3: The Power Of Focus.. pg. 41
Chapter 4: Asking The Right Questions.. pg. 55
Chapter 5: Building Bullet-Proof Confidence...................................... pg. 65
Chapter 6: Your Personal Brand.. pg. 83
Chapter 7: Hitting The Reset Button.. pg. 99
Chapter 8: Being A Successful Entrepreneur...................................... pg. 111
Chapter 9: The Fine Art Of Prospecting.. pg. 121
Chapter 10: Becoming A Master Closer.. pg. 145
Chapter 11: How To Effectively Communicate With Clients............. pg. 169
Chapter 12: Championship Leadership.. pg. 185
Chapter 13: The 5 Fundamental Qualities Of Successful People........ pg. 199
Chapter 14: Leaving Behind A Legacy.. pg. 217
Chapter 15: The Journey... pg. 225
Chapter 16: A Message To My Son... pg. 247
Closing: About The Author.. pg. 255

Forward: The Allegory Of The Cubicle

"The Allegory Of The Cubicle is a disease of the mind that those that dare to dream must fight daily."

-Darren Sugiyama

Thinking Outside The Cubicle

I remember when I first made my decision to be an entrepreneur. I was so excited, I ran out and told everyone, expecting a huge celebratory parade, overwhelming pats on the back, and tons of people that wanted to invest in my soon-to-be empire.

Man, was I wrong. Instead, my news was received with criticism, skepticism and advice about why I shouldn't go for it. People that I thought would be exited and happy for me were negative and sometimes even condescending towards me.

Maybe it was jealousy. Maybe they had a lack of belief in my abilities. Whatever the reasons were, I was left feeling hurt, let down, and quite frankly, depressed. They totally shot my plane down before it even had a chance to take off.

Have you ever experienced this kind of negativity from your friends and family? Have you ever felt *let down* by people that you were counting on to be supportive and encouraging? Most successful entrepreneurs have experienced this emotional *let down* in some form or fashion, and perhaps you have also experienced this as well.

But step back for a moment and consider the demographic of the people that criticized you and tried to talk you out of *going for it*. They probably worked in a cubicle.

It's been my experience that some of the biggest critics out there are people that have never attempted to achieve greatness. All they've ever known is their *cubicle life*.

They show up at their job not a minute earlier than 8:00am. They hide out from their boss in their cubicle, sneaking in as much online shopping, social network texting, and computer games as they can without getting caught. They spend a ton of time taking personal calls throughout the day, chit-chatting with their other *cubicle-minded* friends about meaningless gossip. And at 4:59pm, they're practically out the door. God forbid they spend one minute in the office past 5:00pm.

After work, they meet the rest of their *cubicle-minded* friends for happy hour, spending money they don't have, on drinks they can't afford. They talk about what a jerk their boss is, or about how unfair their company is, or how they deserve a promotion, or higher pay, or more paid-vacation time.

They're in debt, with no financial plans or career plans for advancement. Every problem in their lives is someone else's fault, whether it's the economy, or the government, or their boss, or the fact that Santa Claus didn't give them a million dollars last Christmas.

These *cubicle-minded* people aren't business tycoons, yet for some illogical reason, we as entrepreneurs, feel the need to share our entrepreneurial aspirations with them. And even more illogical, we actually expect them to understand our plans of prosperity. Think about how stupid this is. And it's really not their fault. It's YOUR fault for expecting them to understand your entrepreneurial aspirations. Remember, they're prisoners trapped inside their cubicle.

The challenge that we as entrepreneurs face is that we live in a world predominantly populated by *cubicle-minded* people. You grew up with some of them. You're blood-related to some of them. You're *friends* with some of them. These associations are fine. It's okay to be friends with *cubicle-minded* people, or be related to them, or to love them. The key is to NOT ask them for business advice.

You're an entrepreneur. Whether you started your own company, or you went to work for a start-up company with stock options, or you're working in a straight-commission sales position, you're an entrepreneur-minded individual.

Cubicle-minded people don't understand your mentality. They're trapped inside the cubicle. You, however, are not. You've *escaped*. You've got to *Live Outside The Cubicle*.

Living Outside The Cubicle

Living outside the cubicle sounds easier than it is to do. In a society that is becoming more and more socialistic in nature, where kids now have an entitlement-driven mindset, and selfishness, laziness and complacency have become the norm, it's difficult being an entrepreneur. You're surrounded by people that *don't get it*.

Now, I'm not judging people that work in a cubicle whatsoever. It's not about whether you work in a cubicle versus a fancy corner office with a view. What I'm referring to here is a *mindset* – a mindset of limiting beliefs – which is much different than your entrepreneurial mindset.

Some people think like entrepreneurs, and some people think like cubicle workers. Most *cubicle-minded* people want the perceived security of a guaranteed paycheck and so-called *good benefits*, whereas entrepreneurs like us... we want *opportunity*.

Just understand that no matter how much you try to explain your dreams of grandeur to a *cubicle-minded* person, they won't get it. In fact, the more you try, the more they'll try to talk you out of going for it. It's just like the escaped prisoner's experience in Plato's classic story, *The Allegory Of The Cave*.

Plato's *The Allegory Of The Cave*

Have you ever read Plato's *The Allegory Of The Cave*, circa 380 B.C.? I remember reading this book back in high school, being semi-fascinated by the mindset of the ignorant.

If you've never read this classic, let me paraphrase the concept of the story. Plato writes about a conversation between Socrates and Glaucon. In this dialogue, Socrates begins to describe a scenario in which prisoners are held captive inside a cave.

The prisoners have been bound with chains since their childhood. Even their heads are chained, making them completely immobile, and the only line of sight they have is into a wall directly in front of them. Behind them burns a massive bonfire.

Between the fire and the prisoners is a walkway where people walk by, casting shadows on the wall in front of the prisoners. Essentially, the shadows are the only things the prisoners have ever seen in their entire lives. Due to the fact that they're in a cave, all of the sounds echo, both the footsteps and the voices.

Socrates suggests that in such a scenario, if the only thing the prisoners would have ever seen with their own eyes were shadows, they would interpret the one-dimensional shadows as *reality*. They would have no concept of color, or depth perception, for this is all they've ever known.

Socrates also suggests that the only sound the prisoners would have ever experienced would be echoing sounds. They wouldn't know that non-echoing sounds ever existed. To them, echoing sounds would be the only sounds they've ever heard.

Due to the prisoners being trapped inside the cave their entire lives, they would have developed a belief system exclusively based on what they've experienced in life. Their limited experience would certainly give them limiting beliefs about what existed.

Now, suppose one of the prisoners were to escape the cave and see the real world outside the confines of the cave. Imagine an adult ex-prisoner seeing color for the first time, or seeing light for the first time, or seeing three-dimensional objects for the first time.

Not only would it be overwhelming, but it would also be incredibly exciting. They would be exposed to a world that they never could have fathomed.

Imagine the shock.

Now imagine the escaped and enlightened ex-prisoner going back to his fellow prisoners inside the cave and telling them of his great experiences outside the cave. Remember, these prisoners have no concept of color, light, three dimension, or the outside world.

The other prisoners would probably view the enlightened ex-prisoner as a total lunatic. They may even make him out to be a *liar*. If you were a prisoner, hearing about this new world outside the cave would sound no more ludicrous as someone telling you today that the world is actually flat, and that they've seen the edge of the earth where it drops off into oblivion.

Imagine how you would react to someone telling you a story like this. You might think they've gone crazy, or that they've got an extreme drug problem, or that they're trying to trick you in some way.

In the book, *The Allegory Of The Cave*, that's exactly how the prisoners responded to the news about the *outside world*.

The Allegory Of The Cubicle

The escaped prisoner's experience in Plato's *The Allegory Of The Cave* is probably very similar to your experience as an aspiring entrepreneur. The vast majority of your *cubicle-minded* friends and family members probably haven't been as supportive as you'd hope they'd be. Surprise, surprise. Welcome to the world of being an entrepreneur.

Entrepreneurs are from Mars, and *cubicle-minded* people are from Venus. The two will never see eye to eye. This is something that you must accept.

Cubicle-minded people have a set of limiting beliefs, very similar to the prisoners trapped inside Plato's *The Allegory Of The Cave*. To expect them to understand your entrepreneurial perspective is simply unrealistic. It's just not going to happen.

Evangelical entrepreneurs often become lonely people because once they vocalize their radical thoughts about conquering the universe, their friends and family often become very negative. I remember in the beginning stages of my career, it felt like no one believed in me, and the more I tried to get them to believe in my future success, the more negative they became.

The key to living the life of a successful entrepreneur is to create an unapologetic brand, live a life that is synonymous with your brand, and not seek the approval of *cubicle-minded* people. These principles are all part of successfully *Living Outside The Cubicle*.

So let's get started on putting together your game plan for success. We'll begin with talking about *failure*.

Chapter One: Habitual Failure

"The wise man learns from those more successful than he... and the fool, blind to the facts, remains steadfast in his ignorance as the perennial critic."

-Darren Sugiyama

Habitual Failure

Why would a positive guy like me write an entire chapter about failure? Seems a bit ironic, doesn't it? The reality is that you need to understand what to *avoid*, in order to better clarify what you should *focus on*. You may be unconsciously doing things to sabotage your success right now, and because you're not aware of them, they're holding you back.

One of the biggest reasons for a lack of success in business (and in life) is the habitual pattern of making a series of bad choices. Some of these bad choices are choices that haven't been well thought out, however some of them are choices that you habitually and unconsciously make on a daily basis.

There is a subtle difference – the difference between making *occasional* bad choices versus *habitual* bad choices – but I can assure you that the outcomes are substantially different.

The Curse Of Mediocrity

One example of a *habitual* bad decision for an entrepreneur is the acceptance of mediocrity. It seems like such a minor thing, but it literally shapes your destiny.

If you accept mediocrity, you'll get mediocre results, and even worse, you'll become a mediocre person. You'll have mediocre character, mediocre integrity, a mediocre level of will-power, a mediocre work ethic… and ultimately, you'll have a mediocre life.

Now for some people, that's okay. I know people that have mediocre lives with mediocre jobs and mediocre marriages. They have mediocre relationships with their kids. They live in mediocre houses and drive mediocre cars. They take mediocre vacations, and they accept their mediocre lives. Some of them are actually happy with accepting this mediocrity, and there really isn't anything *wrong* with it, for them.

But if you're reading this book, I would assume that you don't want a mediocre life. The title of this book isn't, *Trapped Inside The Cubicle And Loving It.* The title of this book is, *Living Outside The Cubicle.* You're reading this book because you want to achieve excellence. You want to be more successful.

This being the case, you have to create good *habits*. You have to habitually make good decisions that are based on *success principles*. I'll be sharing with you several success principles that have helped me tremendously in both my business life, as well as my personal life.

But before we go getting all *positive*, let's talk a bit more about the negative stuff. We must understand this repetitive *failure-centric* thought process so that we can extricate it from your mindset.

The Bad Habit Of Rationalization

This acceptance of mediocrity stems from *rationalization*, and *cubicle-minded* people are experts at it. Rationalization can absolutely kill your aspirations and dreams of grandeur. The sad thing is that none of us were born with this terrible habit; the habit of rationalizing the decision to give up on our dreams. We've all *learned* how to do this over the years, which has led us to be very pessimistic in nature.

Think back when you were a little kid. Every new experience was exciting. Everything we experienced created a new experiential opportunity. That's how a child's brain processes new experiences.

My son, Estevan, just turned one-year old this past week. He loves crawling all over me like a jungle gym. Put an obstacle in his way, and he starts smiling and laughing as he climbs over it. Show him a new toy, and he starts reaching for it, wanting to play with it. Put him next to a dog, and he reaches out, wanting to pet it. Put any type of food in front of him, and he wants to eat it.

He looks at everything as an opportunity to experience something new. He has no fear whatsoever, because he was born expecting positive outcomes. Most kids are. As kids get older, they start talking about their *dreams*. They'll tell you that they want to be an astronaut, or a ballerina, or a professional ball player. When you ask them what kind of car they want to drive, they'll tell you they want a *Lamborghini* or a *Ferrari* or maybe even a *Space Ship*.

No 10-year old kid dreams about one day driving an economy car with good gas mileage. Kids don't expect mediocrity. They expect greatness. So what happens along the way? When do we stop dreaming about achieving greatness?

Somewhere along the way, adults start planting negative seeds in kids' heads, saying disempowering things like, *"You have to be more realistic,"* or *"Get your head out of the clouds and stop being such a dreamer."*

When you were growing up, do you remember hearing things like this from adults? I sure do. After years of this type of negative brainwashing and negative mindset programming, we actually start believing all of these limitations that adults put on us, and we begin to *accept* mediocrity, because we've been conditioned to accept these limiting beliefs.

Every time we start talking and dreaming about what *could* be, some stupid adult comes along and kills our dream. One of my favorite songs is from the movie *Rocky III* called *The Eye Of The Tiger*. One of the lyrics says, *"Don't lose your grip on the dreams of the past, you must fight just to keep them alive."*

How true. Think about it.

Even now, as an adult, practically everyone in your life is probably attempting to fill your head with *limiting beliefs*, which is making you doubt your ability to manifest your dream. Yes, you *do* have to fight just to keep your dream alive, and if you don't fight for it, you will surely lose it.

Your dreams, if you really commit to them, will threaten and intimidate other people that have opted to accept mediocrity. The reason they'll try to talk you out of your dreams is that in their little minds, if they can rope you into their mediocre world, they won't feel guilty about being average.

If you rise to the top and become *great*, you'll be a constant reminder to them of their acceptance of mediocrity, which deep down, they will undoubtedly feel ashamed of. Misery loves company, and so does mediocrity.

At some point, you must make a decision to be your own person and fight to hold on to your dreams. If you succumb to negative peer pressure and accept mediocrity, that will be the first decision of a series of *bad* decisions on your part, and these bad decisions will lead to a life of mediocrity.

Again, I'm not judging people that are truly happy living lives of mediocrity. They don't have the stress that I have in my life. Their lives are much simpler. They don't think about work on the weekends. They work far less hours than I do. They get to watch a lot more TV than I do. They just live paycheck to paycheck.

Hey, if they're happy living their lives as such, that's great… for them. But I didn't write this book for people like them. I wrote this book for people like you.

You're a go-getter.

You're an achiever.

You're driven.

And since you're one of these special people that wants to achieve *greatness*, it would be a shame to squander this special gift that you were born with. Not everyone was born with the amount of drive that you possess, and so this book isn't necessarily for *everyone*… but it is for *you*.

The trap that I've seen many driven people fall into, is listening to the advice given to them by mediocre people. It's an easy trap to fall into. Have you ever heard the expression *Majority Rules*? It is absolutely true.

If you spend the majority of your time hanging out with people that accept mediocrity, you will most likely assimilate into their *culture* of limiting beliefs, and this can result in you completely giving up. You cannot allow this to happen.

Never take advice from people that haven't successfully achieved what you are attempting to achieve. They may be nice people, but they aren't qualified to give you advice in an area they are not experts in. If you want to be successful in business, the only qualified advice-givers are successful business people.

The Rich Get Richer, And There's A Good Reason

People that have accepted mediocrity in their lives tend to judge *rich people* harshly. If you aspire to be successful in business, and you want to be *rich*, prepare to face a lot of criticism from mediocre people.

They'll criticize you, both overtly and covertly. Some of them will blatantly tell you that you're a snobby elitist just because you drive a nice car, or because you live in their dream house. But most people are cowards that hide out in their mediocrity. They'll never overtly criticize you directly, but they'll make snide little comments about the evils of materialism and monetary greed.

They'll say things like, "*The rich get richer and the poor get poorer*," implying that somehow it's bad to be rich, and without saying it to your face, they'll lump you into that category as if you're doing something wrong.

Hey, according to their definition, many of my friends, business associates and employees are *rich*, and I think it's a good thing for them to get richer. They got *rich* because they worked hard. They're getting even *richer* because they continue to work hard.

There's a legitimate reason why they're getting *richer*, and it's very logical to a person with half a brain, but jealous idiots will often find fault in other people's successes. Isn't getting *rich* part of being successful in business?

Sure, there are unethical people out there that have gotten rich by exploiting and taking advantage of other people, but I'm not talking about them. I'm talking about the people that started off with nothing more than an idea, a whole lot of ambition, and the guts to build something out of nothing. I'm talking about *true* entrepreneurs.

If you're an entrepreneur, I'm assuming that one of your goals is to become financially successful, right? It may not be the only goal you have, but I'm sure it's one of your business goals, and I think it's a good thing. I believe it's a good thing to be able to give your family a better life, contribute more to charities that you believe in, and empower people you work with by showing them how to be successful too. How is that a *bad* thing?

Truly successful people are successful due to a lot of hard work and developing a set of skills that have enabled them to overcome financial adversities. They've built character and developed resiliency through this process, and one of the benefits of this process is monetary gain.

I've heard several mediocre, so-called *religious* people, say that it's easier for a camel to pass through the eye of a needle than it is for a rich man to get into heaven. The context of this saying implies that the temptations that come with monetary wealth can lead a man to do unholy things. It assumes that a man's faithfulness is solely based on his options, and that his options expand as his wealth expands.

Personally, I believe that a man's *wealth* and a man's *faith* are not in opposition to each other. You can be wealthy and still live a Godly life. In the Bible, there are several stories about faithful men of God that were leaders and kings with incredible wealth, but also had incredible relationships with God.

Now, I suppose that one could argue that with *money* comes *access* to unholy things due to the carnal nature of human beings and the temptation of partaking in these unholy things. Perhaps there is some truth to that, however I've seen a lot of unholy, ugly crimes committed by desperate people whose desperation was due to their *lack* of money, not their abundant wealth.

I even saw a story on the news recently where an armed robber repeatedly apologized to his victim as he robbed him, saying that he lost his job and that he was forced to rob him in order to feed his family. This guy actually felt bad about robbing his victim, but he said he *had* to do it in order to feed his family.

Consider this for a moment. If this man were financially successful in business, perhaps he wouldn't have to commit a crime to feed his family. If he was *rich* and owned a business, perhaps he would have even created jobs for other people, enabling them to support and feed their families too. So explain to me how being *rich* is a *bad* thing.

I would agree that the *love of money* can be destructive, but that has nothing to do with the *money*. It has everything to do with the *character* of the person.

Money is nothing more than a *magnifier*. If you're a greedy person, money will make you *greedier*. If you're a generous person, money will make you more *charitable*. If you're an evil person, money will enable you to do more *bad things*. If you're a good person, money will enable you to do more *good things*.

So you see, all money really does is magnify what is already in a person's heart, both the bad things, but also the good things.

Money Is Not The Root Of All Evil

No where in the Bible does it say that *money* is the root of all evil. It says that the *love of money* is the root of all evil. In this context, the real issue is a *character flaw* and a misappropriation of *values*, not an abundance of money. An abundance of money just magnifies the character flaw.

When someone values *money* over *ethics*, that's where the problem starts, but again, the problem is not the *money*. The problem is the person's *lack of ethics*. All money does is magnify the person's *value system* that already existed, long before the money ever showed up.

Now, for the sake of this discussion, I'm going to assume that you're a *good person*. I'm going to assume that you're a generous, loving person that wants to do good things for other people. Money will enable you to do more of these *good things* that your heart wants to do. Money is a *tool*, and if used correctly, it can be a wonderful tool.

When you go to a hardware store to buy a drill, you don't really want a *drill*. What you want is a *hole*. The hole is the *end result* that you desire. The drill is merely a *tool* to help you get the hole. It's the same thing with money. Money is a *tool* that can help you get what you *really* want.

Some people want more money so that they can send their kids to a better school. Some people want more money so they can afford to live in a safer neighborhood. Some people want more money so they can support a family member. Some people want more money so they can contribute more to a charity they believe in.

Sure, some people want more money to buy flashy cars, jewelry and other material items. There's nothing necessarily wrong with this either. The point is, having more money empowers you to make these decisions based on what you really *believe in*, versus what you can *afford to do*.

Personally, I think that living an empowered life that's governed by your personal beliefs and values, as opposed to living a life governed by your bank account, is a more righteous way to live.

You see, living a life based on *fear* and *worry* is no way to live, and that's what you do when you're always stressed out about not having enough money to pay your bills. Try explaining this to a broke, *cubicle-minded* person and you'll be sure to start an emotionally-charged argument. I highly recommend that you do not enter these types of conversations and debates with *cubicle-minded* people.

It's like being a capitalist having an argument with a socialist about money. All you'll do is piss off each other, and if they catch you on an off-day, they may even cause you to doubt your own values regarding this issue.

Entrepreneurs and cubicle-minded people have different perspectives on the world, on money, and on careers. They have different value systems.

Neither one is necessarily right or wrong, but they are indeed different. You need to make your decision regarding which one you are, and stick to your guns.

It's your life, and thus you need to take responsibility and ownership of your beliefs.

Self-Doubt, Frustration & Worry

It's human nature to doubt yourself... to doubt your abilities... and to doubt your dreams of massive financial success. It's normal to feel inadequate and unsure of yourself from time to time.

If you're currently finding yourself doubting these things, don't beat yourself up about it. It's okay. Regardless of a person's level of success, we all doubt our abilities and our priorities every once in a while, because we're human beings. Human beings are emotional, thus none of us are impervious to self-doubt.

The key to success is to acknowledge these feelings without giving in to them. I certainly had these feelings of self-doubt when I first started my career, but I learned how to change my thought process from being one of self-doubt, pessimism and worry, to one of being optimistic, opportunistic, and solution-centric.

Most people spend the majority of their time focused on their problems, whereas I learned to acknowledge my problems, but then immediately shift my focus to finding solutions. To live a *solution-centric* life, you have to identify the difference between two very similar emotions:

1. Worry.
2. Frustration.

These human emotions are very similar, however they result in two entirely different outcomes. Here are the fundamental differences.

Frustration is an emotion associated with a short-term, temporary problem.

Worry is an emotion associated with a permanent problem that has no solution.

I actually think *frustration* is a healthy emotion. If channeled properly, it can inspire and motivate you to achieve more. Frustration gets your blood flowing and your adrenaline pumping. Frustration can lead to the tipping point in your life where you say, *"I'm going to make it in spite of these crappy circumstances! Nothing is going to get in my way!"* This can be very healthy and very productive.

Frustration can create a fire in your belly. So many people discourage this emotion because they think that happiness in life is about *acceptance*.

But for a driven person, acceptance of mediocrity is the equivalent of complacency, and complacency is synonymous with *giving up*. A person that is driven and committed to achieving success equates *giving up* with ultimate failure. Quitters are cowards, and you are not a quitter.

These so-called self-help gurus that try to get you to ignore feelings of frustration and anger are not only unrealistic, but in my opinion, they're full of crap. Discontent can be a good thing. It shows that you aspire to achieve something, and that you stand for something.

Is it wrong to have feelings of frustration and anger toward unrighteousness? Is it wrong to have feelings of anger towards rapists and child abuse? Is it wrong to have feelings of anger towards injustice? Personally, I don't think so.

The key is to channel these feelings into finding a solution. You see, some of my greatest moments where I felt like a phoenix rising came out of situations where I was incredibly frustrated, and sometimes, downright angry.

I worked hard to find a solution, and I poured my heart and soul into working on that solution, relentlessly. Often times, I not only solved my problem, but I actually put myself in a better position than I was previously in, before the so-called *problem* ever arose.

Frustration Can Also Be Dangerous

Although frustration can be very productive, it can also be slightly dangerous, depending on how you channel it. If you allow yourself to be overtaken by the emotion of frustration (instead of positively channeling it), it can cause you to make stupid, irrational decisions.

You've got to be aware that you are emotionally frustrated, and say to yourself, *"This pisses me off... but watch me crush this adversity and overcome this situation like a champion."*

I've learned to view every frustrating situation in life as an opportunity to grow as a person, and also as an opportunity to create yet another great story of triumphantly overcoming an obstacle or challenge.

However, the danger of *frustration* is that it can lead to *worry*. You see, frustration can empower you, but if you let it, it can lead to emotional weakness in the form of worrying. When you *worry* about something, you're basically saying, *"Oh my God, what if I never get out of this situation, and what if it gets even worse?"*

This anguish that comes with the emotion of *worry* makes you weak and prone to make stupid decisions that are not well thought out. You can lose your clarity of thought, and end up making *emotionally-driven* decisions instead of *principle-driven* decisions.

You see, as long as you say to yourself, *"Although I'm pissed off about this situation, it is temporary and short-term, and I have a way to potentially make my situation even better than before,"* then you are practicing the fine art of turning lemons into lemonade.

Don't feel bad about feeling frustrated. It means you care about the outcome, which is what driven people care about. If you didn't care, by definition, you'd be indifferent and complacent, accepting a life of mediocrity. That's not who you are. You're better than that.

So let's say you're slightly *frustrated* with where your business is right now. Congratulations. This means you're driven. Let's start planning your rise to the top.

The first step to your *Phoenix Rising Moment* is to implement the proper goal setting program.

Chapter Two:
The Ultimate Goal Setting Program

"Time is a fixed entity. It is our allocation of it that is variable."
-Darren Sugiyama

Running Out Of Time

We all have the same number of hours in a day. The question is, how do you spend them? I used to feel like I ran out of time trying to get everything done each day. I used to feel overwhelmed and stressed out all the time.

But when I truly understood how to design a great *Goal Setting Program*, things became crystal clear to me. I stopped doing tasks that didn't directly move me closer to my ultimate goal. I stopped doing tasks that I could delegate to other people. And I stopped doing tasks that didn't contribute to quantum growth.

Basically, I set very specific goals, and I mapped out a very detailed process of what I needed to do to make these goals come into fruition.

I'm sure you've set goals before, and you've probably read about the importance of setting goals. I'm not going to sit here and tell you about all the statistics regarding people who set goals versus people that don't set goals. Instead, I want to clarify what a productive *Goal Setting Program* looks like.

I've seen so many goal setting programs out there, and quite frankly, most of them are absolutely worthless. The reason I say that most of these goal setting programs are worthless is that many of them don't give you anything tangible to focus on *doing*.

So many of these goal setting programs tell you to put pictures on your wall of material things that you aspire to acquire. So you get all excited and cut out pictures of luxury cars, mansions, expensive watches, and exotic vacation destinations and pin them up on your wall. I'm not saying that there's anything wrong with doing this. I think it's great.

However, the problem is that if this is *all* you do, it's nothing more than *wishful thinking*. Yes, I am a believer in visualizing your success before it happens, but you need to understand *how* to execute your game plan, and then actually *execute* it.

You have to perform the proper tasks that are going to get you there. Part of effective goal setting is to identify what specific tasks are required, and to do so, you need to make sure each task and each goal contains five specific elements. Your goals must be:

1. Physically Attainable.
2. Specific.
3. Controllable.
4. Measurable & Quantifiable.
5. Understood.

We'll discuss each of them in great depth.

Component #1: Your Goals Must Be Physically Attainable.

You must understand the process of achieving success within your specific industry. For example, one of the benefits of owning a business (or being an entrepreneur-minded person in a commission-based position) with a steady client base is long-term, stable, ongoing cash flow.

It's only logical to expect that it will take a several months, or even years, to accumulate enough clients to build up steady, ongoing, monthly revenue and commissions. This doesn't happen overnight.

It would be illogical to expect to *get rich quick*. If you have this unrealistic expectation in this type of business structure, you'd be setting yourself up for disappointment. Now, that being said, I'm a big believer in building your own empire, or being an independent contractor with a residually-based commission structure.

One of my companies currently does $37 million in annual sales, and the majority of it is residual. The benefit to me is that this sales volume, and the commissions associated with it, keeps coming in every month... month after month. Some of my sales producers that work for me in this company are making over $220,000 in residual commissions per year now. It took them a few years to build up their client base, but after several years, they're now enjoying the fruits of their labor.

They understood the ramp up period of a straight-commission sales position. They understood the process of gradually accumulating a client base, and they accepted the fact that it would take some time to start earning a substantial income.

Sure, they could have gone out and taken a *cubicle job* and started drawing an immediate guaranteed salary, but they wanted more out of life. They understood that a career with me in a straight commission-based capacity could have huge, long-term rewards... and they knew not to expect a huge income right off the bat.

The challenge is that most entrepreneurs have too many *so-called friends* that work in cubicles, and their *cubicle friends* start judging them. Please understand that when I use the term *cubicle friends*, I'm not judging people that work in cubicles. I'm merely using this term to describe a certain *mindset*.

Remember, this book is entitled, *Living Outside The Cubicle*, and so my ideas presented in this book represent a very different perspective regarding business, careers and money. I'm representing the *Outside The Cubicle* perspective.

Your cubicle friends don't understand the concept of *building an empire*. They prefer to just *work a regular job*. You see, your cubicle friends don't understand why you'd work so hard for such low pay in the beginning, because they don't realize that you're not working for a *paycheck*. You're working to build an *empire*, and they seem to forget that Rome wasn't built in a day either.

While your cubicle friends are out spending their cruddy little paychecks on silly, depreciating items like shoes and fancy cocktails at cool restaurants, on the surface, it looks like their life is better than yours. Hey, temporarily, it *is* better than yours. But I assure you, it is *temporary*.

If you're an aspiring entrepreneur and 100 percent of your income is commission-based, in the beginning, you'll have even less money than your cubicle friends, and you won't be able to afford to have *fun* like them. Hey, I've been there myself.

In the early stages of my career as an entrepreneur, my friends would be going out to dinner, having a good time. They weren't *rich*, but they had decent *cubicle job salaries*.

I, on the other hand, was a struggling, aspiring entrepreneur with no money. I would agree to hang out with them, but I would meet them at the restaurant *after* I knew everyone had eaten. I would eat oatmeal at home to fill me up because I couldn't afford to eat out. Then I'd show up strategically late and just order water, because it was free.

From time to time, I would be envious of my friends. I wanted to be able to afford to eat out with them, and I couldn't. But I stuck to my game plan, buried my head, and worked my butt off. Today, I make more in a month than most of them make in a year. It paid off for me. Thank God I didn't quit.

Even though your cubicle friends are living paycheck to paycheck, in the beginning stages of your career, you may say to yourself from time to time, *"At least they have a paycheck."*

This is the emotional struggle that every aspiring entrepreneur goes through in the beginning stages of their career. You have to sacrifice *short-term* fun in order to reap a *long-term,* rockstar lifestyle of wealth and luxury. If you want to be successful, you've got to *give up* something in the short-term. This is just a basic success principle.

Many aspiring entrepreneurs lose sight of this because they're too easily influenced by their cubicle friends. All of a sudden, they start comparing their cubicle friends' lifestyles to their immediate lifestyle. It looks like their cubicle friends have it better, and they start questioning their decision to take on this risky, *pie-in-the-sky*, entrepreneurial project. What happened?

They've lost their enthusiasm about being a successful entrepreneur because they're looking at short-term results. They've lost sight of their long-term game plan. They've lost their clarity of thought and their vision of the future because their stupid cubicle friends have convinced them that their aspirations of being a successful entrepreneur are never going to happen.

They'll say things like, *"If your business opportunity is so great, how come you're not making any money yet?"*

Because we live in a microwave society in which most people want to see results instantaneously, and very few people understand the concept of paying dues up front for a long-term reward, this is the type of stupid question your cubicle friends ask you when you're an aspiring entrepreneur in the beginning stages of your career.

I call them *stupid* questions not because your friends are literally stupid, unintelligent people. I'm not even saying there's anything *wrong* with being a cubicle worker either.

All I'm saying is that their advice is *stupid* because it's not based on any facts, wisdom-through-experience, or expertise on the topic. These people have never succeeded at what you're attempting to do, and so in my opinion, they're not *qualified* to give sound advice on this particular subject, due to their lack of knowledge and expertise.

In actuality, *they're* not the stupid ones. *You're* the stupid one if you listen to them and take their ignorant advice. You can't expect a business to do something it wasn't designed to do, and any legitimate business is going to take some time to build up.

You can't expect fine wine to age overnight. You can't expect a workout DVD to make you into Mr. Universe overnight. And you can't expect to build a multi-million business empire overnight and get rich quick.

So before you start setting goals, you have to ask yourself, *"Is this goal I'm setting attainable, given what the business model was designed to do?"*

Setting a goal that is physically or mathematically unattainable is not only worthless, but it is counter-productive. Make sure you understand the step-by-step process of what it takes to achieve your goal, and execute it with precision. That's why I'm a bigger fan of setting *activity goals* as opposed to *results goals*.

If you find that mathematically, you'd have to meet face-to-face with 500 prospects per day in order to reach your annual income goal, logic would tell you that it is physically impossible to meet with 500 prospects face-to-face in one day.

Set your goals based on what you know you can physically do (your activity). If you know your process well, then you should be able to mathematically calculate what your results (income) should be.

Focus on how many prospecting calls per week you're going to make, or whatever your marketing/prospecting method is. You can control how many hours you spend prospecting.

It's just like establishing an exercise program. You can't necessarily control how much muscle mass you add to your body, or how much fat you lose off of your body, but you *can* control how many times per week you go to the gym. You can control how many exercises you do while you're there. These are *activity goals*. You probably do this right now if you workout on a regular basis.

Sure, you should set certain *results goals* for yourself. You may say, *"My goal is to lose ten pounds by this summer."* That's great, but in addition to that *results goal*, you'd better set *activity goals* regarding exactly what you're going to *do* to get there. This leads us to the second component of my Goal Setting Program. Specificity.

Component #2: Your Goals Must Be Specific.

Both your *results goals* and your *activity goals* must be specific. The need for your results goals to be specific is pretty obvious. You're looking to accomplish something specific. In the previous example, the goal is to lose ten pounds by this summer.

This goal is specific. You want to lose a specific amount of weight by a specific date. All *results goals* should have a specific desired outcome, as well as a specific amount of time to accomplish the desired outcome in. I've heard people say things like, "*I want to make a lot of money,*" or "*I want to be successful,*" or "*I want to be rich.*"

These are all nice things that most people want, but they are not *goals* because there is no specific dollar amount and there is no specific deadline attached to the goal. It would be like asking an Olympic runner, "*What's your goal to run the 100-yard dash in?*" and the runner saying, "*I don't know. I just want to run really fast.*"

This type of athlete would never break any records because they don't even know what they're attempting to accomplish, thus their training regimen wouldn't be designed to hit a specific target goal.

All world-class athletes have a very specific goal they're shooting for. They're generally attempting to break a world record, and all world records have a specific measurement, whether it's time, distance or some other unit of measurement.

On top of that, every world-class athlete has a trainer. It's the trainer's job to design a training program. Every great training program has a well thought out process of what specific exercises or drills the athlete is required to do, as well as how much each exercise or drill is required to be performed, usually measured in units of time or repetitions. This athlete's training program is based on the concept of *activity goals*.

Think about your own exercise habits. When you go to the gym, do you know how many sets of a particular exercise you're going to do? Of course you do. Do you know repetitions you're going to do in each set? Of course you do.

But in your business, when you start each month, do you know exactly how many prospecting calls you're going to make? Do you know exactly how many prospects you hope to meet with? Do you know exactly how many sales you hope to make?

Don't just say, *"I'm going to work really hard this month."* Instead, say, *"My goal is to make 2,000 cold calls, generate 28 face-to-face sales opportunities, and acquire 7 new clients."* Set specific goals, both activity goals and results goals, and do whatever you have to do to achieve them.

Component #3: Your Goals Must Be Controllable.

This is an area that so many people overlook. Whether you're in sales, or you're the Executive Vice-President, or you own the entire company, you're probably spending too much time worrying about things that are outside of your control.

Being a type-A personality, I'm a self-admitted control freak. I want to control everything in my life. But as I have painfully learned over the years, I cannot control everything in the universe (believe me, I've tried), and thus, I have learned to only attempt to control those things that are controllable.

When it comes to setting goals, some of them I can *influence*, but I can't *control* them, usually because the outcome is partially affected by what other people do. Neither you nor I can control what other people do, and so we can only do our best to *influence* them.

However, there are some things in life that I *can* control. I can control what percentage of my time I invest in a particular area of my business. I can control the spirit in which I do things in, and the attitude that I choose to have. I can control the decisions I make.

Basically, I can control my *actions*. In goal setting, we call these *activity goals*. I keep coming back to the importance of activity goals because it answers the specific question, *"What exactly do I have to do in order to be successful?"*

This is the most important question to ask yourself. Once you have your answer, the ball is in your court. You'll either decide to do it, or you'll decide not to do it. If you do it, you'll be able to celebrate your achievements. If you don't do it, you'll have no one to blame but yourself. It all really comes down to *action*.

I remember a single friend of mine was in a bit of a dating dry-spell. He hadn't gone on a date in a while, and his confidence was beginning to wane a bit. One day, he called me up and told me about this really hot girl he saw at the beach over the weekend. He told me, *"Darren, I saw her, and even though I was kind of intimidated, I just decided to walk up to her and talk to her."*

I said, *"Man, that's great. So how'd it go?"*

He replied, *"Well, I just DECIDED to talk to her. I didn't actually do it."*

Intentions are nice, but they don't produce results. *Actions* do. Control your goals by controlling your actions.

Everyone can control their actions. You might not be able to control your results, and you can't control what other people do, but you can control what activity goals you set, as well as whether or not you actually execute them.

You can also control what step-by-step strategy you use to accomplish your goals, and you can control the level of discipline you have to execute your strategy. Control these things, and you'll accomplish greatness.

Component #4: Your Goals Must Be Measurable & Quantifiable.

We've already talked about the necessity of your activity goals being specific and controllable, but in addition, they must be *measurable* and *quantifiable*. Each activity goal must be tracked and measured against a set expectation.

For example, if you want to make a certain level of income, you've got to reverse-engineer the process all the way down to what you have to *do*, weekly.

In the example I gave you earlier regarding cold-calling, you must understand your numbers. You must know your expected prospect contact rate. In other words, of all the cold-calls you make, what percentage of them are you actually going to reach on the phone?

You must know your expected booking percentage. In other words, of the decision makers you talk to, what percentage of them are you actually booking appointments with?

You must know your expected closing percentage. In other words, of the decision makers you meet with, what percentage of them are electing to become clients of yours?

Of these clients, what is the average commission you make per client?

You see, once you know what dollar amount of commission you make from your average sale, assuming you know the expected success percentages in each of these categories above, it's fairly easy to calculate how many sales appointments you need to execute per month.

You can then reverse-engineer the process all the way down to how many prospecting calls you need to make per month, per week, and per day. Now you know exactly what you need to *do* each day, on a consistent basis, to reach a specific income goal. You're getting closer and closer to fully understanding how to turn your nebulous wish list into a clearly defined Goal Setting Program.

There is one last component to my Goal Setting Program that is absolutely paramount. Without this fifth component, none of this works, and it has to do with some of the concepts we talked about earlier regarding your mindset and your expectations.

Component #5: Your Goals Must Be Understood.

You must understand your goals. This may sound simple, and it is. However, it is one of the easiest things to screw up. You've got to understand the process of achieving your goal, which ultimately comes down to a mathematical equation. Sounds simple, right?

All you have to do is figure out exactly what to do… how much to do it… how often to do it… and how long to do it for. Once you have that, you'll have your formula for success. All you have to do now is *do it*. As simple as that sounds, I've seen people screw this up royally. How is this possible?

The reason this is such an easy area in which to fail, is that we are all emotional human beings. From time to time, we all temporarily lose the proper perspective. Hopefully, this loss-of-perspective is temporary, and hopefully, it doesn't last for too long. Some people never regain the proper perspective, and they start believing the lies that their emotions tell them.

Over 90% of what your emotions tell you is wrong. Think about decisions you've made at the height of emotional extremities. Whether you were overly excited, overly depressed, or overly angry, those decisions you made in the heat of the moment probably ended less than favorably.

You probably let your emotions get the best of you, and your decision was made without fully calculating the pro's and con's. As human beings, we are all susceptible to the negative affects of letting our emotions dictate our perspective, as opposed to being guided by the proper principles.

Understanding what specific numeric results constitute success in your specific business is one of the most important components to achieving success because numbers don't lie. Emotions lie, but numbers do not.

Going back to the baseball analogy, a baseball player that bats over .300 (a 70 percent failure rate) is an All-Star, but if he has a 30 percent fielding percentage (also a 70 percent failure rate) he'll get cut from the team. If a baseball player didn't understand these methods of evaluation, he would have no idea why he was being praised or criticized.

In most sales environments, a 70 percent failure rate (a 30 percent closing rate) is pretty darn good. The irony is that in almost every other area of life (outside of baseball and sales), a 30 percent success rate is terrible. If you miss 70 percent of the questions on your math exam in college, you will fail the course. When driving your car, if you get in accidents 70 percent of the time, they'll take away your license.

But if you're a baseball player, and you fail 70 percent of the time at the plate, you're an All-Star. In business, you've got to know what success percentage constitutes success in your chosen field. But that's not all. The other variable that affects your success is *volume of activity*.

I've had sales reps work for me that had high closing percentages, but they were lazy. They didn't generate very many sales appointments. Sure their closing percentage was high, but the results that a 50 percent closing rate generates on 10 appointments (5 deals) is less than what a 30 percent closing rate generates on 30 appointments (9 deals).

One of the top money earners that works for my insurance consulting firm is a guy named George. George started off with very little skill. He was an ex-professional basketball player from Bulgaria. He had a thick Bulgarian accent (because English is his second language), and he had absolutely no insurance, sales or consulting experience.

His closing percentage was one of the lowest I've ever seen in my organization, however his work ethic was among the best I've ever seen. What he lacked in *finesse* and *talent*, he made up for in *volume of activity*.

His volume of activity generated more than double the number of sales appointments compared to an average sales producer. This allowed George to practice and hone his skills in maximum capacity due to the fact that he created more field time with prospects through his work ethic. Today, George is one of our most talented and most skilled sales producers at my insurance consulting firm.

One of the key principles I taught George when he first started with me was to crank out as much volume as humanly possible, and yes, I gave him a specific number to hit that was:

1. Physically attainable.
2. Specific.
3. Controllable.
4. Measurable and Quantifiable.
5. Understood.

I told him that what he initially lacked in *finesse*, he could make up for with *muscle*. I told him to make twice as many cold-calls as everyone else, and that it would pay off. My rationale was that in almost any type of sales, there is a certain percentage of prospects that are almost predestined to buy from you.

Perhaps their previous vendor dropped the ball, and you just so happened to call them at the right time. Or maybe they've never bought before, but they've been thinking about trying your product recently, and you just so happened to catch them at the right time. Timing can often times play a big role in a prospect buying from you.

In one of my businesses, I have estimated that three percent of the prospects we meet with are predestined *yes's*. I would venture to say the same thing applies to most industries. About three percent of everyone out there that agrees to meet with you already wants your product or service, and they want it now. They've already made the decision to buy prior to you even showing up for the appointment.

That being the case, if you meet with 100 prospects, you're virtually guaranteed to close three of them. If you meet with 1,000 prospects, you're virtually guaranteed to close 30 of them.

I also taught George that 50 percent of the people he meets with were never going to do business with him in the first place. These were predestined *no's*, so there was no need to worry about them. I told him that whenever a prospect rejects him, just chalk them up being one of the 50 percent predestined *no's*.

Of the remaining 47 percent, 10 percent are going to be a pain-in-the-butt. You wouldn't want them as clients, even if they begged you to be your client. Let them go too. They aren't even worth thinking about.

This leaves 37 percent that are sitting on the fence and they could go either way. The better your skill, the more of them you will convert to becoming your clients.

The remaining three percent are going to be lay-downs. Maybe it's timing. Maybe it's the color of your tie. Maybe you have the same first name as their favorite uncle. The reasons don't matter. These are the *easy ones*. I told George to focus on getting as many *easy ones* as humanly possible. So what was *humanly possible*? What activity goals were achievable?

We looked at how many hours were available during the work week. We separated *Green Time* (time during the day that he could reach business owners on the phone) from *Red Time* (time after the work day when business owners were not able to be reached on the phone). He did all of his emails and administrative work after 6:00pm during *Red Time*. If he answered emails during *Green Time*, it would cut into the number of cold-calls he could make.

I wanted to maximize the number of sales opportunities for George, and so I really stressed the importance of *only* doing *Red Time Activity* during *Red Time*, because *Green Time Activity* can only be done during *Green Time*. You can't reach a business owner on the phone at 8:00pm during *Red Time*, but you *can* send emails and put together client proposals at 8:00pm.

I also calculated how many phone dials George could make per hour, and multiplied that by the total number of hours he could dial the phone per week. Of course, I had to factor in time to go on sales appointments. Once the math was done, I put together a Goal Setting Program that included both *results goals* and *activity goals*. Here's what happened as a result of George's Goal Setting Program.

By his fourth year with me, he made $128,747 in annual commissions. In his fifth year with me, his commissions increased to $187,125 per year. In his sixth year with me, his commissions reached $206,910 per year. This past year was George's seventh year with me, and he made $221,649 in commissions. Because George is on a residual commission-structured compensation plan, his income will continue to rise, each and every year. George is currently only 31-years old.

You must understand both the immediate numbers of what constitutes success, and you must also understand the long-term financial benefit. Don't lose sight of your dream, and don't let your cubicle-minded friends talk you out of it. They know absolutely nothing about your business, and so listening to their opinions is just plain stupid on your part.

Just remember, I was once bombarded with the negative opinions of my cubicle-minded friends too, but I never quit. Cowards quit, and you're not a coward. If you were, you wouldn't have picked up this book in the first place.

This type of Goal Setting Program will enable you to stay on track and properly evaluate your progress. Design your Goal Setting Program and stick to it like it's a religion. You've got to treat your goals like they're *laws*. The easiest way to self-govern your *laws* is to have an accountability partner. You need to create formal *punishments* for breaking your *laws*.

These *Self-Imposed Punishments* must be things you abhor doing, and your accountability partner must be the type of person that would enforce the punishment, in your best interests, of course. For example, good punishments would include washing the other person's car or cleaning their toilets.

Punishments must be things that you don't want to do, where there is no benefit to you whatsoever. Don't institute a punishment like taking your accountability partner out to dinner. You'd probably enjoy it as a social event, thus making it a non-productive punishment. They must be punishments that you hate to do.

You'll do more to avoid the punishment (because you abhor the punishment) than you'll do to achieve a reward. Use the proverbial *stick* instead of the proverbial *carrot*. The *carrot* is a reward, using the *greed for gain* as a motivator. The *stick* is the punishment (analogous to getting hit with the stick), using the *avoidance of pain* as the motivator.

Human beings will do more to avoid pain than they will to gain pleasure, and thus due to this understanding of human behavioral patterns, it is best to use this method of self-governance as opposed to any other motivator.

To recap, as you're designing your Goal Setting Program, make sure your goals are:

1. Physically Attainable.
2. Specific.
3. Controllable.
4. Measurable & Quantifiable.
5. Understood.

In addition, as just discussed, create your *laws* as well as your consequential punishments for not following your own self-imposed laws. And make sure you report to an accountability partner that will enforce the punishments.

Have A *Not-To-Do List*

Not only do you need to have a clearly defined list of your goals, broken down to a daily *To-Do List*, you also need to have a *Not-To-Do List*. You need to identify what things you should *not* be doing. I'm not talking about a list of vices to steer clear of. I'm talking about a list of things that aren't necessarily *bad* things to do, but they're not high-priority items.

I've seen a lot of people claim to be consistently overwhelmed, bogged down by massive *To-Do Lists*. Have you ever noticed that people that are always emotionally overwhelmed with too many tasks never seem to accomplish much? It's because they're lazy.

Now, I know that may rub you the wrong way, especially because you yourself might actually feel overwhelmed right now. Before you start hyperventilating and gasping over my statement about laziness, consider what I'm about to say.

Being *busy* is a form of *laziness* when it is based on *indiscriminate action*. What I mean by this is that if you get caught up in trying to resolve every little imperfection, especially regarding semi-inconsequential issues, you'll never get to the game-changing action items. You have to accept that nothing is going to be perfect 100 percent of the time.

As a self-described perfectionist, I find myself often struggling with this concept. I want everything to be perfect. But what I've realized, is that in business, as well as life in general, is that:

1. Nothing will ever be perfect.
2. Sometimes *good enough* is good enough.

The key is to be able to discern which issues are major game-changers, and which ones are semi-inconsequential.

For example, I know a businesswoman that does the majority of her work from home. She has somewhat of an obsessive-compulsive personality, and there are certain semi-inconsequential things she just can't seem to let go of.

Here's an example of what I'm talking about.

Her kitchen has beautiful soapstone countertops. Soapstone is very expensive, but also very high-maintenance. Every time she walks into her kitchen, she starts polishing her countertops. Because she works from home, she's constantly going into her kitchen to get a glass of water or find something to snack on... and every time she does this, she starts polishing her countertops. She literally can't help herself.

So what happens? She's constantly getting distracted from her work, and because of this distraction, she isn't as productive as she could be. This lack of productivity leads to projects backing up on her desk. This backlog of projects leads to her feeling overwhelmed. Once she feels overwhelmed, she flees in search of something to do that gives her the false feeling of immediate accomplishment, which is polishing her soapstone kitchen countertops. And thus, the cycle continues.

She's always *so* busy. Whenever I talk to her, she's always complaining about how busy she is, but she never gets anything done. She's *lazy*. It's not that she doesn't want to be productive, but due to her indiscriminant actions, which by definition, is a form of laziness, she is very unproductive. She lacks clarity and focus.

That's why most people cannot work from home and be effective. They get too easily distracted by non-essential action items, and in the process of feeling overwhelmed by how *busy* they are, they never get anything substantial accomplished.

For those people that work from home, in order for them to be productive, them must have a *Not To-Do List*. Here are some things that should be on your *Not To-Do* List if you work from home:

1. Do not do any housework during your workday hours.

2. Do not take any more personal calls than you would if you were in an office working with your co-workers.

3. Do not watch TV as you work. You're fooling yourself if you think you can be as productive without 100 percent of

your focus. (How would you feel if your doctor was performing surgery on you while watching TV?)

As I said earlier, I myself have been guilty of this type of indiscriminant action. I remember one of the first offices I had. I was obsessed with having my office space perfect. Each Saturday, I would walk through the entire office with a can of touch-up paint and a small paintbrush, and I would fix every little mark on every wall. My office space just *had* to be perfect.

On one hand, my office looked spotless. But I had to ask myself, *"Did the time I spent doing paint touch-up work translate into more profit? Did it result in relevant, substantial revenue growth? Did it make a substantial positive impact on my company's operations?"* I think you know the answer to these questions.

If you were to prioritize every action item that you're currently doing, most likely, you'd reap better results if you let the bottom 20 percent of these items fall by the wayside, and place a heavier emphasis on those items that actually produce substantial results.

Perfection, often times, is the enemy of good enough. Now, I'm not promoting half-ass, lack-luster efforts and results. Not at all. All I'm saying is that there are certain areas of your business that require near perfection, and others that are low-impact items.

If you have enough time to tidy up every little area of your business, then by all means, do it. It's just that most entrepreneurs I talk to complain about not having enough time to do everything they really want to do. I'm assuming you're in this category, just like most entrepreneurs.

This being the case, assuming that you realistically cannot complete every task on your *To-Do List*, you have to make decisions about which items are non-essentials, and elect to *not* do them. This is the only way you can ensure that the essential, game-changing items *do* get done.

Again, it's not that there's anything wrong with prettying up your office, or cleaning your kitchen countertops, but the question you have to ask yourself is, *"If I used this time to execute a different task... a more essential task... would I get better overall results?"*

It's a concept I call the *Alternative Of Choice*. If the alternative is to execute a task that will result in a better outcome (such as a quantum leap in your business development, substantial increase in revenue, etc.), is your time better spent on the alternative choice?

You will probably struggle with this, as I still do, but in order to take quantum leaps in your business, there are some things that you just have to let go, enabling you to execute the core essential must-do's.

Chapter Three:
The Power Of Focus

"Focusing on my problems has never given me better results than focusing on finding a potential solution."

-Darren Sugiyama

Being Task-Focused

As discussed in the previous chapter, implementing proper goal setting strategies enables you to clarify what you should be focusing on, task wise. It also clarifies what your end result should be, relative to how effectively you execute your specific tasks.

Focusing on what specific tasks need to be executed, and directly associating them with desired outcomes, is what goal setting is all about.

Obviously, having the proper *task focus* is necessary, however there is another level to *The Power Of Focus* that we haven't discussed yet, which is having the proper *emotional focus*.

What We Focus On Shapes Our Perspective On What Is Possible

From a very early age, I viewed the world as a place of endless possibilities, both positively and negatively. I remember when I was only eight years old, I saw a man in a wheelchair with no legs and I thought to myself, *"Wow, if it happened to him, it could happen to me too."* I didn't so much fear being physically disabled, but it did make me appreciate being able to walk, run and play. It made me thankful for my blessings.

Conversely, I remember seeing people of great fortune, luck or wealth and thinking to myself, *"Wow, if it happened for them, it could happen for me too."*

Even at the early age of eight-years old, it seemed to me that being incredibly successful and wealthy was possible and attainable. I didn't know how I was going to achieve it, but having this mindset that *anything was possible* allowed me to dream big.

So there I was, as an eight-year old kid, thinking that *anything* was possible, both devastating travesties as well as over-the-top blessings. Perhaps it was because I was exposed to both sides of the tracks when I was growing up.

I learned how to count my blessings, acknowledging those less fortunate than me, but I also learned to work my butt off and be the best I could be. Basically, I grew up having positive expectations of myself and my outcomes.

It's like a kid in a car ride, headed to an amusement park. He's excited. He's not on the rollercoaster yet... he's not eating cotton candy yet... and he's not even in the park yet. He's not *there* yet, but he's *excited* about getting there. Why?

Because he has positive expectations. He's excited about the fun that he's *going* to have. He's emotionally filled with the anticipation of having a great time. That's how kids are.

The sad thing is that during the course of growing up, we lose this positive expectation mindset, and we become afraid to hope and dream. Basically, we become pessimistic, fear-ridden wimps. It's really quite sad. That's the bad news.

Here's the good news. This is nothing more than a conditioned mindset, which means we can recondition our mindsets and reprogram our brains to think differently.

Approaching Life From An Optimistic Point Of View

As we discussed earlier in this book, *positive thinking* only takes you so far. Positive thinking alone is worthless, however when used in combination with a solution-based, proactive plan, it can be very powerful.

Winston Churchill once said, "*The pessimist sees difficulty in every opportunity. The optimist sees opportunity in every difficulty.*" How true that is. Living your life with the expectation of great outcomes is a much healthier, more productive way to live. In fact, I don't know any successful people that don't expect to succeed in everything they do.

I truly expect to have massive success in every single, individual venture I touch. Obviously, that doesn't always happen, but I always expect it to. When a venture fails, I merely chalk it up to a learning exercise that I take into the next venture.

You see, there's a difference between expecting every individual venture to be successful (which I do) versus expecting 100 percent of every venture you touch to turn into gold (which is just unrealistic).

There is a distinct difference between these two expectations, and most people are unable to distinguish the two. I would be a fool to think that 100 percent of everything I touch will turn into gold. In fact, I would be setting myself up for perpetual let downs and a life of misery if those were my expectations. No one bats 1,000. You and I are going to strike out more than once along the way. That's a given.

Now, that being said, every time I step up to the plate on an individual basis, I am expecting success on each individual occasion. I don't start a project and say to myself, "*I think this is going to be a failure, but I'll try it anyway.*" If I thought that, I'd never succeed.

But I do say to myself, "*I know I won't succeed at 100 percent of everything I do... and I don't know exactly what's going to happen with this particular venture... but I do believe this one's going to be successful.*" If I didn't believe it would be successful, I wouldn't be doing it.

Basically, I go into every venture expecting a positive outcome, which is why several of my ventures have succeeded triumphantly. Again, I don't succeed 100 percent of the time, but I personally haven't found any benefit in approaching anything in life from a pessimistic point of view.

One of my surfing buddies that grew up in Indonesia surfing big waves has told me about some of the treacherous spots around the world he's surfed. Some of these surf spots have 20-foot waves that break in only a few feet of water, where the ocean's floor is made of coral and jagged rocks. He said something that is ironically analogous to this idea of having positive expectations in business. He told me that when surfing big waves, "*Hesitation breeds destruction.*"

Being an avid surfer myself, I know that you've got to drop into every wave *expecting* to make it without wiping out. That's why they call it *charging* big waves. You've got to *charge* that wave. You can't hesitantly ease into it. If you do, you'll surely wipe out, and in certain surf spots in Indonesia and Hawaii, you could get seriously injured, and in some cases, lose your life. The same thing goes in other competitive sports.

If a baseball player got up to bat while thinking to himself, *"Gee, I hope I don't strike out again,"* or if a basketball player, while preparing to shoot a free throw, said to himself, *"Geez, I hope I don't blow it like I did last time,"* these athletes would surely fail in their athletic careers.

But how many times have you had these very same thoughts about your career? Are you going into every deal haunted by fear? Are you almost *expecting* to fail? If so, you're setting yourself up to fail on so many levels. Stop it!

Sure your situation may be uncomfortable, and may even be adverse. I'm not implying that you should ignore the severity of your current adverse situation, but I *am* saying that it is absolutely imperative that after you size up the situation, that you must immediately work on developing a solution.

It may not be possible to be positive about the situation, but you can be positive about the potential *outcome* of your solution.

Overcoming Adversities

A lot of people think I'm immune to depression and heartache because I rarely obsess about adverse circumstances. Believe me, I've had plenty of adverse circumstances I had to overcome in my career, but after overcoming a few, my confidence grew. Over time, I built up a tolerance for adversity because I've been in so many adverse circumstances, and have triumphantly come out on top.

In a slightly masochistic way, I actually enjoy the challenge now. I absolutely revel in the idea of being dealt a crappy hand, and still coming out on top. I may not come out smelling like a rose every time, but I still come out on top, nonetheless.

Challenges create opportunities, and it is in these opportunities where *greatness* is born. So perhaps you're in an adverse circumstance right now. Maybe it seems like everyone is against you and things are going wrong all over the place. Maybe it feels like you can't seem to get a break. Hey, I've been there many times before, so I feel your pain.

My advice to you is to look at your circumstance as an opportunity to create a great story of triumph that you can tell other people about one day. Whenever I'm confronted with a major problem, I think to myself, *"When I rise out of this pit of hell, the angels will celebrate my success, which makes the victory that much sweeter."*

Some people call this a *testimony*, and a great testimony only comes as a result of being greatly tested.

Some of the most inspiring stories, or *testimonies* if you will, come from people being subjected to incredibly adverse circumstances, and overcoming their challenges. These testimonials give people hope and encouragement.

The greatest people I know have gone through the greatest challenges. Ironically, the lessons they've learned in the process have directly contributed to their ability to multiply their successes and create unbelievable wealth.

This is the value of being tested in life, whether it be in your business life, or in your personal life. It gives you the opportunity to create a powerful testimony that you can use in the future to help and encourage others. But that's not the main value of the testimony.

The main value of creating strong testimonies in your life is for you to cathartically relive them during times of great adversity in your own future. If you're going to be massively successful in business, you're going to go through many adversities throughout your career.

But if you've been faced with challenging times before, and you've been able to come out on top triumphantly, you will have built up a library of testimonies that you can reference during future adversities. You will draw massive self-encouragement and power by drawing from this library of experiences.

This is what builds your *character*. This is what makes you *strong*.

Character, Wisdom & Integrity

Men and women of great character have developed their character by going into battle when things were tough. That's the thing about character. You can't *buy* it, no matter how much money you have. You have to *develop* it.

That's why I say that you can be *rich*, and not necessarily be *successful*. In order to truly be *successful*, you have to have built *character* over time. Your character is what gives you the emotional strength to have positive expectations and approach life as an optimist.

Every time you find yourself in a less-than-favorable circumstance, you can say to yourself, "*This circumstance sucks, but*

I've been here before and I still came out on top. I'll do it again and prove everyone wrong."

If you've ever experienced such a triumph, you know that there is no sweeter victory, especially when you've been a victim of an unscrupulous person. If you're going to be in business, you're going to deal with a significant number of unscrupulous, unethical, malicious people. This is just par for the course. You're going to have to swim with the sharks, and if your character is strong, you can actually beat the sharks without sinking to their level.

Some of these *sharks* will look good on the surface, but you'll find that they are selfish liars with very little integrity. Many of them have *situational ethics*. They only adhere to their self-righteous ethics when it benefits them, and as soon as they find themselves in a situation where they have to choose between what is *right* versus what *benefits them* the greatest, the ethics they once claimed to have had go right out the window. This type of person lacks character, and eventually, they'll attempt to take advantage of you if you let them.

Have you ever been a victim of a shark, where after you got burned, you said to yourself, *"But this person seemed so nice. I thought they were my friend."* Once you become a victim of a shark's situational ethics, you'll realize they weren't so *nice* after all. You've got to watch people over a significant amount of time to see what their behavioral patterns are.

This doesn't mean that you should live your life jaded and not ever trust anyone. You need to expect positive outcomes and expect positive business relationships, but also know that not everyone is going to have true character and integrity. Just understand that a person's true character is something that will be revealed to you over time.

Ronald Reagan coined the phrase, *"Trust but verify."* What this means is that you have to enter each business relationship with spirit of trusting the other person. You can't have a healthy relationship if you're constantly consumed with paranoia, fearing that the other person is going to try to take advantage of you. However at the same time, it is wise to observe the person over a period of time to see if they're living up to your positive expectations. Here's what I've learned regarding ethics in business.

Wisdom is knowing the difference between right and wrong. Unfortunately, I've dealt with people that were *wise* in this sense of the word, meaning that they *knew* the difference between right and wrong… but the problem was that in spite of them *knowing* the difference, they *chose* to do the wrong thing and I ended up getting the short end of the stick. Just because a person is *wise*, doesn't necessarily mean that you should do business with them. Wisdom is an intellectual thing, and when evaluating character, you need to focus more on people's *actions* as opposed to their *intellect*.

Character is exemplified by a person *doing* what is right. A person's character is defined by what they *do*, not what they *say* they'd do. That's why I take what people say, regarding their values and ethics, with a grain of salt.

My goal is to observe them and analyze what they do. I've made the mistake in the past of listening to people proclaim how ethical they are. As a rule of thumb, whenever someone tells me that they'd never screw someone over, red flags go up. It's almost as if they feel the need to tell you how ethical they are, in order to mask their unethical actions. Their actions should speak for themselves, so just focus on their actions, not their words.

Another quote I love is from Ralph Waldo Emerson. He said, *"What you do speaks so loud, I cannot hear what you say."* This is ultimately how you must evaluate people's character, including your own. It is what you *do* that matters. Good intentions are nice, but as discussed earlier, my friend *intended to* and *decided* that he should go up and talk to the cute girl at the beach, but he didn't actually *do* it. So what was the result? Failure.

A lot of roads have been paved to hell on *good intentions*. I've dealt with people that lack true character, that actually had good intentions in the beginning, but their situational ethics led them to lie, cheat and steal. Sure they weren't felonies, but their actions were dishonest and unethical, and in my book, right is right, and wrong is wrong, regardless of the legality or severity of the crime committed.

Making Important Decisions

When I make decisions, both in business and in my personal life, I ask myself three key questions prior to making my ultimate decision.

1. Is it *ethical*?
2. Is it *legal*?
3. Is it in line with my personal *values*?

When it comes to the *Power Of Focus*, it's not just focusing on success and financial gain. There is great power in focusing on what is *right*. Let's talk for a moment about these three key questions I ask myself when making important decisions. It's somewhat of a decision matrix I put all of my important decisions through.

Question #1: Is It Ethical?

The first question I ask myself is, *"Is it ethical?"* The topic of *ethics* revolves around *fairness* and *sympathy* towards your fellow man. When contemplating an important decision, I'll ask myself, *"Is this fair to both parties involved?"*

I always want a *good deal*, but never at the expense of someone else getting a *bad deal*. Again, *ethics* addresses the fairness of the engagement or transaction. I don't believe you can feel good about yourself if you know an innocent person got the short end of the stick because you hogged the stick, even if it was contractually binding. That's called exploitation, and personally, I feel that it is wrong, simply because it was unfair to one of the parties.

I'm not talking about competing against an adversary in the marketplace, or battling against someone that is attempting to make your life miserable. I'm talking about dealing with an equally ethical person that has acted in a fair manner towards you.

Ethically, it is proper to treat them with compassion and respect, honoring their ethical behavior towards you. It's about creating a *win-win* relationship. So, if the decision results in a fair, win-win transaction, then most likely it is ethical, relative to my definition of the word *ethical*.

Question #2: Is It Legal?

The second question I ask myself in the decision making process is, *"Is it legal?"* This is pretty self-explanatory and logical, however necessary to discuss. Obviously it is wrong (and just plain stupid) to engage in illegal activity. However, it's important to make a distinction between *ethics* and *legality*.

Just because something is ethical (fair), doesn't necessarily mean that it's legal. Conversely, just because something is legal, doesn't necessarily mean that it's ethical. Let's discuss both scenarios.

Let's say you have a client that you have a long-standing relationship with. They trust you and you trust them. You've become friends. One day, your client/friend calls you and informs you that they're going on vacation and that they'll be out of the country for two weeks.

You have a document that you need them to sign before they leave on their vacation, but you both have busy schedules, and you're located two hours away from each other. Your client tells you, *"Oh, just sign my name for me. It's no big deal."*

You may tell yourself that the request is *fair* for both parties involved, because both parties agreed. Your client tells you that you'd be doing them a favor by making it more convenient for them. You tell yourself that you'd be sympathizing with their plight, thus if you sign their name for them, it would be *ethical*.

Regardless of how I personally feel about the ethics of this decision, it is *illegal*. It may be fair, but it's illegal. If it were me, I would decline the request. I know it may not seem like a big deal to you, but if you're going to build a business empire, careless, reckless decisions like this can destroy your empire in a split second.

Think of it like this. What happens if your relationship with your client goes south one day? What happens if your friendship comes to an end over a future disagreement? You have committed an illegal act: Forgery.

If that ex-client/ex-friend decides to become malicious and seeks revenge on you, all they have to do is pull up their file with your forged signature, and BAM! Lawsuit. You could lose everything. Sure, it was verbally agreed upon, and it seemed fair at the time, but it was an illegal act. That's why I'm so adamant about using this three-question decision-making matrix.

Again, just because something seems fair/ethical, if it's illegal, I won't do it, and I would advise you not to do it either.

Conversely, just because something is *legal*, doesn't necessarily mean that it is *ethical*. I remember hearing about a landlord that leased office space to a tenant, and in the lease agreement, there was a typographical error, requiring the tenant to pay through June, even though the tenant intended to occupy the space through July.

When July came, the tenant stayed through July, but did not pay rent for the month of July. The landlord brought this nonpayment to the tenant's attention, however the tenant pointed out that the lease agreement stated that they only had to pay through June. Obviously, this was a typographical error, but the tenant referred back to the lease agreement contract, and stated that they weren't obligated to pay for July's rent.

So, was the tenant legally obligated to pay? Contractually, no. However, this was an example of a person taking advantage of a typographical error, and in my opinion, wrong. Sure, it was *legal* to deny payment, but it was *unethical*, because it exploited an honest oversight. In my opinion, this was wrong. Legal, but wrong nonetheless.

Question #3: Is It In Line With My Personal Values?

The third question I always ask myself when making an important decision is, *"Is it in line with my personal values?"* As we discussed, *ethics* deal with the issue of *fairness*. *Legality* deals with what the law says. *Values* deal with how you prioritize what is most important to you. Here's an example of what I mean.

Would you rather cure all the sick children in the world, or feed the starving children of the world? If you could choose only one, which would you choose?

If you cure the sick, you're allowing millions of children to starve to death. If you feed the starving children, you'd be allowing millions of sick children to die.

When I asked this question to a group of people in one of my seminars last night, it was a split house. About half of the people said they'd rather let the sick kids die. The other half said they'd rather let kids starve to death. Of course I'm being a bit facetious here about some very serious topics, but you see the dilemma.

When it comes to *ethics* and *legality*, it's relatively black and white. Some people may debate the *fairness* of a transaction, but for the most part, we all know what is truly *fair* when it comes to both parties in a transaction having a mutual and equal benefit. When it comes to *legality*, it's even simpler. It's either legal or it's illegal.

When it comes to *values* however, it's not quite as simple. We all have different value systems. Some of them are based on our spiritual or religious beliefs. Some of them are based on our cultural beliefs. Some of them are based on how we were raised.

In business, you need to have clarity when it comes to what you believe in. You need to know what is most important to you and your company culture. You see, what we're really talking about here is having a clearly defined process of making important decisions.

If you have a *Decision Making Matrix* that you run every important decision through, it's much easier to have confidence in your ability to make wise decisions. Your decisions should always reflect your ultimate goal of where you want to be in the future.

Always Moving Forward

In my own business life, I have a little acronym that I live by: AMF, which stands for *Always Moving Forward*. If a decision doesn't allow me to move forward and doesn't propel me closer to my ultimate goal, then it's the *wrong* decision. So many times, people fight battles that aren't worth fighting, meaning that even if they win the battle, the victory isn't significant enough to make a major impact on their business. If I'm going to fight a battle, winning the battle must:

1. Make me a lot of money, or
2. Save me a lot of money, or
3. Make me substantially more powerful within my industry.

If fighting a battle doesn't significantly accomplish one of these three things, typically it's not a battle worth fighting. However, if fighting that battle *does* accomplish one or more of these three things, and the outcome is significant, then I'll put on my full suit of armor, pick up my sword, and engage in battle, perhaps even turning it into a full-scale war. Sometimes you have to *mop up* the spilled milk in order to move forward.

So when is it unwise to engage in legal battle? The most unworthy reason to fight a battle is *ego gratification*. Fighting insignificant battles doesn't move you forward, and as an entrepreneur, you need to always be moving forward towards your ultimate goal. Often times you're better off focusing on moving forward and cutting your losses, as opposed to getting sucked into an insignificant battle.

Here's a great illustration of what I'm talking about. Think about your physical anatomy. Your eyes are facing forward so you can see what's in front of you, as opposed to focusing on your past. Your mouth is facing forward so you can talk to people in front of you, solidifying new business deals, instead of talking to the idiots from your past.

Your hands are built facing forward so you can handle things in front of you that matter most, instead of trying to handle failures from the past. Virtually every part of your anatomy is facing forward, except for one body part. *Your butt.* And what comes out of your butt? *Crap.*

That's because you're supposed to leave the *crap* behind you. You're supposed to move forward and leave the negative waste behind you, and preferably flush it down the toilet so you don't have to look at it or smell it any longer. Forget about it, and AMF. *Always Move Forward.*

As my attorney counseled me years ago regarding the small legal battle I wanted to fight, he helped me evaluate the monetary cost of fighting the battle (legal fees) versus the amount of money I would recoup if I won the battle.

In this particular case, even if I won, I would have been awarded less money than my legal fees would have cost me. And so he convinced me that going on a Hawaiian vacation and buying myself a *Cartier* wristwatch would cost me less than what it would cost me to fight the battle.

I chose *Hawaii* and *Cartier* over my *ego*, and I assure you, my decision was a much better investment of my money, time and emotions.

Again, in this specific case, a legal victory:

1. Would not have made me any money,
2. Would not have saved me any money, and
3. Would not have made me substantially more powerful in my industry.

In addition to evaluating the potential gains of pursuing a legal battle, it is also wise to evaluate the potential losses in the event of a legal defeat. You've got to ask yourself if you're in a position to weather a loss, both from an immediate financial perspective, as well as a long-term perspective. Remember, there is always the danger of a negative ripple effect regarding a legal defeat, and these ripples always have the potential to turn into tidal waves, destroying your empire.

The concept of *Always Moving Forward* is really what the *Power Of Focus* is all about. It's about having a mindset that makes calculated, objectively evaluated, solution-based decisions.

You may be reading this and wondering to yourself, *"When IS the right time to fight a legal battle?"*

Although there are times to *live to fight another day*, there are also times to fight today and bury your adversary. Obviously, if winning a legal battle will make or save you a significant amount of money, it's probably worth fighting.

But sometimes, it's also worth fighting if it will make you significantly more powerful within your industry. Sometimes, you need to send a message out to let everyone know that you're the wrong guy to mess with.

If you make a strategic decision to do so, it must be well thought out. It cannot be simply to satisfy your ego. The emotional temptation to be *right* is a strong temptation, and you need to be careful not to let your emotions guide your decision-making processes, especially when it comes to legal battles, but you also need to let people in your industry know that you're not a pushover either.

I've engaged in legal battles that I knew would cost me more money than gain me money. In other words, I knew ahead of time that my legal fees would be more than the money I would recoup if I won (and I knew I would win in court).

But the reason I went ahead into battle was to send a message that I knew would spread like wildfire throughout my industry, and that message was, *"Don't mess with Darren. He will bury you if you cross him."*

I have a team of very talented and powerful attorneys that I consult with regularly, and when we collectively feel like burying someone that has done me wrong, we bury them, and we let everyone know we buried them.

One of my good friends is a very talented corporate attorney named Alain Bonavida, based in Beverly Hills. Alain's claim to fame was winning a $370 million court settlement against a VERY well known, international clothing company.

Trust me when I say that Alain is the wrong attorney to go up against. Whenever I tell people about Alain, they realize that due to my relationship with him, I am definitely the wrong guy to f*** with in a legal battle.

And so when it comes to legal battles, or any type of business battle, you must always evaluate whether or not it is a good strategic decision, both short-term as well as long-term.

It is always better to be *smart* and *win* the war (even if it means that you elect to lose a few battles along the way), than it is to be *right* – win every insignificant battle – and *lose* the war.

The Lemonade Business

If you want to be successful in business, and in life, you have to get into the lemonade business. I'm not talking about literally opening up a lemonade stand on the street corner.

What I'm talking about is turning lemons (sour situations and circumstances) into lemonade (cool, sweet, refreshing outcomes). And if you want to become wealthy, you've got to build a *Lemonade Manufacturing Facility.*

The bigger and more successful you become, you will encounter more and more *lemons*. These lemons can come in the form of people, and they can also come in the form of circumstances.

God knows, I've been dealt lemon orchards over the course of my career, but let me tell you, I've made some really kick-ass lemonade in the process.

So when it comes to the power of focus, do your best to focus your efforts on making wise, solution-based decisions, and go into every business deal with positive expectations. And as our buddy Winston Churchill said, there's no benefit to being a pessimist.

Chapter Four:
Asking The Right Questions

"The answers your subconscious mind comes up with are always based on the context of the questions you ask yourself."

-Darren Sugiyama

The Subconscious Mind

The power of the subconscious mind is a resource that most people don't truly understand. Back in college, we talked about human behavior in my Sociology classes and my Psychology classes.

In Sociology, we studied the affect that a person's environment has on their thought processes, value systems, and behavior. In Psychology, we studied genetic influences, physical and chemical influences, and external stimuli influences on human behavior. It was all very scientific, based on case studies and research.

Pavlov's dog is the classic stimulus-expectation study, in which a dog was kept behind a small door. The door was intermittently opened, and food was given to the dog. Soon thereafter, a bell was introduced into the equation. The bell rang as the door was opened, and food was concurrently given to the dog.

Over time, the dog linked the external stimulus of the ringing bell to the end result of being given food. The dog became conditioned to expect food when prompted by the ringing bell. Whenever the scientist rang the bell, the dog would eagerly anticipate being given food, salivating, even when on some occasions, no food was given.

The dog would hear the bell ringing, and consciously say to himself, *"Hey, that's the same bell that the scientist rang the last time he gave me food. I think he's going to give me food again right now. Let me go see."* That was the dog's inner dialogue, and thus the dog would have an emotional reaction congruent with his inner dialogue.

We, as human beings, are very similar in this respect. We have strong emotional reactions to our inner dialogue, which is why it's so important to have the proper, empowering inner dialogue. It all starts with asking yourself the right questions.

Asking Yourself The Right Questions

With every inner dialogue you have with yourself, there is an ongoing exchange of questions and answers. You will ask yourself a question, and then you'll come up with an answer.

That's why it's so important to ask yourself the right questions. If you ask yourself the wrong questions, you'll give yourself disempowering, destructive answers. Here are some examples of bad questions.

If you ask yourself, *"How come I'm not making more money?"* your brain will automatically attempt to come up with an answer based on the context of your question.

This particular question is asking your brain to make a list of all the reasons why you're failing, thus you are programming your subconscious mind to focus on the problem as opposed to the solution. In the context of this question, *"How come I'm not making more money?"* your brain will come up with answers like:

1. Because you're a loser.
2. Because you suck at this business.
3. Because people don't want your product or service.
4. Because the economy is down.
5. Because God hates you.

Have you ever had this type of self-deprecating, self-loathing inner dialogue? You see, it all started because you asked yourself a problem-centric question instead of a solution-centric question. Your subconscious mind will involuntarily come up with an answer in the specific context in which you ask a question.

So if you ask yourself, *"How come I'm not making more money?"* your subconscious mind will come up with problems and excuses to validate why you're failing.

Instead, change the context of the question to be solution-centric by asking yourself, *"What can I do to start making more money?"*

Your subconscious mind will involuntarily come up with answers that are solution-based due to the context of your question. Some of the answers might include:

1. I can increase my prospecting call volume.

2. I can design an effective Goal Setting Program that focuses on activity.

3. I can attempt to find a mentor that can give me good, qualified advice.

4. I can change my attitude about my circumstance.

5. I can watch less TV and work more hours.

All of these answers are solution-centric. Your brain will automatically come up with these types of answers – solution-centric answers – if you ask solution-centric questions.

These two questions are so similar, but the way they are framed and constructed are from two entirely opposite perspectives, thus the answers your subconscious brain gives you are from two entirely opposite perspectives.

Here are some other *bad questions* to ask yourself that result in your brain coming up with *bad answers*, coupled with *better questions* to ask yourself that result in your brain generating *better answers*:

Bad Question: "Why does bad stuff always happen to me?"
Bad Answer: "Because I'm destined to have bad luck."

Better Question: "What can I do to change my luck?"
Better Answer: "I can change my daily routine."

Bad Question: "Why don't people appreciate me more?"
Bad Answer: "Because nobody likes me."

Better Question: "What can I do to make people appreciate me more?"
Better Answer: "I can ask them how I can make their job easier."

Bad Question: "How come I'm not as successful as he is?"
Bad Answer: "Because he's luckier and better than I am."

Better Question: "What is he doing to make him so successful?"
Better Answer: "He uses Darren Sugiyama's techniques, and so can I."

Here are some bad questions that I used to ask myself, coupled with better questions that I ask myself now:

Bad Question: "How could they screw me over like that?"
Better Question: "What can I do in the future to indentify character flaws in people in the early stages of a relationship?"

Bad Question: "How could my employee screw that up so bad?"
Better Question: "Can I develop a systematic process that makes it less likely for an employee to make a mistake in this area?"

Bad Question: "Why does this person talk to me disrespectfully?"
Better Question: "What can I do or say to make this person want to help me in the future? How can I win them over?"

Children And Positive Expectations

Dogs are kind of like children in the respect that they both have positive expectations. It's kind of scary to think that as adults, we once had positive expectations about everything in life when we were children, but somewhere along the way, we were conditioned to become pessimists and see problems in every opportunity, instead of opportunities in every problem.

We have been brainwashed into fearing (and almost expecting) negative outcomes, thus the questions we ask ourselves in our inner dialogue generate negative, problem-centric answers.

The good news is that we can recondition our mindsets. We can consciously change the questions we ask ourselves and become solution-centric optimists again.

Back To Pavlov's Dog

We know that an external stimulus can elicit an emotional expectation, whether it's the ringing of a bell, or a question asked in an inner dialogue. These are emotional reactions, and as discussed, emotional reactions can either be empowering or disempowering. If we can control our external stimuli by proactively asking the right questions, we can virtually manipulate our emotional reaction with a premeditated effort.

That's where most people end the explanation of Pavlov's dog, which is a shame because the study is much more interesting than the mere conditioning of the dog's expectation based on a ringing bell.

The fascinating part of this study is that the scientist was able to measure the dog's level of saliva secretion when stimulated by the sound of the ringing bell.

He found that when the bell rang, the dog's level of saliva excretion involuntarily increased. Not only did the dog anticipate receiving food upon hearing the ringing bell, which was an emotional response, but the dog also responded with an involuntary, physical reaction.

Dogs are not able to voluntarily control their level of saliva secretion. It is an involuntary reaction. This proved that biochemically, the dog changed based on a simple external stimulus.

The same concept applies to human beings. Not only are our emotions triggered by stimuli, but our biochemical make up can be triggered and altered as well. Adrenaline and endorphins start firing when we're stimulated by empowering messages, and we become physically stronger and more powerful. We physically *feel* better, and generally speaking, when we physically *feel* better, we tend to *perform* better.

In athletics, in social environments, and in business, when we feel stronger and more confident, we tend to perform better. Adrenaline and endorphin secretion is an involuntary physical reaction to external stimuli, similar to Pavlov's dog's saliva secretion, leading one to believe that involuntary chemical reactions cannot be controlled.

On the surface, that would be true. You cannot voluntarily control an involuntary physical reaction. However you *can* control the stimuli that triggers the involuntary reaction. In other words, you couldn't teach a dog to secrete more saliva on command, but you could control when you rang the bell, which ultimately means that you can control when the dog salivates.

If you take this concept and apply it to human beings, all you need to do is identify what stimuli triggers the involuntary biochemical reaction within human beings. If you can capture the trigger, you can virtually induce the biochemical reaction on cue.

Does This Mean You Can Control Your Emotions?

Regarding controlling your emotions, I'll speak for myself on this topic. If I'm sad, I'm sad. There isn't a damn thing I can do to not be sad. It's how I feel.

Last year, I lost my Uncle Rich to lung disease. I was very close to my Uncle Rich, and when he passed, I was deeply saddened. If some motivational speaker or therapist came along and told me I could overcome my sadness, I would be offended at such an insensitive claim. They would be devaluing my feelings and robbing me of my need to mourn.

If I've been treated unjustly, I'll get angry. I have a right to be angry. It doesn't mean that I'm entitled to go beat people up or destroy someone's property.

But the emotion of anger is not something that should be controlled. Suppressing your emotions is actually a very unhealthy thing to do. That's where resentment starts, and it can manifest itself into heart attacks and cancer.

So as far as I'm concerned, you cannot control your emotions. You cannot control how you emotionally *feel*. However, you can control what you *do* about how you feel. This is a real game changer.

When it comes to matters of the heart including the loss of a loved one, a romance gone bad, or any type of deteriorating relationship, it can be very difficult, emotionally. *Time* is generally required to heal these types of battle wounds.

But when it comes to performing in business, we're usually dealing with a different set of emotions. Fear and insecurity are generally the two main emotions we need to overcome to perform well in business.

These emotions are both routed in how you feel about yourself and your abilities, and these emotions can both turn on a dime on a day-to-day basis. Actually, they can change on a second-by-second basis, depending on what's going on in your business day.

Logic would tell you that if your emotions can change on a dime for the worse, then they should also be able to change on a dime for the better. We're talking about confidence versus feelings of self-doubt. We're talking about feeling strong versus feeling weak. We're talking about feeling empowered versus feeling vulnerable. Think about this for a moment.

Have you ever heard a song on the radio that reminds you of an empowering time in your life? Maybe it reminds you of winning the championship game, or your wedding day, or when your son or daughter was born, or your favorite movie. You hear that song, and you get pumped up.

Every time I hear the song *Eye Of The Tiger* or the theme song from the movie *Rocky*, I get pumped up. I also remember watching the movie *Wall Street*. When Bud Fox finally *made it,* he bought a million dollar penthouse and he looked out the window and smiled as the song *This Must Be The Place* by *The Talking Heads* played.

Every time I hear that song, it reminds me of how hard I had to work to get where I am today, and it makes me feel good. On the flip side, there are also songs that remind me of disempowering times in my life, including break ups, personal failures, and embarrassing moments. I refuse to listen to them, because these songs take me right back to the emotional state I was in back then.

Music can have an incredibly strong impact on our emotions, usually because certain songs remind us of certain events in our lives. Music has the power to trigger certain emotions, just like the sound of the bell ringing for Pavlov's dog. As we discussed, this type of trigger is so strong that the sound of the bell ringing triggered the involuntary reaction of an increase in saliva secretion.

Have you ever heard a song that reminded you of a heartbreaking period in your life, and you found yourself experiencing an increase in tear duct secretion? We all have. This involuntary reaction was triggered by external stimuli, in this case, a song. Why am I talking about this in such great depth?

The reason is that I have found the secret to programming my emotional reactions, which allow me to put myself in an emotional state conducive to peak performance, and I can do it on command. It's not mystical or any kind of weird voodoo stuff. Athletes do this all the time.

Back in college, I played baseball at Loyola Marymount University. As I walked from the dugout up the plate, I would play a song in my head that put me in the most confident, most testosterone filled, cockiest mindset possible.

The song was called *I Ain't No Joke* by a rap group called *Eric B. & Rakim*. Perhaps you're not a fan of rap music, but don't let this distract you from the message here. For you, maybe your pump-me-up song is the Rocky theme song… or a Led Zepplin song… or a song by Guns-N-Roses.

The point is, athletes use music as external stimuli to put themselves in an emotional state (and a biochemical state) conducive to peak performance.

Even to this day, I still do the same thing when I'm surfing, just prior to taking off on a big wave. I do it just before a big business meeting. I do it whenever I need to put myself in a powerful state of mind.

If I'm driving to a big meeting, I'll play that song as I pull up to my meeting location. But if I find myself unable to actually play the song out loud, I'll play it in my head silently.

Music can be a powerful trigger for you. You can also create your own physical triggers, as long as you *link* or *associate* the trigger to a past experience that empowers you.

Several years ago, I used to be in the fashion industry. Stevie, my business partner at that time, was a successful guy who started his career in the fashion business. At that time, he was living in *Bel Air* (the richest neighborhood in Beverly Hills) in a home that was previously owned by Belinda Carlisle (former lead singer of *The Go-Go's*, a pop band from the 1980's). Needless to say, Stevie did well financially.

I noticed that whenever he was in a sales appointment and he was going in for the close, he started tapping his right foot to the rhythm of his speech pattern. I'd be on the other side of the office, and as soon as I heard his Prada sneakers making that *whap, whap, whap* sound on the office floor, I knew he was going in for the close. That was his trigger. Pavlov's dog had a *bell*. Stevie had his *Pradas*.

Creating Your Own Trigger

In most cases, you probably won't have the luxury of blasting your favorite song every time you need to get pumped up, especially in a professional office environment. That being the case, you need to do what Stevie did and go out and buy a pair of $495 Prada sneakers. Just kidding. In all seriousness, you can create your own trigger.

The trigger that I currently use is snapping my fingers. When I'm talking and I snap my fingers, it literally *snaps* me into a certain persona.

I've had my share of successes in the past, and I literally programmed myself to link the action of snapping my fingers to the feeling I had when I was greatly empowered.

When I snap my fingers, it reminds me of how I felt during a past success. I start walking differently, talking differently, carrying myself differently, and my mindset instantaneously switches over into *game time* mode. It puts me into my *I Ain't No Joke* mode. This is something that everyone can do, including you.

It's a mild form of hypnosis. Just pull up a song that gets you pumped up. Find one that reminds you of a time in your life where you felt unstoppable. Crank it up at high volume and walk around the room in your cockiest swagger. Put yourself back in that mode that you were in when you felt like you could conquer the world. Remember exactly how you felt during that successful experience in your past. Cathartically relive that experience.

While you're in this mode, create your trigger. For me, it's snapping my fingers. For Stevie, it was tapping his foot.

Make sure you don't do something distracting that would draw odd attention to yourself in a business meeting. Pumping your fist in the air while yelling *Whoo-Hoo-Hoo-Hoo!* is probably inappropriate in most business environments, and the people you're meeting with will probably think you're a lunatic. Find something subtle, yet distinguishable to you.

It could be a cracking of the knuckles, or a single clapping of the hands, or a double tap on the desktop. I really doesn't matter what your trigger is, as long as it makes your revert back to a specific past success. You need to find your *bell*, just like Pavlov's dog had.

Once you find it, ring it, and like Pavlov's dog, you'll have positive expectations. And if you ring it often enough, instead of Pavlov's dog saliva secretion increasing, your prospect will be the one drooling at the mouth, dying to do business with you.

Chapter Five:
Building Bullet-Proof Confidence

"The difference between confidence and bravado is belief."
-Darren Sugiyama

Confidence & Success

There are so many theories on building confidence. I'll often ask people, *"What do you think comes first, confidence or success?"* Usually over 90 percent of the people answer, *"Confidence."* This answer seems logical on the surface. Common knowledge would tell you that you need to be confident in order to be successful. However, I disagree.

Think back to the first date you ever went on. Were you 100 percent confident? Of course not. You were probably very nervous and insecure. I certainly was. But consider this.

What was the end result? Did anyone die or get seriously injured? Were there any major lawsuits filed? Did the date end with you hating each other's guts? In most cases, the answer would be no (hopefully). So by definition, assuming you both had a good time, the date was *successful*, even though you weren't 100 percent *confident*.

After a string of consecutive successes, your confidence probably started to increase. This newfound confidence probably made it easier for you to succeed in the dating world as time went on, and perhaps you even reached a level of success where someone actually agreed to spend the rest of their life with you. Imagine that.

In business, the more confident you become, the more successful you'll become, however confidence is not required in the beginning. You can achieve success without being 100 percent confident.

You may not have unshakable, bullet-proof confidence today, but that doesn't preclude you from achieving success today, and it doesn't preclude you from one day building your confidence up to the point where it is bullet-proof.

The question is, *"How do you become confident?"*

This is what everyone wants. Can you imagine how much more powerful you would be in business (and in life in general) if you had unshakable confidence?

People see me today and say, *"Darren, I wish I could be as confident as you are."* My response shocks them, because I always say, *"Well, you can."*

This usually puzzles them because success and confidence takes on the *chicken and the egg* debate. Which comes first?

You need an *egg* in order to hatch a chicken, but you need a chicken to lay the egg in the first place. You need confidence in order to be successful, but you need to be successful in order to build confidence.

My answer to the second statement is that you do not need confidence in order to be successful. You need *bravado*.

What Is Confidence?

Confidence is a feeling. It's how you *feel* about yourself. Bravado is an *action*. It's how you act. You can act as if you're confident, and if you do a good enough job at it, no one will know the difference. This is called *bravado*. Bravado is acting like you feel confident, in spite of your inner lack of confidence.

When you see someone that looks incredibly confident, what exactly are you witnessing that would make you believe that they are indeed confident? If you break it down to the mannerisms and visual qualities of a successful, confident person, you'd find a handful of relatively simple things. Here's a list of indicators that a person is successful and confident:

1. The way they walk.
2. Their overall posture when standing or sitting.
3. The way they are dressed.
4. The way they are groomed.
5. Their tone of voice.
6. The style in which they communicate.
7. Their facial expressions.
8. The look in their eyes.
9. The attitude they exude.
10. Their expectations of the way other people treat them.

These are all *actions*, not *feelings*. Other people cannot see how you *feel*. They can only see how you *act*. I'm sure there are a few other actions that would imply that a person is confident, but these tend to be the major ones. If you look at these qualities, the question is, *"Can they be copied?"* and more specifically, *"Could you copy them?"*

If you can copy these things, you will have bravado, and initially, this is all you really need.

Do What Movies Stars Do

Essentially, when movie stars take on a role, they study how the specific character they are portraying talks, walks, acts, etc. They're merely copying the way that their character would act in real life.

Have you ever seen any of the popular sales movies like *Wall Street*, *The Boiler Room*, or *Glengarry Glen Ross*?

Think about *Gordon Gecko* from *Wall Street*.

Think about the stock broker characters that *Vin Diesel* and *Ben Affleck* played in *The Boiler Room*.

Think about *Alec Baldwin's* rich real estate character in *Glengarry Glen Ross*.

They were beyond confident. But consider this. They weren't confident, super-salesmen. They were nothing more than actors playing a role. They just *acted* confident.

They memorized scripts, which made them sound confident. They walked a certain way, talked a certain way, dressed a certain way, and guess what?

You bought into it.

For the duration of the movie, you actually believed that these actors were the characters they portrayed.

Now, I'm not suggesting you start taking acting classes, but I am suggesting that you study the way confident people walk, talk, look and act… and copy them. You may not *feel* confident inside, but on the outside, you'll *look* confident and successful.

If this is what other people see and experience as they're sizing you up, they have nothing else to base their opinion on. As a result, they will assume you are confident and successful, and they will treat you as such.

When people start responding and reacting to you in this manner, guess what happens? They will defer to you as the expert, and over time, you'll gain more and more clients because they're deferring to you as the expert.

The more clients you attain, the more successful you become, and somewhere along the way, you'll wake up one day, and BAM! You'll be successful.

You'll look at your results (and your bank account) and you'll become confident because you now have the track record to warrant feelings of confidence.

So which really came first, success or confidence?

I would argue that your ability to *act* as if you were confident (even though you didn't necessarily feel confident inside) led you to producing successful results. And once you've consistently produced successful results over time, you'll truly be confident.

So under this assumption, success came long before confidence. Your successes may have come in small, gradual, bite-sized pieces, but they came before you actually felt confident.

After you've racked up enough successes under your belt, you'll start feeling more confident inside, and eventually, you'll become confident. You now have bullet-proof confidence. You now have *true confidence*.

True Confidence

We talked about manufacturing *bravado*, which is step one in building bullet-proof confidence. Now, let's talk about fortifying true confidence. When it comes to confidence, which is nothing more than believing in yourself, you've got to be aware of the pitfalls we as human beings can fall into, causing us to lose our confidence.

Often times, we'll listen to other people's opinions instead of our own. This can be dangerous. True confidence, which resides in our subconscious mind, is based on two things:

1. Self-Esteem.
2. Self-Concept.

Self-esteem is defined as how we feel about ourselves. *Self-concept* is defined as how we feel about how other people view us. A person can have high self-esteem, but suffer from a low self-concept.

For example, I was a late bloomer in the dating world. I was very insecure as a kid. I had a decent level of self-esteem, meaning I thought I was a pretty cool kid, and I thought I was moderately handsome. The problem was that I was very unsure of how girls viewed me. I had a very low *self-concept*.

Growing up as an Asian kid in a social circle that was predominantly non-Asian, I didn't know if non-Asian girls would find me attractive. There were no Asian male teen heart-throb icons in Hollywood. Basically, there were no positive Asian male sex symbols to emulate, so I felt very insecure about my place in the dating world and how these non-Asian girls would view me.

I found out later on in life that several girls that I had crushes on in the 7th grade had mutual crushes on me too, but because my self-concept was so low at the time, I couldn't see it.

Perhaps most 7th graders go through similar tormented adolescent lives, worrying about how the opposite sex views them. For most people, this low self-concept wears off after they've had enough positive feedback and boyfriend/girlfriend experiences.

Personally, once my self-concept got stronger in this area, I became incredibly confident in dealing with girls.

Okay, the truth is, I became downright cocky.

But it didn't happen until I was in college. As I said, I was a late bloomer in this area, and it was due to having a low self-concept. The key, whether in dating or in business, is to have both a high self-esteem and a high self-concept.

Many people suffer in both areas. One option to overcome this problem is to spend thousands of dollars talking to a psychologist or a therapist. There are several different psychological therapeutic philosophies available to you.

Gestalt therapy is a counseling technique in which you take out your frustrations on an inanimate object, projecting your frustrations about your overbearing father onto a table for example. You can yell, kick and scream at the table, telling it all the things you wanted to tell your overbearing, abusive father, but in my opinion, the problem is that it doesn't give you any concrete solutions.

Hey, getting some things off your chest is great, but it isn't going to change your situation. If we're trying to increase your sales, revenue, and ultimately your wealth, yelling at a table isn't going to do it.

Another popular therapy is the *Freudian* technique. In this therapy, you are taught to talk things out, getting things off your chest. The theory is that in hearing yourself say what's bothering you, you'll naturally come to the solution on your own.

Personally, this sounds like nothing more than a *bitching-and-moaning* session to me. In my experience, complaining to someone about your problems rarely does anything to solve the problem.

I used to keep a diary when I first started my career. Every night, I'd write about what happened that day and how I felt about my life and where I was in my career. It was depressing. All it did was reinforce that my both my life and my business was struggling, so I decided to stop writing in a diary.

When I realized the adverse affect of the negative programming I was doing on myself by continuously writing about how depressed and frustrated I was, I wrote one final diary entry… ripped out that one page… and threw away the rest of the diary. Here's what that final page said:

"Today is a new day. Starting right now, I am unstoppable. My whole life has led me to this point and I am about to f***ing blow up. No more living the prevent defense way. Everything from this moment on is going to turn to gold. AMF. Always Moving Forward." – *July 11, 2001*

I realized that writing in a journal was making me dwell on my feelings, which at that time, was not productive. I felt the need to rid myself of all doubt, self-pity and self-loathing.

I'm not devaluing the process of acknowledging and processing your negative past in an attempt to come to terms with your past. I think it's important to process some of your negative past experiences, as long as you don't dwell on your past, allowing it to hold you back from moving forward. This processing of past negative experiences is called *catharsis*.

The Value Of Catharsis

Catharsis is the therapeutic process of emotionally cleansing a negative past experience by reliving it and finding resolve in it. The definition of catharsis is *"the elimination of a psychological problem by bringing it to consciousness and allowing its expression."*

This can be a very healthy thing to do, emotionally. It identifies things that may be buried in your subconscious and brings them to the surface. It allows you to acknowledge that which has haunted you. It brings about *awareness*.

However, the problem with this type of cathartic experience is that *awareness* is only step one. Step one, alone, is not enough. That's why I don't believe in diaries and journals. All they do is make you focus on the negative. They make you focus on your troubled past and the immediate, as opposed to focusing on your glorious future.

If you don't stay focused on your glorious future, the past and the immediate become overwhelming negative, and you'll allow yourself to believe the lie that the immediate is permanent.

In business, the immediate, no matter how adverse, is *temporary* if you're focused on *Always Moving Forward*.

But understand this. In order to move forward in business (and in life), sometimes you have to do things – extreme things – to get extreme results. Sometimes, you have to burn bridges.

Burning Bridges

What are bridges? A *bridge* is basically a structure that provides a pathway over an obstacle, giving you easier access to a particular destination. In the context of burning bridges, these bridges that need to be burned are bridges that provide a pathway backwards, back to your old comfort zone.

Most people are afraid to burn their bridges to the past because they either find comfort in knowing they *could* go back, or they think they'll *have* to go back. They want to leave their options open, which is basically a recipe for failure. If going back is an option, you'll most likely fail because succeeding is not the only option.

If succeeding is the only option, you'll do whatever you have to in order to succeed because you have no back up plan. A back up plan says, *"I plan on failing, so I need something to fall back on when I fail."*

I hate back up plans. You've got to be a *balls-to-the-walls* type of player in order to succeed at a high level. I remember back when I started my career in business, I had come out of a career in education. I have a Master's Degree in Multi-cultural Education, and I was formerly a teacher in the public school system.

I also had *tenure*, which basically means that I'd been in the system long enough to where I could not legally be fired. I had ultimate job security. I also had ultimate low pay. Realizing I was going to be another broke teacher if I didn't change my career path, I took a straight-commission sales position.

To make ends meet in the beginning, I was a substitute teacher. Substitute teachers are on-call, so sometimes I'd get a call the night before, requesting to show up and substitute teach for a particular school. I had the choice, on a case-by-case basis, to accept or decline the offer.

It was a pretty good gig for me at the time because if I needed money, I'd accept the assignment. If I had a sales appointment lined up that day, I'd just decline the assignment. After a while, my sales career started to pick up. I wasn't making a lot of money, but my sales appointment schedule started to get pretty booked up. I started declining the majority of substitute teaching engagements, and finally, I got a call from the School District. They wanted to know why I had declined every substitute teaching request for the last full month.

I told them, *"I've decided to not be a teacher any longer. I've switched careers."*

She replied, *"Oh, okay. We'll just need you to come down to the District Office and sign a form requesting a leave of absence."*

I told them, *"Umm, I don't think you heard me. I've decided NOT to teach anymore."* The lady got rather indignant on me.

She said in a perturbed voice, *"Well if you don't come down here and sign a request form, we'll be forced to TERMINATE you."*

I said, *"Perfect. Terminate me."*

She replied, *"Sir, I don't think you understand. If you get terminated, you won't be able to come back into our system very easily."*

I said, *"Maam, I don't think YOU understand. I'm not going to be a teacher, EVER again. Terminate me."*

A few weeks later, I received a letter in the mail from the District Office. The letter read:

August 23, 1999

Dear Mr. Sugiyama,

This is to advise you that your assignment as a substitute teacher has been terminated effective close of work June 30, 1999, as discussed. This decision was made pursuant to your not meeting Long Beach Unified School District Professional Standards.

Sincerely,

Director Of Human Resources

(Name of HR Director removed for privacy purposes)

I took that letter and taped it to my refrigerator door. I wanted to remind myself everyday that going back was not an option. I wanted to make sure that even if I wanted to go back, that I couldn't. This was a bridge that I felt needed to be burned. In case you were wondering, yes, I still have that letter from the Long Beach Unified School District.

Today, that letter is framed and hangs on a wall in my office. Everyday, I look at that letter and it reminds me that I had the guts to burn that bridge.

Next to that letter on my wall is a framed quote… a quote that I came up with myself. Sure, I know it seems rather self-indulgent to quote yourself, but it's such a great quote, I had to do it. It says, *"I have found that the greatest pleasure in life is burning bridges that lead to a life of mediocrity, and accomplishing things that other people said you could not do."*

You see, when you put yourself in a do-or-die situation, it forces you be obsessed with success. You literally have no other options because you burned all of those bridges, and thus, it's do-or-die, baby.

Not only does it eliminate the option to wuss out, but it also subconsciously plants the seed in your mind that you have guts.

Most people are too chicken to jump in with both feet and totally commit, which is why most people fail. Whenever someone fails in a business venture, I always want to ask them the question,

> *"If you look back to when you first started, can you honestly say that you gave it 100 percent of your effort? Can you honestly say that you did 100 percent of what you were supposed to do, 100 percent of the time, with 100 percent of your best effort?"*

Obviously, the answer is *no*, 100 percent of the time. In order to achieve greatness, you've got to give up something in the short term, which includes back up plans.

Back up plans create the bridge back to mediocrity, and the temptation to use them is too great for most people to ignore. Burn these bridges, and put yourself in a do-or-die situation where there is no compromise.

Whenever I look at that letter from the School District hanging on my wall, it puts a huge smile on my face, because it reminds me of the guts it took to burn that bridge.

By the way, my Master's Degree in Education is not framed, nor is it on display in my office. It's buried in a file cabinet somewhere in my closet.

Obsession And Balance

Being successful in business, athletics, and life in general, is about *obsession*. You have to be obsessed, at least temporarily, to get the ball moving in the right direction.

That's why whenever I hear someone say in the beginning stages of their career that they want to have a *balanced life*, I always know that they're going to fail miserably.

Your ultimate goal, once you've built the foundation of your career and you're established in business, can be about so-called *balance*, but in the beginning stages, you've got to live an unbalanced life. You've got to be obsessed with success. You've got to be obsessed with your business.

Now, if you had to live this obsessed all-work, no-play lifestyle for the rest of your life, I would say that it's probably not worth it. But anyone that's successful in life goes through seasons of unbalance.

Think about an Olympic athlete. Do you think they live a *balanced life* during the year prior to the Olympic Games? Of course not. They're in training. They're obsessed with being the best. They're obsessed with being a champion. They're obsessed with getting a Gold Medal.

Their families understand this. Their families understand that this is just a *season*. If they don't, that Olympic athlete will most likely get divorced. It takes a team effort, both the *Olympic Team* and the *Family Team*, to produce a Gold Medalist. Both the athlete and the athlete's family must make sacrifices in order to win the Gold.

I don't liken myself to an Olympic athlete, but I was an All-Conference NCAA baseball player in college. I understand sacrifice. I understand hard work and dedication. I understand obsession.

If you're going to succeed at a high level in sports, you've got to put in an incredible amount of work, with no guarantee of even making the starting team. It was always my goal to be the hardest working player on the team.

Sure, other guys could claim that they had a better throwing arm than me, or that they could run faster than me, or that they had better bat speed than me... but no one could claim that they worked harder than me.

In business, I'm even more obsessive than I was as an athlete. When I was single, I would work 14 – 16 hour days, 7-days a week. My daily routine was to get into the office at 6:30am, and I would normally wrap up my workday around 11:00pm, and sometimes not until 1:00am in the morning. Nothing took precedence over me building my empire. When you're single, and no one else has a say in what you do, you can do this.

Today, I'm happily married to an incredible woman, and I have a beautiful one-year old son. My wife and son count on me to be more than just a *provider*. I'm a businessman of course, but I'm also a husband and a father now. I can't have my mind on business 24 hours a day, everyday anymore.

That being said, there are times, as a successful businessman with multiple companies, that I work longer hours than my wife would prefer. It comes with the territory. Sure, she gets a little upset from time to time, but for the most part, she understands that I'm building an empire, and sometimes, the *king* has to manage his *kingdom*.

My wife has had a successful career on her own merit, and so she has a better understanding of what it takes to be successful, and she understands that I have a vision of what I want to accomplish in my life, both providing for my family, as well as needing to reach certain personal goals.

I'm not a perfect husband by any means, but I do make an effort to include my wife in important decisions, especially when they affect the amount of time I have to spend away from the family. We're a team. She understands that I'm the captain of the team and that I'm the leader of our family, but every wise king (assuming that he has an intelligent, wise and talented queen), consults with his queen when making important decisions.

We'll talk about the duration of the business project I'm looking at, what the potential returns are, and what the short-term sacrifice is. We'll weigh the risks versus the rewards, and we'll come to a mutual agreement. Obviously, this often takes compromising on both sides, but we're a good team.

I can't think of a time where she has adamantly fought me on anything I've ever wanted to do, and I can't think of a time where I've ever had to put my foot down and forbid her from doing something she really wanted to do.

That's one of the magical things about our marriage. Our chemistry is such that we are always encouraging each other in whatever area the other is excited about.

I'm sure there have been times that she's *let* me take on business projects that she would have preferred that I had passed on, but that's what makes our relationship work. In reciprocation, I've passed on opportunities that I was interested in exploring, but I felt that it just wasn't worth it due to spending too much time away from the family.

Fortunately, I have the luxury of choosing to pass on projects and opportunities now because I have so many successful projects in play, whereas in the early stages of my career, I couldn't afford to pass on ANY opportunities. If you really want to be successful, and you're in the early stages of your career (or you just haven't attained the level of success you want yet), there are very few opportunities you can afford to pass on.

Great opportunities don't fall into your lap everyday. If you've been offered a great opportunity, whether it's a unique company, a unique job offer, or a unique opportunity to work with and learn from an incredibly successful person, chase it obsessively.

What does this have to do with *Building Bullet-Proof Confidence*? As a human being, susceptible to your emotions, you may temporarily lose confidence in yourself, your skills and your abilities. That's natural. But one area that you can control your confidence in is your level of commitment.

When you draw a line in the sand, and say to yourself, *"This is MY life, and I'm calling the shots from here on out,"* that's when you become a *real man* or a *real woman*. You've got to become a *shot-caller* regarding how you live your life and how you prioritize things in your life.

Now if you man-up to this challenge, you must be prepared to receive massive criticism from other people, especially your cubicle-minded friends.

Don't Let Social Rituals Control Your Life

One thing that absolutely drives me crazy is when I see cubicle-minded people place such a disproportionate value on social rituals. For example, I know of people that will take a day off of work to celebrate their birthday.

You may be saying to yourself, *"Darren, you can't blame someone for wanting to celebrate their birthday. It's their BIRTHDAY."* I'm not saying it's a bad thing to celebrate someone's birthday, but is it absolutely necessary to celebrate it on the actual day, especially if that day is on a weekday or workday? What's wrong with celebrating it on the weekend after their birthday, or on the weekend prior to their actual birthday?

You see, cubicle-minded people place such a ridiculously high level of importance on these types of things because they have nothing important to look forward to in life, so they get wrapped up in these temporary things that only last 24 hours. Personally, I think it's wiser to get wrapped up in things that last 24 years instead of 24 hours.

Again, I'm not saying there's anything wrong with wanting to celebrate someone's birthday, but so many people put greater emphasis on planning a birthday party than they do planning a career that would ultimately give them a lifestyle to celebrate everyday.

So many people spend more time planning their wedding day than they do planning for their marriage to be successful. They spend more time planning their vacation than they do planning the rest of their life. Cubicle-minded people are focused on temporary things. Successful entrepreneurs are focused on long-term, bigger-picture things.

For example, my wife and I rarely ever celebrate our birthdays, our wedding anniversary, or Valentine's Day on the actual calendar day, especially if it falls on a workday. We celebrate them on weekends.

You may be reading this and saying, *"Oh my gosh, my wife would never go for that. She's got to celebrate these things on the actual day."* I would argue that the reason you think she'd never go for this is that you don't celebrate these days at the level that my wife and I do.

For our anniversary, we don't have a *nice* dinner at a local restaurant during the work week at a local restaurant. We'll spend the weekend at a luxury resort, getting spa treatments, massages, and pampering ourselves. If you're a married man, ask your wife which option she'd prefer.

1. Having dinner at a local restaurant on her actual birthday, or…

2. Spending the weekend after her actual birthday at a luxury resort getting pampered at the spa, lounging by the pool, and enjoying a 5-Star dinner.

I would be shocked if she chose the crappy dinner at a local restaurant on a weekday at the local restaurant. On the day of my last wedding anniversary, which fell on a Wednesday, I was in North Carolina on a business trip. Some people gasped at the fact that I wasn't even with my wife on our special day. But when they found out that the next weekend, I took her to *Bacara*, a luxury resort in Santa Barbara where movie stars vacation, pampered her with spa treatments and enjoyed dinners at five-star restaurants, these critics pipe down.

What I'm trying to get you to understand is that cubicle-minded people think a certain way. They get caught up in social norms. Social norms are what normal people subscribe to. These are ordinary people's rules, and you don't want to be ordinary. You want to be extraordinary, which means that you have to live by a different set of values. These social rituals weren't developed for people like you and me. They were developed for people that subscribe to the *herd mentality*.

This is where the importance of having your own brand comes in. Your personal brand is more than just what car you drive, how you dress, and how you operate in business. It's a *mindset*. It's a mindset that says, "*I know you cubicle-minded people don't understand why I do what I do, and that's why you'll never have what I have.*" This proclamation alone will give you confidence, because you're standing for something.

Standing For Something

One of my best friends that I grew up with, Thad Balkman, came from a family with different spiritual beliefs than my own, but I always respected the way his family lived. The Balkmans were *different*, but as an adult looking back on how they raised their kids, I find myself mildly fascinated by the indirect impact it made not only on my life, but our entire group of friends' lives.

In Junior High School and High School, Thad used to throw parties at his parents' home. On the surface, these parties looked the same as the *cool* parties that our friends would throw when their parents were out of town, but there were some minor differences.

The music was the same as the cool parties, and they would always have a cool DJ. People danced to *Madonna, DePeche Mode*, and *Prince* on the dance floor in their backyard, just like the *cool* parties where people were getting drunk, smoking pot, doing drugs, and partying.

The difference was that there was never any alcohol served at Thad's parties, and everyone knew not to show up with alcohol. Mr. and Mrs. Balkman would be part of the party, circulating, greeting all the kids. They were never judgmental of any of the kids there, and all of the kids treated Mr. and Mrs. Balkman with respect. The kids actually liked talking to Thad's parents.

These are the same kids that were getting drunk and high at a different party the weekend before. These were the so-called *cool kids*, and they actually loved going to a Balkman party. All of us kids loved Balkman parties. Why was this? On the surface, it didn't make logical sense.

But looking back, I think the reason our friends liked Mr. and Mrs. Balkman was that even though we weren't of the same spiritual beliefs or social values, we never felt judged. At the same time, we knew that the Balkmans stood for certain values, and we respected their values, probably because they never compromised their values. You just had to respect them.

Years later, Thad explained to me that in his spiritual faith, there is a defining moment when a boy becomes a man, where he must deliver a speech to the members of the church in a ceremonious event. He said this gives the young man confidence in his arrival into manhood, because he now has an identity.

In addition, in the middle of a young man's college career, he temporarily stops his education, and spends two years on a spiritual mission, usually overseas. In the midst of his sexual prime, when most young men in college are partying, chasing sorority girls, the young missionary spends two full years in another country, spiritually held accountable by a peer who is in the same boat that he is. They are instructed to go door-to-door, essentially *cold-calling* for their religion. When they return two years later, they complete their college education.

Common logic would tell you that being two years behind in their professional career would hinder their success, however, it is the exact opposite. Think about the sacrifice-minded young man doing missionary work. Think about the massive rejection the young man faces knocking on doors, pitching his religion. Think about the perseverance that is built through this process.

It's quite interesting to me, because their system, if you remove all religious and spiritual context, is essentially training the young man to have bullet-proof confidence. He has an identity that is completely opposite from what the rest of the world sees as being *normal*.

He has an identity. He has a purpose. When someone is confident in their purpose, they naturally become confident in themselves. I am not of the same spiritual faith as the Balkman family is, and so obviously, I am not promoting their religion. However, many of the principles that I've seen taught in this culture are success-oriented principles that I strongly believe in. I will always have an affinity towards the Balkman family.

Though we don't see each other often (due to Thad living in Oklahoma and me living in California), we remain good friends. And guess what... today, Thad is a very successful attorney. Surprise, surprise.

Oh, I almost forgot. Have you ever seen the 1986 movie, *Ferris Bueller's Day Off* starring Matthew Broderick? Ferris Bueller's house in the movie was the house that Thad grew up in. We used to watch them film the movie everyday after school at his house. Needless to say, Mr. Balkman did very well financially as a stockbroker. Surprise, surprise.

In business, and in life, you've got to stand for something, regardless if other people don't agree with you and your priorities. People may disagree with what you stand for, but they'll respect you for your integrity.

As for the people that agree with what you stand for, they'll respect you and most likely, do business with you. Standing for something and being passionate about something shows commitment. In order to have an authentic brand identity, you must be committed to what your brand stands for. We'll discuss how to develop your personal brand in the upcoming chapter.

Chapter Six:
Your Personal Brand

"There is a distinct difference between being controlling, versus being in control of your life. The first will lead you to failure. The second will enable you to develop your own, personal brand and will lead you to great wealth, success and happiness."

-Darren Sugiyama

Your Personal Brand

Think about the following brands. *Nordstrom. Chuck E. Cheese. FedEx. Trump.* These brands have a very specific image, as well as a very specific message about their brand. They evoke certain emotions when you hear their names. They even have a very specific tag line, synonymous with the brand's reputation.

Nordstrom is known for having the best customer returns policy. Chuck E. Cheese is a place *Where A Kid Can Be A Kid.* You choose FedEx *When It Absolutely, Positively Has To Be There* on time. Trump is the *Biggest Real Estate Investor In New York City.* These brands stand for something. They have skillfully established an identity... *a brand.*

This is essentially what you must do, even if it's on a smaller scale. Your target client demographic must know what you stand for. This unapologetic, unwavering stance gives you control. As I'll discuss later in this chapter, I define *Being In Control* as not *Being Out Of Control.*

In order to be in control, or perhaps more clearly described, being able to *take control,* you've got to make sure the message that you're communicating to your market answers these three key questions:

1. Who are you?
2. What exactly do you do?
3. Why should someone do business with you and ONLY you?

You can control the message that you project out there into the marketplace, and so it is only logical and intelligent to project your brand identity in a very calculated manner.

Branding Question #1: Who Are You?

When constructing your brand, you must take some time and really think through who you are. This applies both to your company brand and your personal brand. I would say that the majority of people (and companies for that matter) currently have an identity crisis when it comes to their brand. They really can't answer the question, *"Who Are You?"* They spend so much time chasing the latest fad instead of planting their flag.

Similar to the Balkman family that I mentioned earlier, you've got to decide who you are, what you stand for, and never compromise your brand. If you haven't established a clearly defined, unapologetic brand, people will soon realize that you don't stand for anything, your brand loses all authenticity.

Have you ever met someone or seen someone that you didn't particularly agree with, but because they were so passionate about their beliefs, you had to respect them?

The reason you had respect for them was that their brand had authenticity. Whether you want to be known as the *Green Environmentally Friendly* company, or the *Greed Is Good* company, or the *Philanthropic* company, or the *24-7 Workaholic* company, you've got to make a decision on who you want to be.

Once you know who you are and what you stand for, and you heavily promote your brand, the marketplace will accept you as that brand. Those that don't like your brand will not be attracted to you, but those that do like your brand will view you as being authentic. Always remember that people love authenticity, and they can spot a fake a mile a way.

To use an analogy from the dating world, generally speaking, guys that have a specific identity tend to do well with girls. Jocks get the cheerleaders. Bad boys get the hot party chicks. Rockers get the rocker chicks. Surfers get the beach babes.

Sure, I'm making broad, stereotypical statements, but in each of these examples, these guys know who they are, and they're unapologetic about it. They have a very specific image and personal brand. They have their own lingo, their own style of dress, their own attitudes and value systems. Each subculture has a clearly defined brand.

You know who doesn't do very well in the dating world? Guys with no identity. I'm sure you've seen guys that look uncomfortable in their own skin. They perpetually feel out of place. They lack confidence. And how can you tell that they lack confidence?

You can tell because it is visually apparent that they don't know who they are, and it becomes even more apparent when you talk to them. They don't stand for anything. They aren't passionate about anything. They just *exist*. There's nothing interesting or intriguing about someone that just *exists*. Similarly, there's nothing sexy about a company that that just exists, and has no brand.

People, and more specifically, consumers, want to feel like they're part of a club. They want to feel like they have a cultural home they belong to. That's why when you have no brand identity, no one's interested in you. You don't provide them with a culture to be part of.

Generally speaking, women don't want guys with *money*. What they want is a unique, exhilarating *experience*. It just so happens that when a guy has money, it's easier for him to provide a more unique experience because money typically grants him access to more exclusive resources. And thus, typically, guys with a lot of money do well in the dating world. But it's not just about the money.

The *bad boy* also provides a unique experience simply by getting into trouble and mischief. For some women, the thrill of being rebellious and associating with a rebel is intoxicating. I've seen a lot of broke bad boys with really hot girlfriends. Again, the bad boy has a *brand*, and the average, nondescript, *nice guy* has no identifiable brand. In business, you've got to clearly define your brand. There isn't necessarily a bad brand (depending on your value system and personal beliefs), as long as it's unique, extreme and authentic.

For example, Larry Flynt, publisher of *Hustler Publications*, has a brand. People that are fans of pornography love the *Hustler* brand, and thus Larry Flynt and the *Hustler* brand are very successful, financially.

On the other end of the spectrum, the Reverend Jerry Falwell, has an equally extreme brand. His brand is one of ultra-conservativism, and is in direct opposition to Larry Flynt's brand. Jerry Falwell has a huge following, and so by definition, his brand is also very successful.

The irony is that in the business marketplace, both brands co-exist and both brands have tremendous followings, despite the fact that their brands are in direct opposition of each other. So how is this possible?

The reason that both brands are successful is that both brands are extreme. Both brands stand for something. Both brands have a specific identity and a specific set of values. People want to be part of their clubs. They want to be part of their subcultures. Both brands know who they are.

You may be asking yourself, *"Why does Darren keep going off on tangents about dating, pornography, and evangelical Christian groups?"* The reason is that all of these examples require *Living Outside The Cubicle* thought processes. In both of these extreme examples, both Larry Flint and the Reverend Jerry Faldwell, their success came as a result of making a firm decision regarding who they wanted to be, and they made sure everyone knew it.

So you must be able to answer the question, *"Who are you?"* and perhaps more appropriately, *"Who do you want to be?"* and *"How do you want to be perceived?"* You must make every decision in business based on making sure that your decision is synonymous with your brand. So, we've talked about who you *are*. Let's talk about what you actually *do*.

Branding Question #2: What Exactly Do You Do?

I've sat through sales meetings where I was the prospect, and an hour into the meeting, I still didn't understand what the sales rep was trying to sell me. When branding your company or yourself, you've got to clearly and concisely communicate what it is that you *do,* so that the prospect can clearly see the benefit of doing business with you.

Don't spend an unnecessary amount of time talking about unrelated topics. Just cut to the chase and tell the person specifically what it is that you do, and how they can benefit by using your product or service. The easiest way to do this is by showing them *case studies.* Show them examples of the work you've done for other clients and how they benefited from doing business with you. The goal is to create what I call *positive jealousy.*

When you tell the person you're trying to win over, a story about someone else that got a huge benefit by working with you, they'll get jealous, in a positive way. Basically, their jealousy will make them want that benefit more than you want to take them on as a new client, which is exactly what you want.

Once you've created this *positive jealousy* within the prospect, you have all the power. They want *you* more than you want *them*. This is the same reason that typically, in the dating world, women have all the power. Typically, the guy wants the girl's phone number more than the girl wants him to call her. Every guy knows that an attractive woman is in demand, and that she's got plenty of other suitors besides him. This typically makes the man jealous, thus *positive jealousy* has been created in the woman's advantage.

I say *typically*, because this is not always the case if the man repositions himself in the same way that you need to reposition yourself in a business transaction.

When I was single, I mastered this art. On a first date, I would ask the girl, "*What's the most thoughtful thing you've ever done for a boyfriend?*" This was a great question to ask because it made the girl subconsciously feel the need to validate herself to me, proving to me that she was thoughtful. This would put her in a position of trying to impress me, whereas typically, the guy is the one trying to impress the girl. Right off the bat, I've taken control of the first date.

The second reason this was a great question to ask is that after she got done trying to validate (sell) her worth to me, she would ask me the same question. Of course I already knew this question was coming, so I'd already have a great *case study* to share with her. This would give me the stage to talk about how thoughtful I was without coming off like a braggart. She asked me the question, so it would be rude not to answer it, right? This was all in the set up.

Using this format of communication allowed me to answer the question, "*What exactly do you do?*" which is Part Two of solidifying your brand. In addition, whenever you are the one asking the questions, you're in control.

In a sales or business environment, whoever is asking the most questions is leading and controlling the tempo of the meeting, as well as the direction of the conversation. If the other person is asking most of the questions, they feel empowered and will subconsciously feel that your sole purpose in life is to answer to them, which is obviously not how you want to be perceived. You need to regain control by having premeditated questions that allow you to control the direction of the conversation.

In an interrogation, the interrogator is in control. In a deposition, the deposing attorney is in control. On a talk show, the host is the one in control. In each of these three examples, the one who's asking the majority of the questions is the one in control. It's the same in both dating and in business.

This leads us to the third question that your brand must answer, which is, *"Why should someone do business with you and ONLY you?"*

Branding Question #3: Why should someone do business with you and ONLY you?

I love this question. The answer to this question is the crux of success in branding, sales, marketing, and business in general. It basically asks, *"What makes you so great?"* The answer to this question should really be your U.S.P., or your *Unique Selling Proposition*.

Your *U.S.P.* must be unique. That's what the *U* in the acronym stands for, right? Unique does not mean cool, or great, or fabulous. The term *unique* means one-of-a-kind. In order to be successful in the competitive world of business, you've got to be able to differentiate yourself from your competition.

You've got to have an undisputable reason why you're not only the *best* option, but the *only* option. This is actually a very simple thing to do. All you have to do is recall the most frequent complaints that you've heard prospects and clients complain about regarding people that do what you do, and make those the areas that you specialize in. Then, pick the one that none of your so-called competition can do, and focus your message on solving that one problem.

If you're the only one that can provide a solution to that particular problem, you've made yourself indispensible. That's when you know you've found your U.S.P.

In my consulting practice, especially when consulting in the insurance industry, my message is focused around one major thing. Sure there are a lot of very talented sales coaches, motivational speakers, and marketing consultants out there, however, I always make sure that people remember one main thing.

I am the only one in this line of work that has actually done what I teach. None of these other so-called sales gurus have ever built a mega-insurance brokerage like I have. Sure they may be very intelligent people, and they may have some great ideas and strategies... but I've never met any of them that have built an agency to the level I have, in the short amount of time that I built mine.

Essentially, my message is this:

> *"I built a $37 million insurance agency in less than seven years. If you want to build a super agency, I'll show you exactly what I did, and how I did it. If you want to learn from a guy that's never done it, go ahead and work with him, and you'll see what happens."*

So think about what you can produce for your clients that no one else can, and focus on brilliantly communicating that message. In fact, do it shamelessly. People want to know that your conviction in your abilities is rock solid. Sure, I get accused of being arrogant from time to time, but it's almost always by people that were never going to do business with me in the first place, and they're typically not very successful themselves. But those prospects that fall right in my target market demographic… they want to know that I'm confident in my abilities.

I've never been accused of being arrogant by other successful people, or by people that aspired to be successful. The only ones that have ever labeled me as arrogant were jealous losers who had given up on their dreams, and my personal brand threatened them, because it highlighted the fact that they didn't have the guts to go for it.

Develop your brand and only target prospects that identify with your brand. Don't waste time, energy and emotion in trying to win over everyone. First, you'll never win over 100 percent of the people, 100 percent of the time. And second, in the process of trying to be all things to all people, you'll lose your identity and become nondescript. Stick to your brand and stick to your U.S.P. These are things that you have 100 percent control over.

Being In Control

Often times, when people hear me talk about being in control, they assume I'm a control freak. Guilty as charged. But when I talk about being in control, I'm not talking about trying to control the universe. What I'm talking about is not living a life that is *out of control*.

Most people are living a life that is literally spinning out of control. They have no direction, no plan and no vision. Of course you can't control everything in your life, however there are some things that you *can* control, and controlling these key things is the foundation of being successful in life.

Before we discuss the things you can control, let's discuss the things that you cannot control. You cannot control:

1. Your genetic disposition.
2. Your emotions.
3. The economy.
4. What other people do.

These are things that change from day-to-day. However, there are some things that you must commit to never changing, regardless of the circumstance. Things that must never change are:

1. Your effort.
2. Your principles.
3. Your vision.

Let's discuss these three things that you must control.

The First Thing You Must Control: Your Effort.

Regardless of what's going on in your life at any given time, you must always give 100% of your best effort. So many people use excuses to give a poor effort, but successful people's effort is always at *Level 10*.

I remember being hit with food poisoning, and having several interviewees lined up to interview with me. This was within the first year of me starting my insurance firm, and I couldn't afford to take a day off. Now, if you've ever had food poisoning, you know that it is a terrible feeling. I would be right in the middle of the interview, and have to excuse myself for a few minutes as I ran to the bathroom down the hall from my office, vomiting so hard, it felt like I was going to vomit a major organ into the toilet bowl. Sorry to be graphic, but I want you to understand just how sick I was.

I would rinse my mouth out with mouthwash, and walk right back into the interview like nothing happened. I'm not saying this because I feel like I should receive some sort of valiant award for my efforts. Athletes do this all the time.

Successful athletes play when they're sick or injured. This is just standard for an athlete, but for some reason, when it comes to nonathletic careers, they aren't even close to being as committed, which is why they aren't even close to being as successful as some of the big hitters that work for me. My top producers are tough, and they don't allow minor setbacks and adversities to get in the way of their success.

Some days, you're going to be physically fatigued. Some days, you're going to be emotionally down due to something that happened in your personal life. Some days, you're just not going to feel good. But on these days, the key is to never let other people know you're weak that day, and to operate as close to 100 percent of what you can do on your best day. You may not be able to deliver 100 percent of your normal performance, but it is imperative that you give 100 percent of your effort.

The Second Thing You Must Control: Your Principles.

Last night, I posted a message on my Facebook page that said, *"I know a lot of rich people that are not successful, but very few successful people that are not rich."*

What I meant by this is that being rich is a natural and logical bi-product of being successful in business, however being successful is not necessarily a bi-product of being rich. You see, I define success as *"The achievement of overcoming overwhelming adversities, and the development of character used to overcome future adversities."* Under this definition, being *rich* doesn't necessarily mean that any character was developed during the process of accumulating wealth or riches.

For example, if one's riches were attained through inheritance or marriage, there would have been nothing of merit done to earn their riches. Or, if one's riches were obtained through taking advantage of other people through lies, cheating and deceit, there would not have been any character developed in the process either.

That's why your principles must never be compromised. Your principles must remain steadfast and unchanging. Sure, your moods might swing and vary on a day-to-day basis, and certainly your circumstances will change on a case-by-case basis, but your principles must not. Have you ever had to deal with someone whose principles and ethics waivered based on their circumstances? These situational ethics exist in people that have a lack of character and integrity. Let this not be you.

A person's true character is often revealed by the circumstances they find themselves in, especially in times of adversity. Again, circumstances change, as do your emotions, but your character and integrity are defined by your principles and how committed you are to them. This is something that you can and must control.

The Third Thing You Must Control: Your Vision.

Think back to when you first decided that you wanted to be financially successful. What specifically did you hope to accomplish? Why was it so important for you to accomplish this?

If you're like most driven people, you probably had a *vision*. I'm not talking about some mystical, weird vision that involved burning incense or smoking an illegal substance in the desert while sweating it out in a teepee.

I'm talking about a big-picture goal that you set out to accomplish. For some people, their vision is as shallow as driving a Bentley, living in a mansion, and flaunting their wealth, making a spectacle of themselves. I'm not judging these types of people. I like driving a luxury car, and I like living a life of luxury. But my vision goes far beyond material wealth.

I've found that for the large majority of extremely successful people, their vision usually has something to do with a worthwhile cause, whether it be a charitable cause, or involve some aspect of service to others.

Typically, these visions are grand visions. They tend to be larger than life. In other words, they allow people to dream. The thing to be aware of is that all dreams and visions are susceptible to dream-killers, especially the ultimate dream-killer.

The ultimate dream-killer is *rationalization*. When things get challenging in business, it's easy to give up and turn into a wuss. Now, because no one wants to be called a wuss, people will rationalize why their vision is no longer a necessity.

Most people, when they first begin their quest to achieve success in business, set semi-superficial, material goals along the way. There's nothing wrong with this, in fact, I still do it to this day myself. These little goals act as temporary benchmarks, or *scorecards* if you will.

Take something simple and superficial, like driving a luxury car. Some people start out fantasizing about driving a luxury car, but once they realize that success in business doesn't happen overnight, they start rationalizing why they don't *need* a luxury car. I recently had someone tell me, *"Darren, I'm just not that into cars. All I need is something to get me from point A to point B. Luxury cars are gas guzzlers, plus, they're too expensive to maintain. And I wouldn't want to have to worry about it getting scratched or dinged in the supermarket parking lot. I wouldn't want the stress."*

Hey, I agree with the fact that no one *needs* a luxury car. However, I personally like driving a luxury car. It gets me from point A to point B more comfortably. Sure it doesn't give me the gas mileage of a hybrid car, and sure, it's more expensive to maintain than an economy car, but I can afford it, so it doesn't bother me. And no, I don't worry about it getting scratched or dinged because I flip cars every three years anyway. So what's my point?

My point is that this person is lying to themselves. Deep down, everyone wants the finer things in life. Everyone may not obsess about it the way that ultra-driven people do, but you can't tell me that if a certain wealthy celebrity talk show host offered them a $100,000 luxury car with free maintenance and free gas, that they'd request to be given a $13,000 economy car instead.

The only reason that this person claims that they wouldn't want a luxury car is that they perceive that they'll never have one, so they've rationalized why they don't want one. It's the same thing with living in a mansion or a luxury estate.

I've had people marvel at my house, but then retract their statements and say, *"I wouldn't want to live in place this big. It would be too much work to maintain it."* Umm, hello! I pay a gardener to maintain the grounds. I pay a housekeeper to clean the house. I pay a pool service to clean my pool.

You see, these types of people become very defensive in their rationalization because their subconscious, cubicle-minded brain is forced to come up with an excuse as to why they don't have these finer things in life. It's a defense mechanism that has been hard-wired into their system to preserve their egos.

About a year ago, I had an interesting conversation with one of my employees. When she started working for me about six years ago, she was a top producer. In fact, she still holds two production records at my insurance firm. However, about two years ago, I noticed that her production level (and her level of drive) began to slowly diminish. So we talked.

I asked her if her vision for her career had changed. She replied, *"Well, when I first started working for you, I thought I wanted to be rich. But now, I realize that my husband and I are really just simple people. We're fine driving an economy car, living in a modest apartment. In fact, we could probably survive off just my husband's income."*

I was shocked. It was like I was talking to an entirely different person than I originally hired. I knew something had changed and I suspected that she fell victim to the evil enemy called *rationalization*. I racked my brain, trying to come up with a solution to rekindle her original vision.

Coincidentally, I was having a business dinner party at my home a few weeks later. I do this every year as a gesture of appreciation towards all the important people I do business with. I usually have about 80 to 90 guests. I thought it might be a good idea to invite her to this event, just to expose her to the *good life*.

From the time she stepped into my home, her eyes lit up as she explored every detail of my home. It's a hacienda-style estate, however the interior décor is very eclectic, pulling influences from my Asian culture as well as my wife's Latin culture. There are elements of both modernity as well as elements of antiquity in its interior design. As my employee wandered through my home, she told me, *"Oh my gosh, this is exactly my style. I love it."*

Okay, remember what she previously said about being *simple*? A *simple person* doesn't have a *style* of interior décor. Basically, she's been lying to herself, rationalizing why she doesn't need to be rich and successful. In a discussion with her following the event, I asked her about her experience at the event, and if her previous vision became a current desire. It had, and she told me, *"Darren, I want to get back into the game."*

I was elated. My excitement wasn't based on getting one of my sales producers back in action, as much as it was seeing someone rekindle their vision. You must not allow your vision, whatever it may be, to be stifled by limiting beliefs that lead to rationalization.

It's easy to convince yourself that you don't need to achieve greatness. There will be no cataclysmic tragedy in the world if you decide to succumb to the curse of mediocrity. However, the real tragedy will be the fact that you allowed your dream to be killed by self-doubt, emotional weakness, and rationalization. In most cases, you'd be able to get away with it, and no one would ever know, but the problem is that you would know.

My Uncle Rich, who I mentioned passed away last year, once told me that of all the business ventures he ever tried, he never regretted any of them, even the ones where he lost money. He said to me, *"Darren, the only business ventures I ever regretted were the ones I never tried."*

I often think about my Uncle Rich's wise words. These words gave me the hope, encouragement and confidence I needed to stay positive on my journey. What my uncle was trying to teach me was to dream big, and to never lose sight of my vision. I'm almost positive that half of the crazy ideas I used to run by my Uncle Rich probably gave him a good chuckle, but he never tried to talk me out of any of them.

I think he understood the power of having a vision and committing to it, even if it may have seemed over-the-top. When he looked back on his life, just one year before he passed away, he saw all of his business pursuits as one big adventure. He used to tell me, *"Darren, most people have only seen the successes I've had in business, but they never saw any of my failures. I've lost millions of dollars on business ventures that never panned out, but had I not had those experiences, I would have never gotten to my mega successes."*

To further illustrate this concept, hockey legend Wayne Gretzky once said, *"I missed 100 percent of the shots I never took."* Sometimes, you have to put yourself in a situation where there is a chance of failure, because then and only then, are you in a situation where you have a chance to succeed. If you never put yourself out there, you're guaranteed not to succeed.

I would say that most people think success is about *not failing*. Nothing could be further from the truth. Success is not about failing the least. It's about working until you hit it big, regardless of how many times you fail.

If you look at Michael Jordan, who is arguably the greatest basketball player of all time, he admits that his success came with many concurrent *failures*. He says, *"I've missed over 9,000 shots in my career... I've lost almost 300 games... 26 times, I've been trusted to take the game winning shot, and missed... I've failed over and over and over again in my life... and that is why I succeed."*

What so many people fail to realize is that sometimes, the greatest successes come after several repeated failures. With Michael

Jordan, his so-called failures happened concurrently with his many successes, but he isn't remembered for his many failures. He's remembered as one of the greatest players of all time.

Many people that never achieved great success in their lives just quit too early. They got too emotionally attached to the short-term lack of success, instead of just persevering.

There's a great story about an archeologist that fell victim to having a lack of perseverance. It goes something like this:

> *An archeologist spent a good majority of his life in search of finding a long, lost treasure. Though it was thought of as a myth to the archeologist community, he believed it was a reality. His dream, which practically turned into an obsession, was to find this buried treasure. After much research and calculation, he believed he had found the exact coordinates of where the treasure was buried several civilizations ago. He began digging... and digging... and digging. He spent his entire life's savings on this adventure, and he was excited beyond belief. This would be the greatest excavation in the history of the world, and would bring him riches beyond his wildest dreams if he found it.*
>
> *But after a year of digging, he began to wonder if he had made a mistake. His friends and family all told him that he was crazy, and that he was chasing a pipe dream. Over time, people that supposedly loved him were talking behind his back and making fun of him.*
>
> *At first, this ridicule didn't phase the young archeologist, but after months and months of being ridiculed, it began to wear on him, emotionally. He dug and dug, digging over 500 feet deep. But after 500 feet, he threw up his hands in despair saying, "I can't believe I did all this work for nothing! I'm such a fool!" And so he quit.*
>
> *The day after he quit, a young teenage boy, against his mother's instruction, rode his BMX dirt bike down into the ditch with some of his friends. It looked like a cool place to build a race track, so they took some*

shovels and rakes down into the ditch. As they began shoveling dirt to make their race track, one of the boys' shovels hit something hard. The rest of the boys ran over to see what the loud sound was, and they pulled a huge treasure chest out of the ground, just six inches under the surface. It was filled with gold and fine jewels. The boys marveled at their finding, and decided to keep digging.

As they kept digging, they uncovered the greatest hidden treasure ever found, and as a result, became billionaires.

You see, the moral of the story is that in life, as well as in business, finding your treasure often takes time. So many people quit just inches before their major breakthrough. They do a significant amount of work, but they don't stay at it long enough. They give up too soon.

Giving up and losing hope often happen when a person is both physically and emotionally fatigued. If you want to be successful, you're going to have to deal with physical fatigue. It's just par for the course. The danger is that when a person is physically fatigued, it is easy for them to fall victim to emotional fatigue. Football coaching legend Vince Lombardi once said, *"Fatigue makes cowards of us all."* I would tend to agree with coach Lombardi's statement, and so the key to persevering in business is to not let your emotions become fatigued.

It's easier said than done. Repetitive failure can be emotionally exhausting if you don't have the proper perspective on the process of success. Success, in most cases, comes as a result of repetitive failure... as long as you keep moving forward, without quitting. Sure, your failure rate (percentage of failure, relative to your number of attempts) may be high, but so what? Unlike scholastic test scores, success in business (and in life) isn't about percentages. It's about aggregates.

In baseball, a batter is evaluated based on a batting average, or a percentage of success. In school, we're graded based on a percentage of answers we get correct on an exam. But in the real world, we're rarely graded on the percentage of our successes relative to our failure rate. We're graded based on the aggregate level of success we accomplish, monetarily. It's the same thing in relationships.

Let's say you have two married couples, both in their 60's. One couple has been married for over 30 years, and is blissfully happy in their marriage. The other couple went through a series of bad relationships, including several divorces, but today, they are blissfully happy in their marriage.

If you were to evaluate both couples solely based on their marriage relationship today, is the couple that has been married for over 30 years any happier than the couple that had to strike out several times before they hit their grand slam into marriage bliss? No, not at all.

In fact, one could argue that the couple that found each other after a series of bad relationships might even enjoy their marriage more so, because their negative past makes them appreciate their current wonderful relationship on a deeper level. They know how fortunate true love is, because they've experienced relationship hell.

The point is, in life and in business, it's never too late to achieve massive success, even if you've had a negative past. It's never too late to reclaim your original vision of grandeur. It's never to late to hit the *reset button*.

Chapter Seven:
Hitting The Reset Button

"Once you die, it's too late to start over. Up until then, you are granted an unlimited number of times to hit the Reset Button."

-Darren Sugiyama

It's Never Too Late

I've interviewed thousands of people over the course of my career, and one of the most common complaints I've heard people say regarding their career is *"I wish I could have gotten in sooner."*

Even worse, I've heard numerous people use *timing* as an excuse to not start a new career or a new business, as if to say that it's too late for them to start. This is just plain stupid.

It's never too late to start a new venture, unless you're dead. I find it to be such a shame when I see people that have so much life ahead of them choose to just live out the rest of their existence in mediocrity.

Again, not that there's anything wrong with living an average lifestyle, but when a person chooses a life of mediocrity due to the belief that it's too late to start over, it's a sad misperception of what's truly possible.

Hitting The Reset Button

Maybe you've had some setbacks in your life. Perhaps you're starting over right now, rebuilding your career, and maybe even rebuilding your life. Maybe you're recovering from a severe illness or injury, or a devastating divorce, or a traumatizing bankruptcy.

Or maybe you're walking away from a semi-successful career to follow your dreams of being a mega-successful entrepreneur. Whatever the case, it takes guts to start over.

I've had to start over several times in my life, both personally and professionally, and each time, I had to overcome a major adversity. Sometimes these adversities were financial, and sometimes they were emotional. If you've been beaten up as much as I have, then you know how draining starting over can be.

For example, I got married and divorced at a relatively young age. My ex-wife and I were both college athletes at Loyola Marymount University in Los Angeles, California. I played on the varsity baseball team, and she played on the varsity tennis team.

When I graduated, we talked about getting married. She was originally from Hawaii, and she really wanted to move back to Hawaii and start our family there. That being the case, I left all of my friends, family and career aspirations behind in California and moved to Hawaii in an attempt to get established there. I went back to school to get a Master's Degree from the University of Hawaii and planned on being a high school teacher in Hawaii.

While getting my Master's Degree, I worked as a bouncer in a nightclub three nights a week. I also worked as a counselor at the Honolulu Detention Home, working with troubled teens on Saturday mornings. I also had a part-time afterschool job helping elementary school kids with their homework. And on top of all these part-time jobs and going to school, I worked as a runway model for DKNY, Hermes, Armani, Dior, and several other top designers.

That's part of the reason why I don't have much sympathy for people that say they're too busy to take on another project. In life, you just have to do whatever it takes to make things happen. And so there I was, trying to make things happen.

Once I completed my Master's Degree program, I began teaching full-time. I now had a career, and felt it was time to get married. At age 24, I got married. At age 25, I got divorced.

I remember growing up in Southern California, being somewhat connected to the Hollywood scene, and seeing these celebrities that would get married and get divorced a year later, and I would think to myself, *"What could possibly go so wrong in a year? What's wrong with these idiots?"*

Well, one year and three months into my marriage, I realized I had married one of these idiots. One day, my ex-wife came home and told me that she didn't want to be married to me anymore. I was shocked and totally caught off guard.

I begged her to go to marriage counseling with me, but a couple of weeks later, she was gone. I was absolutely devastated. It was as if a big piece of my manhood was taken away from me, and I lost a lot of my self-confidence. There are several stages to the grieving process when something like this happens to you.

Stage #1: Denial.

The first stage is *denial*. I didn't spend much time in this stage because I got kicked out of the house and had to move in with a buddy of mine in order to get back on my feet.

When you're packing all of your belongings in boxes and signing divorce papers, there's no denying what's happening. I got kicked to the curb, and there's no denying that.

Stage #2: Sadness.

The second stage of the grieving process is *sadness*. Believe me, I spent a lot of time in the sadness stage. I spent many nights crying myself to sleep.

I couldn't listen to love songs on the radio. I felt completely disempowered and weak. I felt like a total failure.

Sadness is a very dangerous emotion, especially if you spend too much time in this emotional state. I'm not saying that mourning the loss of something important to you isn't necessary, however you've got to move forward as fast as possible, or you'll end up drowning in your own misery. I knew that I had to move on with my life, as heartbroken as I was.

There's a great final outcome to this story, so don't feel too bad for me. It was ultimately the best thing that ever happened to me. So how did I ignite the process of moving on? I quickly moved into Stage #3. I got angry.

Stage #3: Anger.

The third stage of the grieving process is *anger*. Believe me, I was ANGRY. Man, was I angry. I had given up my entire life for this girl, moved to a place where I didn't know anyone, and had completely changed my career path to accommodate her dream of living in Hawaii. I felt like I had been stabbed in the back and betrayed at the highest level possible.

There are very few things in life that are more important to me than loyalty, and when someone is disloyal to me, it can push me to a level of anger that you can't imagine. But remember what I said earlier about the ability to use feelings of frustration and anger to motivate you to move forward in life? Anger can be channeled in a way that becomes very productive.

One of the biggest motivators that works for me is anger. Now, I'm not talking about walking around pissed off all day, everyday. And I'm not talking about carrying a chip on my shoulder. I'm talking about reaching a point in life where you proclaim that no matter what has happened to you, and no matter what else may happen to you in the future, you will win at all costs.

Once you make the proclamation that you will never allow someone or something to stand in your way of happiness and the pursuit of success, you become stronger emotionally, and that's exactly what happened to me. I realized through my divorce that I have no control over what other people do. If your happiness is dependent on other people's loyalty, love or acceptance, you will surely live a life of perpetual let downs.

People, unfortunately, will let you down on multiple occasions. In order to be strong and ultimately happy, you need to be able to create your own happiness. And so, I got angry.

Sounds contradictory, doesn't it? I got angry so that I could be happy. I know, it sounds completely nonsensical, but finally understanding this concept is what led me to become happy and free.

You see, when you embrace anger in a positive way, that adrenaline and adamancy gives you the strength to draw your line in the sand and finally stand for something… or in my case, stand against something. So what did I have to stand against?

I had to take a stance against letting the wrong people influence my decisions. I finally said to myself, *"Darren, you're a talented, intelligent guy that is destined for greatness, so stop listening to people that aren't where you want to be."*

I learned to trust in my own instincts and follow the path that I knew I needed to follow. I had to look at myself in the mirror and say, *"I'm a leader, and leaders lead. Screw what all of these cubicle-minded people are telling me to do. I'm a real man, and real men make their own decisions."*

When you decided to be an entrepreneur, you probably had people advise you to take a more secure job with good benefits. They probably told you that your crazy aspirations of financial freedom were too risky. What you have to realize is that they're not going to pay your bills. They're not going to buy you a multi-million dollar mansion. They're not going to buy you luxury cars. They're not going to pay for your kids' education. They have absolutely no responsibility to support you financially, so by definition, isn't it incredibly irresponsible for them to give you any career advice or financial advice?

You need to make your own decisions about what you want to accomplish in your life, regardless of whether or not you get the emotional support from your so-called friends and family. This is never an easy thing to do, but it is a necessary thing to do. When I got divorced, I promised myself to never allow anyone to influence the direction I wanted to take my life in, ever again.

Once I entered the dating world again as a single man, I had a different perspective on my relationships with girlfriends. I remember telling a friend about a new girlfriend I was seeing. It was right around Valentine's Day, and my friend asked me what I was going to buy my new girlfriend for Valentine's Day. I told him that I already had the *New Girlfriend Talk* with her.

My buddy said, *"What's the New Girlfriend Talk?"* The New Girlfriend Talk went something like this:

> *"Listen sweetie, here's the deal. I work everyday, all day, even on weekends. Every dollar I make has to get reinvested back into my business because I've just started a new venture. This means no expensive dinners, no vacation trips together, no lavish birthday gifts or Valentine's Day gifts. If you're cool with this, we can continue and we'll have a lot of fun together. But if you're not okay with this, then you should probably find someone else."*

My buddy's wife overheard this conversation, and she said, *"Darren, oh my gosh! You're so harsh on these girls!"* I replied, *"Listen, my future wife will thank me for it."*

Today, I am married to an incredible woman. My wife Emilia is a self-made, successful entrepreneur, completely self-taught. She came from a poor immigrant family from Mexico, growing up in Northern Nevada. At twelve-years old, she was out slumped over in the garlic fields, picking garlic to help support her family.

At age seventeen, she left home and lived in her uncle's garage in Watts (a ghetto in South Central Los Angeles), working as a receptionist at a garment manufacturer in Downtown L.A. She worked her way up to office manager, and within a few years, she was practically running the operation.

To make a very long story short, she landed in the insurance industry, and eventually got into sales as a 1099, independent contractor, working in a commission-only life insurance position.

When I met my wife Emilia, she was a polished, successful insurance sales executive, making six-figures. And I, having obsessively worked and reinvested in my companies, was deserving of such a high-caliber woman.

Last year, she gave birth to our first son, Estevan. As I write this chapter, the three of us are vacationing at our oceanfront place in Hawaii. We live a truly blessed life. A few weeks ago, I received a call in the middle of the day from Emilia, thanking me for working so hard, providing such an amazing life for her, our son, and her parents. That simple three-minute conversation made my entire day.

It made me think of the *New Girlfriend Talks* I used to have years ago, back when I first started my business conquest. Thank God I didn't conform to popular demand back then. Sure, those talks were uncomfortable to have, but when I look at the business I have today... the lifestyle I have today... and the family I have today... it was all worth it.

Stage #4: Revenge.

Wait a minute! Revenge? I thought Stage #4 of the grieving process was *acceptance*! Most psychologists and counselors will tell you that you have to accept what has happened in your past in order to move on. Perhaps there is some truth to that.

I remember having dinner with a pastor friend of mine as was going through my divorce. He told me, *"Darren, what happened to you was unfair. No doubt about it. But what you need to focus on is what you're going to do with your life from this moment forward."*

I suppose what he was trying to tell me was that I needed to just accept the fact that I was where I was, and that there was no turning the clock back on time. He was trying to tell me to accept the reality, but focus on the future. There was a lot of wisdom in that piece of advice.

The problem was, it didn't make me feel any better emotionally, and it didn't empower me.

Most people in my life were trying to get me to peacefully go on with my life and love my enemies. Well, let's just say that I'm not a *love thy enemies* type of guy. At the same time, I'm also wise enough to know that *getting even* in the traditional sense of the phrase doesn't improve my life either. Moving forward is about personal empowerment, putting yourself in a better situation.

Seeking revenge can be dangerous and can lead to a life of bitterness filled with grudges. I, however, have a different perspective on how to use revenge as a very positive motivator. When I got divorced, I went back to Reynold, the jeweler who I purchased my wedding rings from. He was a childhood friend of Earl, my ex-wife's father, and so it was a very uncomfortable feeling to ask him to buy back my wedding band.

As I walked into Reynold's store, I didn't know what to expect. I didn't know if he'd welcome me, or throw me out. Well, my conversation with Reynold went very differently that what I expected. He welcomed me into his store, and said to me, *"Look Darren, I know what happened. Earl and I have been friends since we were kids, and we'll always be friends. But you're a stand-up guy, and you're always welcome here. I'm happy to buy your ring back, but the price of gold is low right now. Come back when the price of gold is up, and I can give you a better price."*

I gladly took Reynold's advice, and thanked him. One year later, I had decided to leave Hawaii and return to Los Angeles, California and start my life over again, focusing on business. I went back to see Reynold before I left to see if he would honor his promise of buying my ring back.

Reynold told me that the price of gold was still low, but that he'd be happy to buy it back from me. I gladly accepted. He asked me what I was going to do back in California, and I told him I was going to start my own business.

Reynold stopped what he was doing and got very serious. He looked me in the eyes and said, *"You want to know what the best revenge is?"* I thought to myself, *revenge*? Where did that come from? Reynold was dead serious.

He said, *"Hey! Listen to me. You want to know what the best revenge is?"* I stared at him sheepishly.

"*Success,*" he replied. Now, I think Reynold was talking about financial success. He was a successful guy himself, owning a couple of companies in the jewelry business. Reynold understood something. A man can only be happy when he feels like a *real man*... and a man can only truly feel like a *real man* if he is financially successful.

You can argue with me, but every man knows what I'm talking about when I say this. It's just part of what is hard-wired into our DNA, going all the way back to the beginning of our species' existence.

I'm not saying it's right, or good. I'm just saying that it's true. Most male entrepreneurs, including myself, are empowered by being financially successful. Perhaps it's part of fulfilling our role as a provider for our family. Whatever the case, it is what it is. So Reynold knew what made me tick.

But I took Reynold's advice to have a deeper meaning. He didn't say that the best revenge was to get rich or to rub it in anyone's face. He also didn't say that the best revenge was even to make a lot of money. He said that the best revenge was *success*.

When I thought more about Reynold's words of advice to me, I realized that what he was really talking about was regaining my *Belief In Self*. I think he knew that my confidence had been shaken through the process of divorce, and that I needed something to make me feel good about myself.

So I poured everything I had into my work, which included a lot of internal work on myself. I was broke at the time, so I used to go to used book stores and buy self-help paperback books for $1.50 each.

As I've said before, success in life is not so much about what you accomplish, but rather what you overcome. And so I set out to overcome my self-doubt. That would be the way I would avenge myself; to become successful. I look back on that five-minute conversation with Reynold, and I realize now that it was a major defining moment in my life. It's amazing how something so simple can have such a dramatic impact on a person.

I remember surfing at one of my favorite surf spots the day before I left Hawaii to pursue my entrepreneurial aspirations in California. I was filled with two very strong emotions: Excitement and Fear. I was excited about finally pursuing my dreams, but I was also deathly afraid of failure. This reminds me of an old story about a Native American Chief. The story goes something like this:

A young warrior went to seek advice from a legendary Native American Chief. Upon finally finding and meeting the Chief, the young man tells the Chief that he always feels conflicted.

He says, "Chief, sometimes I do everything I'm supposed to do. But other times, I don't do what I know I should be doing. Sometimes I'm driven, and sometimes I'm lazy. Sometimes I work hard, and sometimes I procrastinate. Sometimes I'm courageous and sometimes I'm a coward. Why is this?"

The Chief replied, "Young man, inside your heart lives two dogs. One dog is the master of courage, discipline and honor... and the other dog is the master of cowardness, laziness and selfishness... and they are always fighting each other."

The young warrior then asked, "Which dog will win?"

The Chief answered, "Whichever dog you feed the most."

And so that's where I was... fighting to feed the good dog that would make me courageous. I think all entrepreneurs and aspiring entrepreneurs have been in this same predicament. It's never easy to feed the good dog, but if you're passionate about seeking the kind of revenge that Reynold inspired me to achieve, you'll choose to consistently feed the good dog.

When I finally *made it*, I started going back to Hawaii to vacation once or twice a year, and always made it a point to surf that same surf spot I surfed the day before I left Hawaii to pursue my entrepreneurial dreams. I remember when I was a kid, I'd hear about celebrities and movie stars living in hotels, and I always thought that was cool, and so as a *revenge-inspired trophy*, I bought the Honeymoon Suite at a hotel that sits right in front of that same surf spot I told you about. It's a one-bedroom suite on the twelfth floor, and it sits right on the water. It is literally seventeen steps to the water.

The entire wall on the right side of both the living room and the bedroom is floor-to-ceiling glass, and has an incredible, unobstructed view of the ocean, mountains, and the city, looking straight into Waikiki. The entire wall on the left side of both the living room and bedroom has huge windows that give me an unobstructed view of Diamond Head and the ocean, looking right down on that great surf spot.

My wife and son go there a couple of times a year, and it always reminds me of the day before I left Hawaii. It reminds me of the fear I had that day. It reminds me of what I had to go through to achieve the lifestyle I have today. It reminds me of that conversation I had with Reynold. And it reminds me of how glad I am that I had the courage to hit the reset button.

Sometimes hitting the reset button happens during one momentous occasion. However often times, hitting the reset button is a process that happens gradually. In either case, there is usually a defining moment that sparks the beginning of hitting the reset button. I suppose my conversation with Reynold was that spark I needed, and for that, I will always feel grateful towards Reynold.

When One Door Closes, Find Another One To Open

Going through a setback is never easy, and sometimes it can feel as if your world is coming to an end. Believe me, I've been there. But what I can tell you is that being a solution-centric person, practically every time I've suffered a set back in my life, or when a door has been slammed in my face, I've been able to find a better door to open.

Notice I didn't say that another door opened. Another door did not magically appear, nor did one open for me. First, I had to do the work to find another door, and then I had to open it myself (often times it required prying it open with a crowbar).

Making lemonade out of the sour lemons you've been dealt is rarely an easy or convenient process. It takes work. You've got to squeeze a lot of lemons to get the juice. Squeezing lemons is hard work, and you'll get fatigued in the process, but you must not quit. Keep squeezing and squeezing.

On top of that, you've got to add your own sugar. Lemons don't come with their own sweetener. It's your responsibility to supply the sweetener. Some people think the sugar fairy is going to come along and sprinkle magic fairy sugar dust into their sour lemon juice.

Squeezing the lemons is not enough. It's up to you to change the sourness into sweetness. And then you've got to stir... a lot. I know people that want other people to do all the stirring for them. You're the one that's got to do the stirring, and yes, your arms will get sore from stirring and stirring and stirring, but you've got to keep stirring. No one said this was going to be easy. Always remember that anything worth having, especially a triumphant revenge, is worth working hard for.

So whether you're starting your career, or you're starting your career over (or maybe even starting your life over), always remember that it's only too late to hit the reset button once you're dead. Until then, you still have the opportunity to get your revenge... the revenge of being successful and reclaiming your confidence. And if you're an aspiring entrepreneur... whether you're starting your own business... or you're an independent contractor... or you're working on straight-commission... or you a network marketer... or you went to work for a start-up company, banking on your stock options and the growth of your company... you, my friend, are an entrepreneur at heart.

What I love about entrepreneurs, is that entrepreneurs have the ability to *dream big*. There are no glass ceilings... no boss trying to keep you down... no restrictions on your income potential. As an entrepreneur, the sky is the limit... and here's the best part. You were born this way.

People either have the *entrepreneur gene*, or they don't. If you dream about being a successful entrepreneur, don't take this gift lightly. It's a gift that very few people are given. The ve ry fact that you have this burning desire within you means that this is your destiny. You were made to do this. Let's discuss how to make sure you fulfill your destiny as an entrepreneur.

Chapter Eight:
Being A Successful Entrepreneur

"What you are given is never as valuable as what you earn."
-Darren Sugiyama

Successful Entrepreneurs

Have you ever wondered what makes certain people successful? If you compare two people of similar intelligence, similar upbringing and similar education, how can one person be so incredibly successful in life, and the other person just be *average*? Is it luck? Is it skill? Is it work ethic?

I remember back when I started my career, I'd see these successful people and wonder to myself, *"What exactly are they doing differently than everybody else… and can I do what they're doing?"*

I didn't want to be *average*. I wanted more. I wanted to achieve *greatness*. I'd see these people driving luxury cars, living in mansions, and traveling to exotic places around the world, and I'd ask myself, *"Why couldn't that be me one day?"*

It's not that I was materialistic. I just didn't think these people possessed any superhuman powers that I couldn't develop myself. Maybe I was naïve. Maybe I had an over-inflated opinion of myself. Or maybe, I just realized something that most people never quite grasp. I realized that success is nothing more than preparing for and creating opportunities, and then being able to capitalize on these opportunities immediately.

Sure, being *lucky* can expedite the process of becoming successful, but I've never seemed to be able to create *luck* in my life out of thin air. I've read books about success that implied that all you have to do is think positive thoughts, and expect positive things to happen, and that was the so-called *secret*.

Give me a break. I know of too many people that have used *positive thinking* as a substitute for hard work, which is absolutely ridiculous. The real world doesn't work that way.

I've also heard people talk about how they asked the universe to magically make them rich, and that magically, they opened their mailbox one day and found a big check. Perhaps this actually happened to a few people, possibly through an inheritance. Call me crazy, but becoming rich due to the death of a loved one doesn't seem like something to celebrate.

In addition, inheriting someone else's fortune doesn't make you *successful*. Being *successful* implies that you've accomplished something on your own merit, usually overcoming multiple adversities along the way.

You see, a truly *successful* person is one that has built character through perseverance, dedication and sacrifice. I know a lot of *rich* people that I wouldn't categorize as being *successful*. Sure, they have money, but they didn't accomplish anything on their own merit to get it.

There are so many teachings out there that imply that you can achieve financial success by substituting something mystical in the place of hard work. I even know of people that say that if you have faith in God, that God will take care of all of your needs, almost devaluing the importance of hard work.

These same people will quote the Bible when discussing this issue. Matthew 6:26 says, *"Look at the birds of the air; they do not sow or reap or store away in barns, and yet your heavenly Father feeds them. Are you not much more valuable than they?"*

But let's take this scripture and put it in the proper context. Have you ever seen a bird kicking back in a lounge chair with his beak open, waiting for a worm to crawl in? Of course not.

Birds work hard, all day long, looking for food. One of the fundamental principles of *success* is that in most cases, you have to *create* your own opportunities, just like birds do.

Perhaps God provides the worms for the bird, but the bird still has to do the work to find them. The bird has to work hard. Unless you're a trust-fund baby, or you marry a wealthy person, you have to *do* something in order to *get* something. So-called *luck* often happens when opportunity and the proper preparation meet. In reality, this is not luck at all. This is *planned* success.

The question is, *"If you want to be successful in business, what should you do?"* Most people don't know the answer to this question, and so they look outwardly for answers, which is the beginning of their problem.

Being successful in business, and in life for that matter, is about looking *internally* and reprogramming your thought process. We have all been involuntarily programmed and brainwashed by the media, pop culture and society at large, to think like a pessimist. You need to reprogram your thought process.

Reprogramming Your Thought Process

The first step of reprogramming the way you think is to see things for what they *really* are. I'm not an advocate of being unrealistically positive about adverse situations. That's called *denial*, and denial will not improve your situation. That being said, being unrealistically negative doesn't help things either.

Many times, we see our current situation as being *worse* than it actually is, which will lead to a life of failure. I'm not suggesting that you force yourself to see things as being *better* than they actually are, but I *am* suggesting that you should not see things as being *worse* than they actually are. You've got to objectively see things for what they *really* are.

What we're talking about here is having a realistic, yet optimistic perspective. Your current situation is what it is, but the game changer is your *perspective* on your current situation.

Your perspective shapes what you're going to *do* about your current situation to change the circumstance in your favor. That's why I say that the first step to being *successful* is to do some *internal work*, starting with changing your *perspective*. Your *perspective* is based on how you emotionally *process* an experience... and ultimately, what you *do* about it.

What you *do* is predominantly shaped by your *perspective* regarding the level of difficulty of what it is that you're attempting to *do*. How *hard* or *easy* is the task at hand?

Hard vs. Easy

If you view something as being *hard* to do, you will most likely procrastinate, and possibly never get around to attempting to execute the task. However, if you view something as *easy* to do, you're more likely to just get it done.

In business, we as human beings are very susceptible to our emotions. We abhor the feeling of rejection, which is why most people avoid situations that could potentially lead to feelings of rejection. Now, the obvious problem with *rejection avoidance* is that if you give in to it, you'll never accomplish anything. Usually, when people say their business is *hard*, they're referring to the emotional component of the task, not the task in and of itself.

For example, *sales* is one of the most looked down upon professions, which I find to be incredibly ironic. Without sales people, there would be no consumers. Without consumers, there is no revenue. Without revenue, there are no profits. Without profits, companies lay off employees. Without jobs, well, you know what happens next.

Sales people create jobs for people and stimulate the economy. Whether you're a business owner, or a corporate executive, or a sales executive, or a telemarketer, you're in sales, and you should be proud of it. Without you leading the charge, companies go out of business.

I've heard people say that being in sales is *hard*. But think about this for a moment. It is not a physically difficult thing to do. You pick up the phone, dial it, talk into it, and that's about it.

There really isn't anything else to it. It is not a physically *hard* thing to do. It doesn't require a superhuman skill. The skills required would include:

1. Literacy (the ability to read and memorize your pitch).
2. Vocal Competency (the ability to audibly speak out loud).
3. Minor Dexterity (the ability to physically dial the phone with your finger).

Most people have these skills, and so by definition, being in sales is not *hard*. The *hard* part is experiencing rejection 90 percent of the time, and not allowing the high percentage of rejection to affect your emotions in an adverse way.

Let's face it. Getting rejected sucks. It doesn't make you feel good about yourself, no matter how much someone tells you that it's just a *numbers game*. It still makes you feel like crap. This is just a function of poor *expectation management*.

Managing Your Expectations

In the world of *selling*, you're only going to have a 10 percent contact rate, which means that you're only going to get 10 percent of your prospects on the phone with you. 90 percent of them will be unavailable for a variety of reasons, and you'll get their voicemail.

Of this 10 percent that you actually talk to on the phone, you'll probably only book appointments with about 10 to 15 percent of them. So if you look at your total experience on the phone, over 98 percent of every call you make results in *failure*. If you understand that this is the road to success, then you won't sweat it. But if you lose clarity and get emotional about it, you'll start making a series of bad decisions based on your misinterpretation of your results.

For example, in school, if you score 30 percent on your exam, you failed the exam. But in baseball, if your batting average is .300 (which is a 30 percent success rate), you're an All-Star. It all comes down to understanding what specific results constitute success, and setting your expectations accordingly. If your expectations are not in line with the true definition of success in your specific industry, you could get depressed about your results, when in fact you're tracking perfectly according to the proper success expectations.

If a baseball player got depressed that he only succeeded 50 percent of the time (meaning he was batting .500), that would be ridiculous. But it would be understandable if he was comparing it to scoring 50 percent on a math exam (which would earn him an F grade), thus truly understanding how to gauge success as it pertains to your results in your specific business is paramount.

I've seen people quit careers simply because they misunderstood or lost sight of what constitutes *success* in their particular industry. Understanding the numbers, ramp up time, pipeline building and future gains is what separates *successful business people* from *sales rep burnouts*.

One of the companies I own is a $37 million insurance agency. This morning, I held a meeting with my sales producers regarding this debate of whether the insurance business was *hard* versus *easy*. I asked my sales producers if they thought the insurance business was a *hard* business. I got a wide range of responses.

My goal of this meeting was to help them clarify the actual tasks required to succeed in our particular industry (the insurance industry). I also mathematically illustrated what the actual payoff was per prospecting phone dial. You should have seen their eyes light up.

In my prospecting system, I know the numbers on a very intimate level. I designed my insurance consulting firm to generate sales opportunities exclusively through cold-calling, which *no one* does in my industry. In the initial testing phase of developing my firm, we tracked the statistical results using cold-calling as our primary form of marketing.

Let's say one of my sales producers makes 500 phone dials. We have a 6 percent contact ratio, meaning that 94 percent of every dial we make results in us not being able to generate a conversation with the *decision maker*, due to the fact that they're not available to talk.

This means that 6 percent of these calls result in conversations with *decision makers*. In our case, we define a *decision maker* as a business owner. A 6 percent contact rate on 500 phone dials equals 30 conversations with *decision makers*.

Of these *decision makers* we talk to, our average appointment booking percentage is 14 percent, so 14 percent of 30 decision makers equals 4.2 appointments generated with decision makers.

Of these 4.2 decision makers we generate meetings with, our average closing percentage is 32 percent. So 32 percent of 4.2 decision makers equals 1.3 deals closed per 500 dials.

If we use an average company size of 10 employees, my sales producers' commission is approximately $1,000 per year. If the client only stays on the books for 5 years, the total commission paid to my sales producers would be $5,000.

So this means that for every 500 phone dials my producer makes, at $5,000 in commissions per client, each dial would be worth $10, regardless of the outcome of each individual call. I asked all of my producers, if I changed the commission plan here to $10 per dial, would you think this job is *hard* or *easy*?

They all started laughing, because they finally realized their misperception of making cold-calls. I asked them, *"If I paid you $10 per dial, how much would you have made last week?"*

The average number of dials was a little over 400 dials per week per producer, which means they would have made over $4,000 last week... which would be the equivalent of $16,000 per month... which would be the equivalent of $192,000 per year.

I asked them if they would prefer this commission plan over the one that currently exists. Most of the new producers emphatically jumped at the idea of this proposition. In fact, they said that with this type of compensation plan, this would be the *easiest* job they ever had.

The irony is that George, one of my successful producers that has been with me for almost seven years, made over $221,000 in commissions with me last year. Do you think he wants to switch out commission plans? No way.

You see, once the newer producers compared the two compensation plans, and after discovering what George makes, they all realized that if they work hard for seven more years, they'll be making more than $10 per dial. Illustrating their actual monetary return on their investment per dial helped them understand how easy their job really is.

Sales And Dating Are Both Numbers Games

In my *Success Training Seminars*, I often use examples of human interaction in the *dating world*. The world of dating is so analogous to sales and business.

In most cultures, the man is the one that typically approaches and pursues the woman. Metaphorically speaking, the man is the *sales producer,* and the woman is the *prospect*.

The man is trying to get a date with the woman, and the precursory goal is to get her to willingly give him her phone number. In order for the woman to *want* to give the man her phone number, the man has to build trust, likeability and feelings of attraction with the woman, and he only has a few short minutes to do it.

The initial interaction must make the woman feel comfortable or intrigued, preferably both. If the interaction doesn't go smoothly, and if it feels forced or awkward, it will probably end poorly. So the question is, what can a man do or say that will make the woman attracted to him and intrigued by him?

Most men do not know the answer to this question, which is why most single men experience so much anxiety when it comes to dating. In my previously written book, *How I Built A $37 Million Insurance Agency In Less Than 7 Years*, I actually discuss how to overcome this anxiety in Chapter 9, entitled *Managing Expectations*.

The primary purpose of that chapter was to overcome the fear of prospecting and the fear of rejection, however ironically, most single guys seem to be more interested in utilizing those techniques to talk to women instead of generating sales. Go figure. In a nutshell, the concept of overcoming the fear of prospecting is that if you understand the numbers game, and you map out the mathematics of it all, you'll eventually succeed.

Let's use a humorous, hypothetical example. And single ladies, you can participate in this too. Think about how many people you come within a 100-foot radius to on a daily basis. Is it realistic to say that within this physical radius, you see at least one person per day that you're physically attracted to?

Okay, so consider this. If you just walked up to just one of these people per day and started a conversation with them, and at the end of that conversation, you said, *"Hey, we should hang out sometime. Let me get your phone number,"* what's the worst thing that could happen to you? They could say, *"No, I'm not interested."*

Now, I could sit here and say, *"So, what. It's no big deal,"* but the problem is that it *is* a big deal, emotionally. The feeling of getting rejected sucks, right? So what happens?

You avoid putting yourself in scenarios where you risk the chance of getting rejected. If you're single, and if it's fair to say that you see at least one person per day that you find attractive, what if you forced yourself to talk to that one person, each day?

Sure, you'd get rejected a lot, but think about this. You'd have talked to 365 people per year. Now, let's also assume that half of the 365 people that you find attractive are married. That leaves you with about 182 unmarried people. Let's also assume that of the remaining 182 unmarried people, half of them are already in committed relationships. That would leave you with a pool of 91 people that are *qualified dating prospects* for you.

Let's say that half of these people don't find you to be physically attractive, for whatever reason. Of the 91 people, 46 of them prefer taller or shorter people, or people of a different ethnicity, or people that dress differently, or people with a different hairstyle or hair color, or whatever.

Okay, that means that 46 of the people that you find attractive don't find you attractive. That sounds depressing on the surface, but just look at the *real numbers* objectively.

It means that 45 people *do* find you attractive. It may not make you feel better, but 45 attractive people that also find you attractive… that's a lot of people. Let's say that of this pool of 45 people, you totally screw up the conversation with half of them, and they walk away thinking that you are a total dork. I don't think this would happen, but let's just say it does.

That means you still have 22 people that you find to be physically attractive, that also find you attractive, and they also find you interesting and fun to talk to. That's a run-rate of almost two *first dates* every month. That's a lot of first-dates. Sure, only 6 percent of your efforts ended in success, which means that you had a 94 percent failure rate, but who cares? Your failure rate is irrelevant, as long as your success rate was enough to get you what you ultimately want, in this case, two first dates per month.

Now, think for a moment about a happily married person. How many first dates has the average happily married person gone on in their entire adult life? For most people, it's less than ten.

So based on these numbers in my crazy example, you would have gone on more than double the amount of first dates that the average happily married person has gone on in their entire lifetime, and you did it in just twelve months. Statistically, you would have met at least two people that you would actually consider marriage material, and again, you did it in just one year. Not bad.

You see, success is not about *percentages*. Success is about *aggregates*. It's about what you ultimately end up with, and how you perceive the experience along the way, relative to your outcome.

Monetary Success In Business

You may be asking yourself, *"Why is Darren talking about dating and cold-calling? What does this have to do with being successful and Living Outside The Cubicle?"*

Both the *dating world* and the *cold-calling/prospecting world* are analogous to being successful in business because they both deal with your expectations and managing your emotions. They both deal with a significant amount of rejection. When it comes to finance and success in business, the amount of rejection you experience is only relevant based on the size and frequency of the ultimate reward.

In monetary terms, who cares if you got rejected 99 times out of 100 if it meant you made over a million dollars? The end result was worth the emotional feeling of rejection along the way. This is what I'm talking about regarding truly *understanding* the outcome of your actions. The physical act of prospecting might not be as fun as watching TV, but it certainly pays off financially over time.

You need to understand what the *real* reward is, and then reverse-engineer the mathematical formula to come to a dollar figure that each individual action is *actually* worth. Once you do this, your perspective (in this case, regarding making cold-calls) will change and you'll see what your actual reward is… not your immediate emotional reward, but rather your bigger picture monetary reward.

I've seen so many people lose sight of the bigger picture because they get caught up in their day-to-day emotions based on their day-to-day results and day-to-day experiences, especially early on in the game. This is about as illogical as going to the gym and complaining that you haven't lost twenty pounds and four inches off your waist within the first week, or deciding to build a house, and complaining a week later that you don't have a mansion yet.

Building a successful career or a successful business, generally speaking, takes time. You've got to map out your game plan and create a timeline. Your timeline must be based on a proven model in order to set achievable expectations.

If you're venturing off into unchartered waters, and being a true pioneer, I think that's great, but just remember that although your success *could* manifest overnight, it will most likely take longer than you emotionally want it to. That's where *discipline* and *clarity* come in.

Discipline is obviously important when it comes to being successful, but an equally important component to the success formula is *clarity*. Think of it like this. Discipline is the *muscle* behind your operation. Clarity is the *brains* behind your operation. You need both in order to be successful.

You can have more discipline than your competition, but if you're doing the *wrong things*, or not enough of the *right things*, you'll fail. You've got to do enough of the *right things*, repetitively, over time. This leads us back to the million dollar question, *"What are the right things you should be doing to become successful?"*

As we uncovered in this book, the answer is not a secret, nor is it mystical. It is based on a formula of simple, logical principles that I have used in my own life. My wish for you is that you apply these principles to live a happier, more successful life.

Never despise the days of small beginnings. You have to start somewhere, and usually, the beginning stages are not very glamorous, but they are necessary. Let's talk about step one of the empire building process… the part that few people know how to do properly. *Prospecting.*

Chapter Nine:
The Fine Art Of Prospecting

"Amateurs are in the convincing game, whereas masters are in the identifying game. Which game are you playing?"

-Darren Sugiyama

Identifying Your Target Market

I've heard so many amateurs in sales say things like, *"Most people aren't interested."* No matter what you're selling, statistically, most people will not be interested. But you've got to understand that your target market is not *most people*. Every product or service has a niche market of consumers that wants that particular product or service – a *target market* – and part of your job is to identify that market, and construct your message to speak to that market, and ONLY that market.

So many people in sales attempt to appeal to *everyone*, and not everyone is interested in their particular product or service. For example, most people are not going to buy a Ferrari. In fact well over 99 percent of the people in this world will not buy a Ferrari, however Ferrari does just fine without *most people*.

In consulting multi-million dollar and multi-billion dollar corporations, I've found that the majority of sales executives in these companies are still trying to sell *everyone*. This is a huge mistake. Trying to convert the proverbial atheist into a believer takes a huge amount of work, and unless you're in an evangelical organization, it is a poor business plan, mainly because it rarely works.

You've got to identify your target market, and design your entire marketing campaign around resonating with this target market, instead of trying to appeal to markets that want nothing to do with you.

What Do Prospects Really Want?

Once you've identified your target market, you have to identify what they will respond to. Notice, I didn't say to listen to what they *say* they want, and I didn't say to focus on what they *think* they want. I said to identify what they will emotionally *respond* to. In the world of sales, prospects are like women in the dating world. What they *say* they want is rarely what they *respond to*, emotionally.

I've heard women say they want a nice, sensitive, chivalrous gentleman that likes to take long romantic walks on the beach... but then who do they go out with? The *Bad Boy* in the leather jacket riding the motorcycle, who is neither sensitive nor chivalrous. Men are just as bad. Men think they want a sexy, slightly-naughty, Playboy bunny-type, but once they're in a committed relationship, they get all pissed off when their girlfriend or wife dresses too provocatively in public.

My point here is that people, in general, think they want one thing, but when push comes to shove, what they *say* they want is not congruent with what they *respond to*. So what does this have to do with sales? Oh, just about everything.

Think about your prospects. You probably think your prospects want one thing, usually because they tell you what they want. The problem is that the prospect doesn't even understand how their subconscious mind works, thus they don't really consciously know what makes them tick. They don't know what truly drives their decision-making process, and thus, if you construct your sales message based on what they *say* they want, you're setting yourself up for failure. Let me explain.

Most sales reps base their entire sales message around the lure of saving money... or proving that their product is better than the prospect's existing product. Sorry to break the news to you, but they don't want to save money. They don't want a better product. And I hate to crush your optimism, but they don't want *your* product either.

Offering a monetary savings, or a better product, or a better service to your prospective clients seems logical and rational, and on the surface, I would agree. If you were to ask one of your prospective clients what they want, they would probably say things like, *"If you can save me money, I'd be open to switching,"* or *"If you can prove that your product is better, I'd be open to switching."*

The problem is that they're lying to you. They may not be maliciously lying to you, or even consciously lying to you for that matter, but the reality is that both of these propositions are focused on appealing to their *greed for gain*. Again, this is a logical thought process, so please don't take offense to what I'm saying.

I used to do the same thing. But when I used to use this approach, all I got was a bunch of prospects that smiled at me, saying things like, "*It looks like you have a great product/program/service, but I think we're just going to stay where we're at right now.*"

Have you ever heard this? Have you ever had a prospect that seemed to love your product/program/service, but didn't pull the trigger with you? It's frustrating, isn't it?

I used to have these conversations with myself, saying, "*I don't get it. They seemed so positive. Why aren't they doing business with me?*" When I finally found the answer, my entire business changed forever, and I became wealthy within one and a half years. Here's what I discovered.

I realized that my sales message needed to appeal to my prospects' emotional need to get out of pain. Here I was, with what I thought was a well crafted sales message, but I was blowing it. My sales message was attempting to appeal to the person's logic instead of their emotions.

Understand that logic *solidifies* a prospect's decision to buy, but emotion is what *triggers* the decision to buy. You've got to understand what set of emotions trigger the decision making process. You've got to identify the initial tipping point.

The Emotional Tipping Point

Think about luxury cars for a moment. People don't buy luxury cars for logical reasons. They're depreciating liabilities. The maintenance cost on luxury cars is often times triple cost of economy cars. You have to use higher octane gasoline, which is more expensive. The insurance cost is more expensive.

So how do luxury car manufactures stay in business if their product is more expensive, they're more of a pain-in-the-butt to maintain, and they're more expensive to maintain?

Here's why. People don't buy luxury cars for logical, practical reasons. Consumers in general don't make initial buying decisions based on logical, practical reasons. They make them based on emotional gratification. Here are some reasons people buy luxury cars:
1. Prestige.
2. Acceptance in certain social circles.
3. Recognition for their success.
4. Validation for their hard work.
5. Emotional revenge on their enemies.

The majority of benefits that come with driving a luxury car are emotional. As a businessman, sure I get a strong *Return On Investment* by using luxury cars to enhance my personal brand and image, and sure I get a substantial tax deduction due to leasing the vehicle instead of buying it, and sure, driving a luxury car makes me feel more powerful, indirectly resulting in me closing more business and making more money. All of these points are true and accounted for, and they reinforce the decision to spend over $100,000 on a luxury car.

However, it's easy to argue these points by rationalizing the fact that I don't *need* a car this expensive. That's the problem with focusing your initial sales message on rationality. It doesn't work. You've got to dive straight into the emotional gratification the prospect is going to receive, which is routed in the prospect escaping from an emotional frustration.

A few years ago, the new Mercedes S-Class came out, and I was at the dealership in Newport Beach. The price of the car listed at $93,000. The sales guy came up to me and asked if I needed any help.

I replied, *"I'm not in the market for a new car right now. I'm just looking."* The sales guy asked me what I was currently driving, and I told him that I already had a Mercedes CL 500, and I was happy with it. My car payment at that time was a little over $1,000 per month, which I was comfortable with.

The sales guy said, *"What if I could get you into a brand new S-Class for only a few hundred dollars more than you're paying now?"*

I replied, *"No thanks. I'm happy with my car now, and I don't really feel like spending more money."*

He then asked if I owned my car, or if I was leasing. When I told him I owned the car, he asked me what I did for a living. When I told him that I owned a few businesses, he said, *"If you lease the car, you can get a bigger tax deduction, and your net cost will probably be about the same as you're paying now."*

Okay, I must admit that this caught my attention, so I called my CPA from my cell phone, right there on the spot to verify whether or not this was true.

My CPA confirmed that it was in fact true, and so I penciled the numbers out. The S-Class would cost me about $150 more per month, net. Not bad, but I still went back to the fact that I didn't *need* a new car.

Logically, the extra $150 per month would probably be the savings in maintenance costs (because the car was brand under a factory warranty), and it was a four-door sedan where 500 was a coupe (making it more practical because my wife and I were planning on starting a family).

These were all logical reasons that I could use to justify splurging a little bit. But they still weren't enough to get me to pull the trigger.

Here I was, at the crux of the tipping point. I could go either way. I was open to the idea of pulling the trigger, but no matter how many logical/cerebral reasons that were communicated to me, it just wasn't enough.

Then the sales guy hit my hot button. He said,

> *"Look Darren, you don't drive a $93,000 car because it's a good investment. You drive a $93,000 car because it's a way to reward yourself for working so hard. If you own several companies, then you're probably very successful, and you probably got to where you are today because you worked your ass off, right?"*

Basically, he gave me validation. He made me feel good about what I've accomplished. He gave me recognition, which is something that every human being wants. And then he sealed the deal with these next few words. He said,

> *"You deserve to reward yourself. You can obviously afford a couple hundred bucks more per month, but that's not the issue. The issue is that you're going to drive this car everyday, and everyday you step inside this car, you're going to feel good. You're a successful man, and a successful man deserves to drive a car like this."*

He closed me. He appealed to my sense of entitlement, which is an emotional feeling. He made me want to escape the feeling of having to be *practical*. My current Mercedes was a beautiful car, but when I felt like I deserved to be driving a brand new car, I felt like I was sacrificing my well deserved desire for the sake of being *practical*. Emotionally, being practical sucks.

I said to myself, "*Damn it, I work my ass off! I shouldn't have to feel like I'm sacrificing anymore!*" And that was the tipping point for me.

When you construct your sales message, you have to get your prospect to that tipping point. They must get frustrated with their current circumstance, and feel entitled to being put in a better circumstance.

The easiest way to do this is to identify what your prospects complain about most. If you're pitching a service, identify the most frequently complained about issues that exist in your industry, and position your service as the *only* service that never has these issues due to a unique element of your business.

All you have to do is get your prospect emotionally worked up about problems they encounter that frustrated the heck out of them, and harp on these problems, putting the prospect in the emotional state of wanting to get rid of them.

If you're selling a product, identify the most common complaints that clients have about like-kind products, and position your product as the *only* product that doesn't have these problems. Obviously, you've got to back up that claim, which means you'd better make sure you're representing a great product.

Essentially, in either case, whether you're selling a service or a product, you've got to position yourself as selling a *solution*... a solution to the prospect's problem.

You need to make them want to escape the emotional frustration of their current problem, more so than trying to convince them that your product or service is better.

In other words, get them to focus on *escaping from prison*, as opposed to trying to inspire them to *achieve freedom*.

Now, all that being said, it is imperative that you only focus on hitting your target market. So step one is identifying your target market.

Step two is identifying what your target market really wants, which is to *escape from prison*. Do these two things, and you'll have so many clients, you can afford to fire the bad ones.

Firing Prospects and Clients

In my own companies, I actually fire prospects all the time, and from time to time, I'll fire existing clients as well. Sounds ballsy, right? I'll tell you why this is a smart thing to do, and why you should do it too.

If you were to identify the key characteristics of *good clients*, what characteristics would make your *Top 5 List*? I've identified 5 key characteristics of the types of clients that I want to work with. I only look for clients that are:

1. Smart enough to realize the level of value they receive from me is unparalleled, and appreciative of the quality of work that I do.

2. Ethical, whose actions would not put me in an ethically compromising position.

3. Not looking for the cheapest deal in town, and are willing to pay top dollar for top quality work, giving them top quality results.

4. Patient, valuing long-term, steady growth and progress.

5. Realistic in their desired outcomes.

If I get the slightest feeling that the prospect is missing one of these five essential qualities, I cut bait immediately. If it's a current client that is showing signs of not embodying these essential characteristics, I seriously think about firing them as a client. I've done this several times with substantial clients that were producing me substantial revenue, but they were a big pain in the butt, and my time was better served replacing them with better clients.

Again, there are some clients that are *bad clients*. They're just not your target market, and if you really understand the type of business you're building, you won't want to work with *everyone*. That being said, you need to stop trying to appeal to *everyone*, and just focus in on appealing to your target market.

Your goal should be to identify which prospects are a good fit for your product or service. You've got to be in the *identifying game*, not the *convincing game*. In simple terms, just find the people who want what you've got.

This is the same mistake I've seen people make in dating. It seems like everyone's trying to be something they're not, attempting to be a chameleon and win over approval from the masses. If you just focus on being the best *you* as possible, you'll attract the *right* companion.

And just like in the dating world, in the world of business, you can create whatever parameters you want. You can decide to be whatever you want, which is part of developing your own brand, something we discussed earlier.

The key, however, is to stick to this brand and market yourself accordingly. Your marketing message and selling efforts need to be congruent with your brand, so that you attract the right type of prospect... and when you do this properly... your closing percentage will go up, as will your client retention rate.

But even when you're targeting your ideal client demographic, you've still got an initial hurdle to get over in the world of selling (as well as in the world of dating). Typically, your prospect isn't just sitting around, waiting for you to call. They're busy.

So when you do call them, you're typically going to be calling them at an inopportune time. They're probably right in the middle of something. They're either just stepping out of a meeting, or just about to step into one. Or they're just getting off another call, or just about to answer another one. Or they're right in the middle of working on a project... or stepping out for lunch... or dealing with an important business issue. They're distracted.

By definition, you're interrupting them right in the middle of doing something, and when they're in this distracted emotional state, they're not going to be open to talking to you, in most cases.

Everyone is in a particular emotional state, and this emotional state is dictated by the scenario the person finds themselves in at that very moment. For instance, right now, you're reading this book, which means that you're in a curious, intrigued emotional state. You're open to receiving new ideas because I have your undivided attention.

With prospects, they aren't in a curious, intrigued emotional state when you call them in the middle of their work day, so you've got to put them in this emotional state in order for them to be open to hearing about your idea.

Think about the last time you found yourself in the midst of putting out a fire in your own business. Were you open to hearing about or dealing with anything other than the problem at hand? Probably not, and neither are your prospects... unless you do something to shock them out of their current emotional state. You've got to break them out of their current emotional state, in order to put them in the proper emotional state where they're *curious*, *intrigued*, and eventually, *excited*.

Breaking Emotional States

What I'm about to share with you is a very subtle technique, however the results you'll get by using this technique are absolutely dramatic. I call this *Emotional State Breaking*.

The power of effective sales language is something that I've come to master over the years, and it all starts with breaking your prospect's emotional state. In almost every one of my phone sales scripts, I lead off by saying, "*Hey, I'm glad I got a hold of you!*"

When someone hears this simple line, at the subconscious level, they will either expect *good news* or *important news*. In fact, suppose I called you up at home in the middle of the night and said, "*Oh man! I'm glad I got a hold of you!*" you'd probably think that I was calling you to let you know you either won the lottery, or your car is on fire in front of your house. You'd either expect *good news* or *important news*. Either way, I'd have your undivided attention in a matter of seconds.

When a prospect expects either good news or important news, their subconscious mind shuts down all immediate stimuli, and focuses entirely on what's about to be disclosed.

Once this happens, you've successfully *broken* their emotional state. They're curious and intrigued. YOU are their new distraction, and they are focused on you entirely, at least for a split second. During this split second, you've got to captivate them with a great *hook*.

This hook is what I call *The Benefit*... and you must always lead with the *benefit*.

Lead With The Benefit

The Benefit is what the prospect consciously thinks he wants. The reason I'm making a distinction between what the prospect consciously wants versus what they subconsciously want is that the *master* artfully weaves in language that first appeals to the prospect's subconscious mind, then appeals to the conscious mind, then back to the subconscious mind, and back and forth. This rhythm practically hypnotizes the prospect.

The Benefit is the sizzle of your message. It should typically propose that your prospect can either make a substantial amount of money, or save a substantial amount of money. There should be some sort of monetary benefit.

The Benefit should also be positioned as a new opportunity, whether it's a new *product*, a new *program*, or a new *deal*. The word *new* is one of the most powerful words in marketing to consumers. In fact, in marketing the three most powerful words are:

1. Free.
2. Sex.
3. New.

In the world of consumer products, one of the best campaigns is, "*Buy one, get one free.*" In fact, ask yourself which sale you get most excited about between these three sale offers:

1. 50% Off.
2. ½ Off.
3. Buy One, Get One FREE.

Most people will say that the *Buy One, Get One Free* offer gets them the most excited. Retailers have even turned it into an acronym: B.O.G.O. The brilliant part of this offer is that *Buy One, Get One Free* is essentially the same offer as *50% Off*, which is the same as *½ Off*, however it guarantees double the sales volume (because it moves two units instead of only one).

Any type of FREE bonus offer is generally received with much excitement. But let's say you're not in an industry where it's appropriate to give away a free-bee. In fact, you might be in an industry where it's actually illegal to give away free-bees (typically known as *rebating* in some regulated industries). In this scenario, using the word *sex* is probably going to be inappropriate as well. This leaves us with the word *new*.

People love the word *new*. In fact, I'll share with you a humorous experience I had as a consumer with the word new. I do a significant amount of traveling and motivational speaking, and I usually video record my speaking engagements. About a year ago, I purchased a video camera from the local Super Electronics store here in Orange County, and after a few short months, it broke.

So I took it back to the store, and the customer service rep said, *"I've got some good news for you. It's still under warranty, so I can replace it... and on top of that, they just came out with the new version of this camera, and we're expecting a shipment to come in with the new model on Tuesday."*

I said, *"But I leave on a business trip tomorrow, and I need a video camera for the trip. Can you check and see if any of your other stores might have any in stock?"*

At this point, I'm practically doing a happy dance in the store because I thought I was going to get the *new* model, for *free*. I was getting something *new* and it was *free*, which fulfilled two of the top three marketing offers. You see, even I respond as a consumer to these two words. But then in the middle of my celebration, I was hit with devastating news.

The customer service rep came back and said, *"We don't have any of the new models shipping out to any of our stores until next week on Tuesday, but I found another location about ten minutes away from here, and they have four of the old model in stock."*

"What! The OLD model? I don't want the old, outdated, obsolete model. I want the NEW one, man!" I exclaimed. That's when I caught myself. I was perfectly happy with my video camera before it broke, and I haven't even seen the *new* one. I might actually have liked the *old* model better. So why did I want the *new* one so badly?

The answer is that I'm a human being, and human beings, for whatever reason, like to have the newest version of whatever toy, car, program, or offer that exists. We always want the *new* stuff.

So how does this apply to your business? If you're in corporate sales, you've got to position your product or service as a *new program*. Never sell your product, or your company, or your service. That's what all your competitors are doing, and you don't want to lumped into the same category as them. You don't want to be a *me-too* product or service. You want to represent a *new program*.

Positioning your offer as a *program* has several advantages. The first one is that if you brand your program properly, you ensure that the prospect has never heard of it before. That alone makes your offer unique, simply because they've never heard of it before.

It makes the prospect say to themselves, *"What's that? I've never heard of that before."* As soon as they say that, you've got their attention. You have something that they've never heard of before, and so if what you have is *new* to the marketplace (simply because you've positioned it as such, as a new program), the prospect will want to hear more.

This is under the assumption that you're talking to a prospect that is interested in hearing about everything new in the marketplace. If they're not the kind of person that is intrigued by the thought of getting something new, updated, more efficient, and better overall, then they really aren't part of your target market.

But if they're open to new ideas, not only are they more likely to be the type of client you want, but they'll also be more open to you showing them new, alternative options.

Positioning a new program also puts you in a position of power and demand. You know something that the prospect doesn't know, thus you have leverage. You can even show your program to a zillion other prospects, however the prospect wouldn't even know where to go to find your program if you walk out the door or hang up the phone. If they're curious and intrigued, you've *hooked* them with *The Benefit*.

You've got their ear. Now you've got to keep it, and you do so by telling them a compelling *Inside Story*.

The Inside Story

As human beings, we love to feel like we know something that other people don't know. It's actually rather petty and immature, but let's face it... we like to know other people's *Dirty Little Secrets*.

That's why gossip columns exist. That's why *Reality Shows* are so big right now. Human beings love to feel like they know *inside information*. We love to be in-the-know.

That's why *The Inside Story* is such a key component to your selling approach. *The Inside Story* tells the prospect the story behind why *The Benefit* exists. It basically validates *The Benefit*, which kills the prospect's objection of, *"It sounds too good to be true."* Here's an example.

If I told you that I could get you a $2,000 laptop computer for only $800, your knee-jerk response would probably be, *"There must be something wrong with it,"* or *"It must be a refurbished, factory defect model,"* or *"Is it stolen?"*

These responses are routed in disbelief because the offer just sounds too good to be true. In most cases, if you're offering your prospect something that sounds really good, their knee-jerk reaction is going to be one of disbelief. Knowing this, you've got to immediately kill this objection, and validate WHY your claim is legitimate.

In the example I just gave about the computer, what if I told you that the reason is that a friend of mine, who owns an electronics store, has brand new laptop computers that are last year's model. If I told you that he's just trying to get rid of them to make shelf space for the new replacement model, and that he's dumping them at his wholesale cost, you'd probably say to yourself, *"Well, that makes sense. Cool."*

In sales, you must give the prospect a reason to buy, which is *The Benefit,* however you've also got to validate why your claimed *Benefit* is legitimate, which is where *The Inside Story* comes in.

As you craft your *Inside Story*, you must include some sort of association with a current event. I call this *relevancy*. It must be relevant to something current that everyone knows about.

For example, your *Inside Story* might be somehow linked to the current economic climate, or a current political issue, or some sort of recent event. If the current event is in the news on television, or in newspapers, or on magazine covers, it will most likely suffice.

So now, you've hooked the prospect with *The Benefit*, and you've validated it with a strong, compelling *Inside Story*. The prospect actually believes that you might actually be able to deliver what you claim you can deliver, but they're not 100 percent sold yet. They're *curious*. They're *intrigued*. But they're not *excited* yet.

So the question is, *"How do you get them excited?"* The key to getting a prospect excited – excited enough to book an appointment with you – is to create what I call *Positive Jealousy…* and you do so by sharing a great client testimonial with them.

The Power Of A Great Testimonial

You've probably heard the sales platitude, *"Facts tell, but stories sell."* As cheesy as this saying is, it's actually true… but only partially true.

To illustrate the symbiotic relationship between *The Benefit*, *The Inside Story*, and *The Testimonial*, I'll give you a few examples:

Sales Rep: Works for a hardwood floor installation company.

The Benefit: I have a new program that can save you up to 30% on your hardwood floor.

The Inside Story: My company just did a huge installation job on a 10,000 square foot mansion in Newport Beach. Initially, the client wanted oak floors, but in the middle of the job, they decided to do all bamboo floors, so we got stuck with a ton of oak. So if you want oak, I can get you a killer deal on it.

Testimonial: I just had a client take advantage of this situation... they did a dark, mahogany stain with a distressed finish... it looked amazing... and they saved $6,376.12.

Sales Rep: Realtor.

The Benefit: I have a unique opportunity where I can get you a $2.5 million Spanish hacienda-style home in Beverly Hills for only $1.7 million.

The Inside Story: The seller owned a software company, and he just got sued for patent infringement, so he's got to sell everything he has, and he's got to do it within two weeks. This house hasn't even been listed yet, so you're the first person that even knows about this.

Testimonial: I just put one of my clients in a beautiful home in Bel Air... similar situation... the seller used to own a construction company... and he lost everything with the downturn of the economy. My client picked up this home for $800,000 below market value. These deals come along once in a lifetime. This could be your chance to get *in* and have over half a million dollars in equity, the day you take ownership.

Sales Rep: Life Insurance Agent.

The Benefit: We have a new program specifically designed for business owners where they can have up to 93 percent liquidity of the cash value in their life insurance policies, as early as within the first year.

The Inside Story: Usually, you can't touch the cash value of a life insurance policy until the fifteenth or twentieth year without taking a huge hit in surrender charges... but I have a policy that allows you to have access to over 90% of the cash value, as early as the first year of the policy. A lot of life insurance agents don't show their clients this type of policy. You know why? The reason is that this policy pays significantly lower commissions to the agent in the first year, and most agents want to make a big first-year commission. But my clients are business owners like you, and there's one thing I know about business owners. They need liquidity. So sure, I make less commission on this policy, but in my opinion, it's the right thing to do for the client.

Testimonial: In fact, I have a client... this guy owns a manufacturing company. His old life insurance agent never showed him this type of policy, and when he found out that he could have had this instead of having his cash tied up, inaccessible, he fired his agent and started working with me. Plus, we were able to do a 1035 exchange and transfer his old cash value into the new policy... so now, if he needs access to his cash, he can take a policy loan at any time.

In each of these three examples, the sales rep offered a unique benefit to the prospect with a monetary incentive. What made their offer unique is that in most cases, the prospect would not have ever been offered the program or the opportunity.

The offer was due to a unique set of circumstances that recently occurred, and would most likely not occur on a regular basis, or it was due to information that was not general, public knowledge.

Lastly, in each example, the prospect was told about a client that received a similar benefit due to this unique set of circumstances, which both further validated the legitimacy of *The Benefit*, as well as creating *Positive Jealousy* within the prospect, making them want the offer even more.

At this point, the prospect is curious, intrigued, and excited. The iron is hot, so it's time to strike. You must quickly transition into booking the appointment. The sales language you use here will dictate whether or not the prospect decides to meet with you, and so you must use the proper *Suggestive Sales Language*.

Suggestive Sales Language

This is where most amateur sales reps blow it. They'll make one of two tragic errors in the process of attempting to book the appointment.

On one end of the *Pendulum Of Sales Mistakes* is what I call *Desperately Asking For Permission*. I've heard sales reps say weak, desperate things like, *"Would it be okay with you if I stopped by your office for a few minutes to show you the benefits of my product?"* or *"If you would just give me fifteen minutes of your time..."* or *"With your permission, may I show you how I could help you?"*

These are all pleadings of an unsuccessful, desperate sales schmuck, begging for a meeting. Never ask a prospect for permission. You might as well ask for the appointment by ending with, *"Pretty, pretty please, which sugar on top."*

The problem with asking for permission, is that it implies that you're asking the prospect to grant you a favor. Do you really think the prospect is doing you a favor by meeting with you? If you believe this, you should get out of sales immediately. I'm serious. You should just quit, immediately.

If you have something that can truly benefit the prospect, who's doing who the favor? If you can save your clients money, they should be thanking you. If you can improve the efficiency of their company operations with your product or service, you're the one doing them the favor. You need to show them that you're bringing them value, and you'll never be perceived as such if you're desperately begging for an appointment.

On the opposite end of the *Pendulum Of Sales Mistakes* is what I call the *Selfish Command*. I've heard sales reps give prospects selfish commands, saying stupid things like, *"What I'd like to do is set up a meeting with you."*

Listen, the prospect doesn't care what YOU'D like to do. They only care what THEY'D like to do. So when you tell them what YOU'D like to do, subconsciously, they interpret your command as being very self-centered. They don't feel like you're there to *help* them. They feel like you're there to *sell* them. So don't ever tell the prospect, *"What I'd like to do…"*

Instead of desperately asking for permission… and instead of giving your prospects selfish commands… give them suggestive propositions. Make a logical, sensible, convenient suggestion. In almost every phone script I author, I use the phraseology, *"What probably makes the most sense is to get together to see if we can <insert The Benefit>, and if we can, it'll be a no-brainer, and if we can't, then just keep doing what you're doing now. Does that make sense?"*

This is a suggestion. It's logical. It makes sense. And most importantly, it asks the question, *"Does this make sense?"* Notice, it doesn't ask the prospect if they want to meet or not. It asks them if the suggestion makes sense or not. Are they really going to say, *"No, it doesn't make sense to save money, get a better deal, or learn about a new program?"* If that's really how they feel, they're an idiot, and I don't do business with idiots.

So when booking the appointment, simply suggest what the next step should be. Don't beg for permission. Don't tell them what you'd like to do. Just suggest what the next logical step should be, and ask them if your suggestion makes sense to them. Simple, but very powerful.

Schedule Appointments Like A Doctor

Weak, amateur sales people often ask their prospects, *"So, when would be a convenient time for us to meet?"* or they say something equally as stupid like, *"What does your schedule look like next week?"*

Think about the last time you scheduled an appointment with your doctor. Did they say, *"So what does your schedule look like?"* No. They probably said, *"The doctor can see you on Thursday the 24th at 10:30am,"* and you probably jumped at that time slot and exclaimed, *"I'll take it!"* In fact, you probably thought this was the soonest available time slot the doctor had available. You might have even felt *lucky* to have been blessed with this time slot.

So why is it that doctor's appointments are coveted in this manner, but most sales appointments are not? It's all in the way the appointment was positioned. Human beings covet scarcity. Whenever we perceive that something isn't special, exclusive, or in demand, we

137

aren't as interested. It's kind of a psychological sickness that we all have. We all want what we fear we cannot have.

In sales, the *Master* understands how to position his offer in a way that is so compelling, that it is perceived as something to be coveted. Think back to the way the doctor's office positions the doctor's *availability* to meet with you. They typically only give you one option up front. If, for some reason you cannot accommodate the doctor's schedule on that particular day at that particular time, they give you a secondary option.

The entire process is based on when the doctor can bless you with his presence. The reason the doctor can get away with this is that he knows you want to see him. You *want* that appointment. That's his power.

In sales, especially on an initial cold-call, you've got to make that prospect *want* the appointment. We talked about how to make that happen, right?

Step 1: Hook them with a unique benefit/offer.

Step 2: Tell them an inside story that explains why the benefit exists.

Step 3 Make them jealous by giving them a client testimonial.

After this three-step process, they want to meet with you. They *want* that appointment, just like you *want* that doctor's appointment. You now have leverage, meaning you have something that they want.

Once you've created this *positive jealousy* in them… this *want*… now you have the power to take the opportunity away from them. You can do this by creating *scarcity*, which is exactly what the doctor's office does with you. You perceive that the doctor has a limited amount of openings, and you want one of them. You want to get *in*. The fact that they only give you one available time slot up front makes you want it even more.

So in sales, when you're booking the appointment, don't ask them about *their* availability. Tell them what *your* availability is. In most of my phone appointment setting scripts, I'll say, "*Let me take a look at my schedule here… let's see… This week is really booked up, but I do have an opening at 10:30am this coming Thursday. How does that work for you?*"

I'm creating scarcity with this approach, and I'm also dictating when we're going to meet. Subconsciously, the prospect responds because inside, they're saying to themselves, *"Wow, this guy is in high demand. There must be a reason everyone wants to meet with him."* I want that prospect to feel *lucky* to have gotten *in* with me. It's the old law of supply and demand.

Whether you're at the point in your career where you're in high demand, or you're just starting out, it is absolutely imperative that you create the perception of high-demand, limited access, and exclusivity. This must be part of your brand if you want prospects to beg you for your product or service. This is the *mastery level* of sales.

Once you have achieved this level, and you have prospects desperately wanting to meet with you, it's time to make them want it even more. You do so by never thanking the prospect for their time.

Never Thank A Prospect For Their Time

This is one of the worst habits that sales people develop... the habit of ending every prospecting call with, *"Thank you."* The majority of corporations that have hired me to coach their sales teams absolutely cringe when I teach this at first pass. I don't blame them. I know it sounds completely counter-intuitive... perhaps even rude. However, once I explain the rationale behind this philosophy, they start to come around.

The reason it's a mistake to end a prospecting call with *"Thank you"* is that it's only logical to thank someone when they've gone above and beyond what would be normally expected to help you. In other words, when someone graciously does you a favor, then and only then, is it appropriate to thank them. Under this logic, if you thank a prospect for agreeing to meet with you, it implies that they somehow did you a favor.

If you really believe that the prospect did you a favor by granting you a sales appointment, you're not going to be very successful in sales. It actually has very little to do with what you believe about what I'm saying. It has everything to do with what the prospect believes. You see, if the prospect believes that they're doing you a favor by granting you a meeting with them, subconsciously, they believe that the main purpose of the meeting (as well as your focus) is to sell them, entirely for the purpose of you making a commission.

Consciously, they may not be thinking this, but subconsciously, their emotional filter of suspicion is in full effect. At the subconscious level, their defense mechanism is activated, because they perceive that you are there to *sell* them, instead of being there to *help* them. That's why it's so important to establish the proper relationship dynamic between you and the prospect from the very beginning, starting with how you communicate with them on the initial prospecting call.

At the end of your prospecting call, instead of saying *"Thank you,"* tell them, *"I think I'm really going to be able to help you guys out."* It's no less cordial, and it's no less polite. It's also interpreted by your prospect's subconscious mind that your true intention is to help them. At the subconscious level, it completely changes the prospect's perception of who you are and what you do. You're no longer the *salesman*. You're the *consultant* that is going to help them. Right off the bat, you're positioning yourself completely differently than your competition, and your prospect will react to you accordingly.

In fact, when you say, *"So I'll see you on Thursday at 10:30am... I think I'm really going to be able to help you guys out,"* the prospect will often say, *"Okay, thanks for calling."* Think about how the prospect subconsciously feels when they hear themselves thanking you for calling them. They're appreciative that you may have something of value for them. They have positive expectations regarding meeting with you and working with you. But most importantly, they have feelings of respect for you and the product or service you provide.

Who's Got The Power?

One of the key fundamentals in sales is to work directly with the decision maker. I've seen a lot of sales reps waste their time by meeting with non-decision makers. For example, you need to exclusively deal with people that have *check-signing authority*. So many times, I've heard people in sales talk about how great one of their sales appointments went, but when I asked them what the result was, they say things like, *"Well, they were really interested, but they said they have to run it by their boss first."* Basically, they met with someone that didn't have check signing authority.

There are several problems that this mistake creates. The first one is that they're meeting with someone that doesn't have the power to say *yes* and write the check. However the *do* have the power to say *no*. Have you ever met with someone that you realized didn't have the power to say *yes*, but they had the power to say *no*, and they exercised their power to say *no* to you? You set yourself up for failure.

Prior to booking the sales appointment, you must confirm who makes the final decision, and make sure they're in that appointment. However, every once in a while, you'll speak with a decision maker on the phone and they'll try to pawn you off on a non-decision maker, expecting the non-decision maker to screen your proposition before it gets to the real decision-maker. Don't fall for this.

If you meet with *Sally*, she doesn't have check-signing authority, which means she's going to have to talk to her boss about the meeting you just had with her. Basically, you're relying on *Sally* to communicate to her boss the benefits of doing business with you, and you know damn well, *Sally* ain't no *Super Saleswoman*. So you effectively outsourced the sales process to the worst sales rep in the world: *Sally*. You've elected to make the deal contingent on *Sally* closing her boss for you, which as you can imagine, is a losing proposition.

In several of my businesses, we market to small business owners, and from time-to-time, they'll try to redirect the call to their Office Manager or their HR Director. Tell the decision-maker,

> *"Look, I know Sally usually handles this for you, and I'm sure she does a great job, but she's never going to have the same perspective as you, the business owner. She's just not a business owner, like you are, and so we just need fifteen minutes of your time on the front end, and fifteen minutes on the back end, just to make sure we're on the same page. Other than that, Sally can handle the rest. Does that make sense?"*

If they won't spend that time with you, generally speaking, it's better to just walk away from the deal. If they agree to meet with you for fifteen minutes on the front end, and your message and your offer is compelling enough, they'll stay for the full hour.

Penciling In The Appointment

In some cases, you'll have a prospect that seems interested in your offer, however they might say, *"Why don't you call me next week, and we'll set something up."* Amateurs will get all excited at this response because they think they have a *hot* prospect. Nothing could be further from the truth.

Have you ever experienced this type of scenario? Let me guess. You called them the following week, but got their voicemail. You left a voicemail, requesting a callback, but after a few days passed, you received no callback. So you called them again, being the diligent person you are. Of course you got their voicemail again, and left another friendly, polite voicemail. You tell yourself that the prospect is just really busy, but you have faith that they're a viable prospect because they said that they were interested. They even asked you to call them back, so you don't feel *desperate*, nor do you feel like you're *chasing* them.

But here's the problem. They generally won't call you back, even if they're interested, because they're busy. So what do you do when they haven't called you back yet? You call them a third time. Of course, you get their voicemail again, and that's where the dilemma starts. If you leave a voicemail, that's three voicemails you would have left in a week's time. That's overkill.

However if you don't leave a voicemail, and they have caller ID, you'll look like a stalker. So what do you do? Regardless of your decision, you've made three attempts to follow up with your prospect, which by definition means that you're in the *chasing game* now.

Now the weekend comes, and you are totally obsessed about this prospect that seemed so interested when you first talked to them. You spend the entire weekend talking to your spouse about it... then you talk to your friends about it... then you even talk to your dog about it (because they're the only one that will listen to you).

Monday morning comes, and you are completely screwed. The reason I say you're completely screwed is that you don't know what to do now. Should you call them? Should you wait for them to call you? You're just like that insecure high school kid that isn't getting a callback after their first date, and you're completely desperate. Can you relate to this? Have you ever found yourself in this position with a prospect?

That's why I'm such an advocate of solidifying the next appointment, whether it be a face-to-face meeting or a teleconference, before you end the first conversation. The primary goal of any conversation with a prospect is to book the next appointment. You must do this on the spot.

You're probably thinking to yourself, *"Darren, I tried to do this, but the prospect insisted that I just call them back next week."* Hey, I don't doubt that the prospect told you this, but you've got to take back control of the conversation.

If they tell you this, just respond by saying, *"You know what, my schedule usually books out a couple weeks in advance, so let's just pencil you in a date to reserve you a spot in my calendar, and if you have to reschedule later, it's no problem... let's see... I've got an opening on Wednesday at 10:30am. How does that work for you?"*

Using the phrase *"Pencil you in a date"* is extremely effective because it sounds very noncommittal. It makes the prospect feel like they aren't making any huge commitment.

However, when you say this, they don't actually put down their pen, pick up an erasable pencil, and write the appointment in their calendar. They use a pen, or they input you into their Outlook calendar, Blackberry or iPhone calendar.

What happens is that after a few days, they forget that the appointment was *penciled* in, and they will rarely cancel on you.

Thou Shalt Not Convince

All of this said, with all of the communication techniques and positioning strategies that I'm teaching you, the bottom line is that the prospect is either interested in hearing you out, or they're not.

Sure the language you use is important, but you must understand that this high-impact sales language is designed to uncover whether or not the prospect is truly open to hearing about your idea. It's meant to *identify* if the prospect falls into your target market. It's not designed to *convince* anyone to do anything. The goal is to clarify the offer to the prospect, so that if they truly are interested in your offer, you can deliver the benefit to them.

I've seen some people brag about how many appointments they booked with prospective clients due to them *winning them over* or *talking them into it*, but the problem is that those appointments are going to be unqualified appointments. They will be a waste of time to meet with, because they were never really interested in the first place.

Again, your entire goal in prospecting should be to find as many prospects as you can that want what you've got. This being the case, the key is to make a tremendous amount of volume of calls, and just cherry pick the easy ones. That's what the *Master Prospector* does. The *Master* is a volume player.

Always remember, you want to be in the *Identifying Game*, not in the *Convincing Game*.

Chapter Ten:
Becoming A Master Closer

"Clarity and brevity are lost arts. Master them, and wealth shall follow."

-Darren Sugiyama

Don't Try To Build Rapport. That's what suicide negotiators do.

So many sales trainings teach you to build rapport with the prospect by starting your sales meeting off by identifying a common interest and chit-chatting about that common interest. Most of these trainings will teach you to look around the prospect's office and find something to talk about that makes you relatable.

For example, if you see a picture of their kid's football team, you could talk about your kid's football team, or how you used to play football. This is just plain stupid.

Do you really think the prospect booked the appointment with you, in the middle of their very busy workday, to talk about football?

In today's world, people are busier than ever, especially business owners. They're not sitting around all day eating Bon-Bons, watching soap operas, bored out of their minds. They're working, trying to make the best of these economic trying times.

If they wanted to talk about their kid's football team, they'd be doing that with their friends, not you. This rapport-building strategy also assumes that if the prospect *likes* you, that they'll do business with you. Wrong again.

In today's world, *performance* trumps *likeability*. In all of my companies, our goal is always to outperform the competition. If the prospect elects to not do business with us, they will either lose money or overpay for an inferior product or service. That being the case, our primary goal is to communicate this message to them in as clear and concise manner as humanly possible. When we do this, the prospect may or may not say, "*I like Darren*," however they do say, "*I need Darren.*" Ultimately, that's the goal... to have the client feel that they *need* you. Once we perform for the client, they will automatically *like* us.

After we have solidified a commitment to do business with us, I have no problem with chit-chatting about non-business related topics, assuming you really want to do that. You see, if you have these friendly chats after you transact business, these chats are genuine, because you're not trying to butter them up to close them. But if you do this prior to transacting business, it can come off as being very disingenuous, because the only reason you're showing interest in their personal life is to set them up for a close. Personally, I have a problem with any type of disingenuous set up.

So cut to the chase and communicate your offer, focusing on the value that you're bringing to your prospective client. It's a refreshing approach, and in the long run, your clients will respect you more for it.

Breaking Trust And Gaining Trust

Dovetailing off what I said earlier regarding the stupidity of attempting to start off a sales appointment with rapport building, we need to discuss the issue of client trust. The biggest disadvantage you have in sales is not your product, or the economy, or the marketplace. Your biggest disadvantage is centered around *time* and *trust*.

In most cases, the prospect that you're trying to acquire is currently doing business with your competition, and the advantage your competition has over you, in this particular case, is trust and familiarity. This trust and familiarity has been developed over time.

Think about this. How long does it generally take you to trust someone? It usually takes years to build trust within a relationship. So the *Incumbent* (your competitor that the prospect is currently doing business with) has this edge over you, and there's no way you're going to be able to trump them in this area.

For example, let's say a guy meets a girl in a bar. The guy is a nice, trustworthy, charming guy. The girl, however, already has a boyfriend. In fact, she's in love with her boyfriend. They've been together for over three years. No matter how nice the guy in the bar is... no matter how likeable he is... no matter how trustworthy he appears... he cannot win over more trust than what the boyfriend has been able to build over the last three years.

So we said that trust takes a long time to build. But how long does it take to *break* trust? Trust can be broken in a split second. If this guy in the bar showed the girl digital pictures of her boyfriend snuggled up in a dark corner of a nightclub with a hot blonde chick, trust would be instantaneously broken. She would no longer trust her boyfriend (and maybe even fall out-of-love with him right there on the spot).

Now, I'm not saying that this would make her trust the new guy in the bar more, but he's a least neutral in the trust department... whereas the boyfriend is actually distrusted now. So if one guy is neutral, and the other is distrusted, by definition, who is going to win in the trust department at that given time? By default, the new guy in the bar wins.

This is essentially the exact same situation you're in when you're selling. Your prospect is in a monogamous relationship with your competition, and they trust them due to the longevity of their relationship. In fact, they may even be *in love* with them. This being the case, you can't beat your competition by trying to win over more trust. That's why I say that attempting to build fake, bullshit rapport is useless. You can't win when you play that game. You can't win over more trust.

However, just like the new guy in the bar, you can strategically and tactfully break the trust between the client and your competition. You may not be able to show them digital pictures of your competition cheating on them with a hot blonde, but you CAN show them how your competition has been cheating on them by not offering them the best solution at the best price.

I call this *The Incumbent Character Assassination*. The goal is to expose all the wrongdoings of your competition, and show the prospect better alternative options. You want to position these better alternative options as the very things that you specialize in doing, and you can do it in a way as to imply that you are shocked (and almost mortified) that your competition didn't offer them these better options.

Orchestrate A Bad Break-Up

Think back during your young, single days. Have you ever broken up with a boyfriend or girlfriend on good terms, and at a later date, gotten back together again? Most people have done this at least once in the life.

But think about relationships that ended with you cursing each other out where you broke up hating each other's guts. I'm guessing you probably didn't ever consider getting back together with them. In fact, maybe you made it a point to never cross paths, ever again.

You may be asking yourself, *"Why does Darren keep going off on these tangents, talking about dating?"* I assure you that this is not a tangent. This principle is one of the most important principles in terms of closing the back door to your new clients. If your new client leaves your competition being angry at them, because they feel victimized by either an incompetent or unethical sales rep, they will never be tempted to go back to them. Perhaps *angry* is too strong a word, but you get the idea. You must orchestrate a bad, ill-willed break up between your client and the competition, thus solidifying the relationship with your new client.

Many people will argue with me, saying that you should win over the business without bad-mouthing the competition. This is just stupid.

When you're in business and sales, it's competition. If the client is getting a sub-par deal from your competition, you should point it out. People will generally only take action when there is a substantial amount of pain associated with not taking action.

Have you ever had a friend in a bad relationship… maybe even an abusive relationship… and they stay in it? Typically, the reason they stay in it is that they associate more pain with being alone, than they do with being in a bad relationship. Whichever situation is perceived as generating the least amount of pain, wins. Again, that's why your prospects may be procrastinating with you right now, because making a non-decision seems less painful than proactively making a change and doing business with you.

To drastically reduce the amount of prospect procrastination in your business, you must show the prospect that they will suffer far more pain by staying in their current relationship. I want you to really understand this part, because most people don't internalize this concept at the level that they need to in order to be successful. They try to win over the prospect by convincing them that they will experience more pleasure by leaving the incumbent and working with them. This is like the nice guy in the bar trying to convince the girl that she should fall in love with him, and that his love would be greater than her boyfriend's love. This may be true, but there's no way you're going to be able to convince this prospect or girl of these claims in less than sixty minutes.

You have to assassinate the character of the incumbent boyfriend/competition and break trust as fast as possible. You need to highlight the pain they're currently experiencing, and if they're unaware of the pain, you need to identify it and magnify it so the prospect can see just how bad of a situation they're in, comparatively.

Please do not misinterpret what I'm saying here. It is never appropriate to trash talk your competition with lies and slander. But if the client isn't getting a good deal, you need to be honest and tell them, and communicate to them why they're getting a bad deal... and show them better options. Essentially, my point is that we need to tell our prospects the raw truth, without sugar-coating it.

Think of it this way. If you weren't going to earn a commission from the transaction, and your best friend was getting a crappy deal on something and didn't know it, would you tell them the truth and try to get them a better deal? Of course you would. And why would you do this? Because it's the right thing to do... to help someone get the best deal available.

That's what I do in business. I help people get the best deal their money can buy, and I have no problem showing them that their current situation is not getting them the best deal money can buy. By definition, whose fault is it that they're not getting the best deal? It's my competition's fault... and I make sure my new clients recognize this. If anything, it actually deepens the trust and further develops my relationship with my clients, because they know I'll:

1. Tell them the truth.
2. Protect them from getting screwed.

If this seems simple, that's because it *is* simple. Serve the client and put their needs first. Protect them from incompetent and unscrupulous competitors, and you'll make yourself indispensible.

Acknowledge The Pink Elephant

Have you ever heard this expression? If not, allow me to explain. If you were in a room, and in that room, there was a giant pink elephant, it would be impossible to ignore, right? I mean, it's a freaking elephant... and on top of that, it's pink! You can't ignore it.

In sales, the *Pink Elephant* in the room is the incumbent... your competition that is currently selling to your prospect. Most people in sales will try to ignore the *Pink Elephant* by not addressing the existence of the current relationship. This is just plain stupid.

You've got to acknowledge the *Pink Elephant* by addressing the current relationship. Very few people in sales do this, so if you pull this off properly, you're going to stand out in a sea of nondescript sales schmoes. Usually when you're attempting to win over someone's business, you're competing against an incumbent (a competitor that already has a relationship with your prospect). When you really think about it, what is the number one reason a prospect doesn't retain you and become your client?

It's usually due to an existing, comfortable relationship with one of your competitors. The question is, do you currently address this existing relationship with all of your prospects? Probably not.

This is a big mistake. Don't try to ignore the *Pink Elephant* in the room. Here's an easy (and very powerful) way to do it.

Right off the bat, in the beginning of the initial sales appointment, ask your prospect, *"On a scale of 1-10, how would you rate your current _____ based on performance?"*

The reason this is such a great question is that it:

1. Addresses the fact that you know they're already using someone else.
2. Sets the table to discuss what's lacking.

Most people in sales would be too *chicken* to ask this question, because they would be afraid that the prospect would come back with too high a rating, reinforcing the fact that the client is happy and has no incentive to change over to you.

Nothing could be further from the truth.

Now, obviously, if the prospect gives your competitor a low rating, you'd be thrilled. You'd be surprised how often this happens. So if this happens, you've just set the stage to crush your competitor's incompetence.

You would respond to the prospect's low rating of your competition with, *"Well no wonder you wanted to meet with me... So tell me, what problems are you currently having with your _____?"*

Notice, I didn't ask them what problems they're currently having. I specifically asked them what problems they're currently having with their current guy.

The goal here is to subtly place 100 percent of the blame on their current guy, not on any of the other potential variables of their current circumstance. You need to associate all of their problems and frustration with their current guy. This is part of the *Incumbent*

Character Assassination I discussed earlier. This is the only time you should ever ask an open-ended question. I will discuss the importance of asking close-ended questions in a moment.

The reason you want to ask an open-ended question in this particular stage of the appointment is that you want them to verbally assassinate the character of the incumbent for you, so that you don't have to do it.

Let them rant and rave, and take their side in the process. Once they're done venting, that blame-oriented feeling they have towards their current guy will linger, thus making them want to escape into your camp.

But let's talk about what happens if they give the incumbent a high rating. If the prospect gives the incumbent a rating of a *Level 8* or a *Level 9*, don't lose your enthusiasm. You see, they just told you everything you need to know.

Even if they rate them at *Level 9*, that's not *Level 10*, which means they perceive that there's room for improvement. All you have to do is get them upset that they don't get *Level 10 Service*. Just ask them, "*So what's missing? What would you need to feel like you're getting Level 10 Service?*"

All you're looking for is one little thing they're upset about that they're not currently getting. If you can position yourself as the *only* one that can get them this one little thing, the deal is yours.

Okay, I know what you're thinking. What if the prospect rates the incumbent at *Level 10*? If this happened to you, you'd probably be devastated and crawl out of their office with your tail between your legs.

That's only because you haven't been taught one of the key fundamentals about sales, which is this: The prospect wouldn't have booked an appointment with you if they weren't somewhat interested in giving you a shot.

Do you really think they have nothing better to do than spend an hour with you? Trust me, whatever you said on the phone got them thinking about the possibility that their current deal isn't so great. That's why they agreed to meet with you. Here's all you have to do if they rate their current guy at *Level 10*.

Tell them, "*Well if that's the case, maybe you should just stay with your current guy and not use me,*" and start packing up your briefcase. Watch their jaws drop and hit the ground. They will be in a state of shock. They'll probably say, *"Wait a minute. I thought you said you can help me."*

You'll reply, *"Look, all of my clients rate me at Level 10, but you said your current guy is also Level 10, so if I'm Level 10, and your current guy is Level 10, then according to you, everything is perfect... unless there's something you feel that you're not getting. I mean, let me ask you this... If I gave you a magic wand, and you could waive it, and change ONE LITTLE THING about your current situation, what would that one thing be?"*

Again, always remember that the prospect agreed to meet with you for a reason. They want something. If they perceive that they can only get it from you, who has the power? You do.

Once you identify that *one little thing*, ask them, *"Have you addressed this problem with your current guy?"* If they say *no*, then you've got them right where you want them.

If they say *yes*, ask them, *"When?"* Their answer to this question is somewhat irrelevant. You're basically just calling *bullshit* on them. But let's say they stick to their guns and tell you they just met with them to discuss the issue.

If this is the case, ask them, *"So what solutions did they propose for you?"* Now, you know damn well that if the incumbent actually did propose some solutions, that they must not have been very good, because:

1. The prospect hasn't implemented the proposed solutions.
2. The prospect has agreed to meet with you, which means their current guy hasn't found any viable solutions for their problem.

Once you've identified these two key facts, your goal should be to hit them with a strategy/solution they've never heard of before. This highlights the fact that:

1. They have a problem.
2. It's their current guy's fault.
3. You have the solution to their problem.

This process of communication puts you in control, and it sets the groundwork for making yourself indispensible.

Ask Closed-Ended Questions

Most sales trainers promote asking open-ended questions. They'll tell you to get the prospect talking, and that you should focus on listening instead of talking. This is absolutely stupid.

In a first-meet with a prospective client, you only have about thirty to sixty minutes to *wow* them. You've got to captivate their attention and keep it throughout the meeting. If you ask open-ended questions, you're giving up control of both the content of the meeting as well as the tempo. Open-ended questions allow the prospect to babble on and on about unrelated subjects, which leads to an unfocused, unrehearsed sales appointment.

However, when you ask closed-ended questions, you're able to maintain control of the meeting, if you format them properly. For example, if you ask *yes or no* questions, the prospect is forced to only choose from two options:

1. Yes.
2. No.

Now, if you're going to ask questions that cannot be answered with a *yes* or a *no*, they should be multiple choice questions. In other words, you need to format your questions in a manner where you give your prospect two to three options to choose from instead of asking an open-ended question. Here's an example.

Have you ever called up your friend and invited them to dinner? You probably asked them, *"Where do you want to go?"* They probably responded, *"I don't care. Where do you want to go?"* Then you probably said, *"I don't care. What do you feel like eating?"* And then they probably said, *"I don't care. What do you feel like?"*

You see where I'm going with this? When you ask an open-ended question, it requires the other person to think, and when people are required to think too much, they make *non-decisions*. Very rarely will you get a straight-up *no* from a prospect. You'll usually get a *non-decision*, and the reason is that you didn't make it easy for them to buy. You required them to think too much.

Going back to the scenario of asking your friend out to dinner, if you asked a closed-ended, multiple choice question, it would have been easier for them to answer. For example, if you said, *"Let's grab some dinner tonight. Which sounds better... Mexican food or Italian?"* They'd probably pick one of the two, and you'd be done, as opposed to going through the shenanigans of the back and forth *"I don't care... Where do you want to go?"*

Here are some examples of what to do, and what not to do:

Bad Question: *"So what do you think about the product?"*

Better Question: *"Can you think of any reason why you wouldn't want to try the product?"*

Bad Question: *"Which one do you like the best?"*

Better Question: *"Do you like the red one better, or the blue one better?"*

Bad Question: *"What does your schedule look like next week?"*

Better Question: *"I have some openings next Thursday. What works better for you, mornings or afternoons?"*

Consistency Of Content

Consistency Of Content (*C.O.C.*™) is a communication concept I developed years ago. It's basically routed in the fact that human beings are emotional beings, and this being the case, we tend to have *On Days* and *Off Days*. What this means is that our ability to construct and perform *A-Game Level* sales presentations is only as good as how we are emotionally feeling that day. When a sales rep is not scripted, and doesn't have a rehearsed, premeditated pitch, the prospect is likely to get a fragmented message.

Part of my *System-Driven Business*™ process is reliant on creating consistent client experiences, regardless of which one of my sales reps is pitching the deal. This is the only way to ensure that my brand is perpetual. It's also the only way to monitor and quantify sales production results. You've got to know what is being communicated and how it's being communicated in order to evaluate the effectiveness of your brand.

So many sales coaches teach you techniques on how to read the prospect. They'll teach you psychological interpretation techniques, telling you, *"If the prospect is a visual learner, you should ask them if they can SEE the benefits of working with you."* Or if the prospect is an auditory learner, ask them, *"Does this SOUND good?"* Or if the prospect is a kinesthetic learner, ask them, *"Do you FEEL like this would work for you?"*

This is absolute nonsense. You're not a clinical psychologist, nor should you aspire to be one. There is no way you're going to be able to consistently guess what kind of learner they are... and what if you guess wrong? Don't try to shrink their head. Just create a message that communicates exactly what you do, and how your offer is unique. Point out the deficiencies of their current provider, and highlight your ability to deliver solutions in these areas of deficiency.

If you've done your homework, you should already know what areas your competition is deficient in, and you should obviously know what your strengths are. Go into each sales appointment with a premeditated message about why the prospect should do business with you and only you. Show them a handful of case studies – examples of other clients you've helped – and create that *positive jealousy* we talked about earlier.

Again, your goal should be to:

1. Dazzle them with your brilliance.
2. Point out the deficiencies of their current situation.
3. Blame the incumbent.
4. Create positive jealousy by showing them your capabilities by using case studies to substantiate your claims.

So far, I've talked about the beginning of your sales appointment, as well as the body of your appointment. The next stage of this appointment is *The Close*, however it's imperative to set up your *close* properly. There are two things that will absolutely kill your close.

The first is obvious. If you don't have the guts to go for *The Close*, and you exit the appointment leaving things up in the air, you're weak. Period. So many people in sales are too chicken to ask for the order, right there on the spot. What's the use of going through the process of the sales appointment if you don't even ask for the order? Isn't that the whole point of a sales appointment? I'll give you some great closing language and discuss closing strategies in a minute.

The second thing that will kill your close is going in for the kill too abruptly. If you spring a hardcore close on the prospect too abruptly, you'll most likely shock them into freezing up. Their guard will go up, and once their guard goes up, it is very difficult to coerce them into lowering it.

You've got to strategically gain momentum, and carry it into *The Close*. It all starts with *The Bucket Brigade*.

The Pre-Close (AKA: The Bucket Brigade)

Have you ever seen one of those old black-and-white Western movies where the saloon catches on fire? All the townspeople line up between the well and the saloon-on-fire. The one closest to the well dunks a bucket into the well, filling it up with water, and passes it to the next person. The bucket gets passed down the line, as the person closest to the well continues to fill up buckets and pass them down the line.

As the buckets reach the last person closest to the fire, that last person dumps bucket-of-water after bucket-of-water onto the fire. Bucket after bucket, over and over, until the fire is put out. In these Western movies, they called this *The Bucket Brigade*.

In sales, you must use a similar type of strategy. As you transition into *The Close*, the goal is to refresh their memory of all the things that they said they liked about your product or service, as you communicated in your sales appointment. As you remind them of these things the format should essentially look like this:

> *"Mr. Prospect, based on our time together today, you said that you liked <benefit #1>... and <benefit #2>... and <benefit #3>... and <benefit #4>... and <benefit #5>... and you also said that your current supplier/broker/agent/rep isn't offering you any of these benefits. Is that right?"*

This is *The Pre-Close*. Essentially, you're recapping all of the areas of interest that the prospect had, which prepares them to make a decision in favor of working with you, exclusively. What makes this technique so powerful is that the prospect is the one that told you that they need these key benefits, not the other way around. You see, the prospect will not contradict themselves and change their mind, which is why it's better to position the necessity of doing business with you as something that *they* said, versus something that *you* said.

The concept of *The Bucket Brigade* is powerful because when you hit them with benefit after benefit after benefit, it becomes overwhelmingly obvious that you have a bunch of stuff that they want. Plus, *they're* the ones that told *you* that they liked/wanted/needed all of these things.

In addition, you reminded them that they're not receiving any of these benefits from their current product/service/provider, thus it just seems logical that they should start doing business with you.

It's important to understand that as you're building your case and building your momentum into The Close, your case must be substantiated with indisputable facts. These facts (void of subjectivity and personal opinions) appeal to their logical brain; their conscious brain.

Ultimately, *The Close* comes during a crescendo of emotional excitement, but setting yourself up for *The Close* (building your case) is a strategic process that relies on solid, logical, indisputable facts. You now have what I call *leverage*.

The Leveraged Close

Having *leverage* means that you have something that the prospect wants, and the prospect knows that you know they want what you have. It's like knowing that someone likes you before you ask them out on a date… you have *leverage*. The reason this is so important is that you can use this fact to your advantage by asking them a hypothetical question.

If you know the prospect wants a particular benefit or set of benefits that you (and only you) offer, you can ask them, *"So basically, you said that you want all of these things we talked about… and you said that you're not getting any of these things right now… so if I can deliver all of things, which I will, can you think of any reason why you wouldn't want to work together?"*

Notice that I didn't ask them if they would sign on the dotted line of my proposal yet. I asked them a hypothetical question. The format of the question is designed to make the prospect feel like they don't have to answer the direct question of whether or not they're ready to make a commitment.

The question is designed to essentially challenge them to come up with a rational reason why they shouldn't work with you. When they can't come up with a valid reason, they're essentially admitting that they should work with you, exclusively.

The mistake a lot of people make in attempting to *close a deal* is that they make the prospect feel like they have to make a huge decision. Human beings are terrified of making big decisions and commitments.

The Master leads the prospect down a logical path that results in them saying, "*Since I can't think of any reason why I shouldn't do this, heck, I might as well do it.*" If they have to decide if it's the *right decision*, you're requiring them to get caught up in the fear of the unknown.

However if they feel like it's definitely not the *wrong decision*, there's nothing to lose, thus the fear subsides, making it easier for them to pull the trigger with you.

In addition, as I often teach all of my people, it is easier for someone to say "*no*" than it is to get them to say "*yes.*" Saying "*no*" is the standard default answer that is programmed into human beings when presented with a new idea. If you asked your single friend, "*Would you like me to fix you up on a blind date?*" their response would probably be, "*No, not really.*"

But if you changed your approach to, "*If I had a really hot friend, would you have a problem if I fixed you up on a blind date with them?*" they'd probably say, "*No, that would be cool.*"

In both cases, the answer was "*no,*" but in the first example the *no* meant *no*, whereas in the second example, the *no* meant *yes*.

Another example would be if your friend called you up and said, "*I want to go on a road trip. Do you think you could get away for a few days?*" you'd probably say, "*No, I'm just too busy to go on a road trip.*" But if they said, "*If I asked you to go on a road trip with me, can you think of any reason why we shouldn't have some fun and get away for a few days?*" you might just say, "*No, I can't think of any reason why we shouldn't go. We work hard man. We deserve it!*" Again, the *no* ended up meaning *yes*.

Once you have agreement in *The Pre-Close* stage, your chances of closing the deal are greatly enhanced. Again, the prospect doesn't emotionally feel like they made any commitments. All they did was agree that there isn't any reason why they *shouldn't* do the deal with you.

Now, since they couldn't come up with a logical reason why they shouldn't do the deal with you, your next step is to transition into *The Assumptive Close*.

The Assumptive Close

Based on their very logical reasoning behind coming to the conclusion of, *"What the heck, I've got nothing to lose... only to gain,"* your goal is to parlay that positive momentum into *The Close*.

The beautiful thing about the way you've set up this moment is that you never really have to ask them to make a commitment. They've come to a logical conclusion, which is better than forcing them to make a huge decision. The logical conclusion was developed through a process, whereas a huge decision is not a process.

A huge decision requires that a trigger on a *starting gun* be pulled by the prospect, whereas a logical conclusion never required a trigger to be pulled... or more specifically, it never required a *decision* to pull the trigger.

The Assumptive Close requires that you smoothly transition from the *Leveraged Pre-Close* into the client taking the next action step. This is actually a relatively easy thing to do, if done properly.

All you have to do is, after they tell you that they can't think of any reason they shouldn't work with you, you direct them to take the next step by saying, *"Great. So here's the next step..."* and give them two to three action items that are required to get the deal going. It's usually a combination of them giving you a few of their documents... them signing a few of your documents... and scheduling the next time to get together with them.

It's important to lump these three action items together so that none of them *feel* like a big deal to them. If you break apart each one, separating them, the first one (having them dig up a few documents from their file) is not that big a deal. Neither is scheduling the next time to get together.

However, signing the contract/application/agreement can feel like a huge decision that should be contemplated, if you put it on a pedestal. This is why you must lump it in with the other two action items, making it seem like the signing is just a formality, rather than a high-pressure commitment.

When done correctly, it is a beautiful thing to watch happen. However, every once in a while, you'll face client objections. For the *Amateur*, objections can stop them dead in their tracks, and they immediately turn into a *Deer-In-The-Headlights*. However for the *Master*, objections are crushed by premeditated rebuttals.

Rebuttals

Having premeditated, rehearsed, canned rebuttals will turn a weak, desperate, insecure *sales rep* into a confident, cocky, bulletproof *consultant*. *Sales reps* sell and convince. *Consultants* indentify and advise.

I teach my people to have two, rock-solid go-to rebuttals, and if neither rebuttal works, I teach them to transition into a new offer, which I'll discuss in a moment.

The reason you don't want to go more than two rebuttals deep is that after this point, your discussion turns into an argument... an argument that you will never win. You need to choose your battles wisely. Here are the two conceptual rebuttals that you should use, regardless of your industry.

Rebuttal #1: The *What The Heck* Close

If your prospect objects, regardless of what the objection is, you should respond with,

> *"Whoa... let me take a step back here. Is there anything you're getting right now that you're afraid of losing?"*
>
> *"Okay, well, you told me that you wanted <benefit #1>... and <benefit #2>... and <benefit #3>... and <benefit #4>... and <benefit #5>... right?"*
>
> *"And you also said that your current supplier/broker/agent/rep isn't offering you any of these benefits. Is that right?"*

Of course, you already know the answer to the question, *"Is there anything you're afraid of losing?"*

The answer is *"no."* You've also *Re-Bucket Brigaded* them, and you've reconfirmed that they have nothing to lose. So follow it up with,

> *"I'm telling you, you're going to love this. If you don't like it, you can yell at me and throw rocks... but seriously, everyone that I've worked with loves this, and you will too. Does that make sense?"*

Essentially, in *The Pre-Close*, you want their *no* to be a *yes*. In *The Assumptive Close*, you don't need a *no* or a yes. You just assume that the answer is *yes*. But when you're in the *Rebuttal Stage*, you initially lead off with another *Pre-Close* by asking them if there's anything they're afraid of losing.

However, after you *Re-Bucket Brigade* them, you quickly transition into gunning for the *yes*. The key is to make their *yes* be a *"Yeah, okay. What the heck, let's do it"* kind of *yes*. Most people are not going to verbally say, *"No, that doesn't make sense"* unless they're irrational. So once they say, *"Yeah, I guess that makes sense,"* BAM! You've confirmed the deal.

Now, if the prospect still has reservations, and they tell you that they need to think about it, or that they're just not ready to make a decision just yet, you need to uncover the real reason they're hesitant. Often times it is fear of the unknown, and fear of the unknown is usually a symptom of *lack of clarity*.

Rebuttal #2: Clarify What *The One Little Thing* Is

There is usually *one little thing* that's keeping them from pulling the trigger with you. You need to do two things to provide ultimate clarity for your prospect:

1. Reconnect them with the reason they agreed to meet with you in the first place.

2. Identify what that *one little thing* is that's holding them back.

Never forget that the prospect *wanted* to meet with you, which means there is a certain level of dissatisfaction regarding their current situation, and they perceived that you might have a solution to their problem. Otherwise, they wouldn't have agreed to meet with you in the first place. You need to reconnect them with their feelings of discontent and remind them that they have a *pain*, and that you have the proverbial *aspirin* to make their pain go away.

The second thing you must do is you must identify what the *one little thing* is that's holding them back. Often times, they'll have an area of concern that they're too embarrassed to confront you about, so in an effort to avoid confrontation, they'll say, "*Let me think about it.*"

You would be amazed at just how many people are too embarrassed to say, "*I don't understand this. Can you explain it to me again?*" These same people are also too shy to tell you, "*I'm afraid that if I pull the trigger with you, <this> might happen.*"

When you encounter this type of scenario, use the *Feel, Felt, Found* technique. First, identify what the real area of concern is by telling them a story about one of your clients that had the same concern you think they may have. Tell them,

> "*I had this one client that was really excited about working with me, but they were afraid that <insert what you think they're concerned about>.*"
>
> "*Is that what you're concerned about?*"

That's the *Feel* part. Once you've identified the prospect's concern, tell them, "*Look I understand. My client felt the same way.*" That's the *Felt* part. Then tell them,

> "*But once they started working with me, what they found was that their operations functioned much smoother and more efficiently... their employees were happier with the new program... and with the amount of cost savings I generated for them, they were able to take a family vacation to Hawaii.*"

That's the *Found* part. So the three-step technique here is:

1. Identify and acknowledge how the prospect *feels*.

2. Confirm that they're not the only one that initially *felt* that way.

3. Share with them the benefits that your client *found* by working with you, putting all of their concerns behind them.

Once you've done this, tell them,

> "*I know you're a little afraid of making the switch, but I'm telling you, you're going to love this so much, you're going to tell all your friends that you wish you would have switched years ago. Does that make sense?*"

When they say *yes*, go right back to the *Assumptive Close* and tell them,

> "*Okay so here's the next step... The first thing we'll do is <insert action item #1>... then the second thing we'll do is <insert action item #2>... and the third thing we'll do is <insert action item #3>. So let's start with action item number one.*"

If It's Not Necessary To Say, It's Necessary Not To Say It

I'll close out this chapter with one of the most important elements of selling, closing and communicating in general, and that is *brevity*. William Shakespeare was quoted as saying, "*Brevity is the soul of wit.*" What a brilliant quote. Even the quote itself is brief, which is part of why it is so witty.

Brevity, in sales, is paramount. It is also what most people in sales lack. So many people in sales fill their sales message with nonessential, filler material that does not directly make a contribution towards closing the deal. It clouds and dilutes the core message.

Every word that comes out of your mouth must have a purpose. Every word you utter must be necessary... and if it isn't absolutely necessary to say, then it is absolutely necessary not to say it.

I met very talented marketer years ago, and he shared with me a very vivid image. He said, "*Every word that comes out of your mouth is like a little soldier going to battle.*" The analogy he was making was that if you were taking an army into battle, you wouldn't take weak soldiers. You wouldn't take your 87-year old grandma. Why? Because one weak soldier can lose the battle for you.

One of my favorite movies is *300*, a fictionalized retelling of the *Battle of Thermopylae*. In this battle, Spartan King *Leonidas* leads 300 Spartan warriors into battle against the Persian God-King *Xerxes*. This Spartan army was comprised of the elite Spartan warriors, and their battle strategies were as calculated as my business strategies. I was fascinated.

In one scene, a Spartan man with a major physical deformity begs *King Leonidas* to allow him to join his army. But due to the courageous man's physical deformity, he is unable to raise his shield high enough to meet the king's requirement, and so the king graciously declines the man's request.

There is a level of counter-intuitiveness in this decision because the Spartan king only has an army of 300 warriors to take on the massive Persian army of thousands of warriors.

However, once you understand the strategic fighting techniques of the incredibly efficient Spartan army, you realize just how important it is to not have any weak links. I highly encourage you to watch this movie and draw parallels between the Spartan war philosophies and my selling philosophies.

In sales, if you bring weak soldiers to battle, you will surely lose the battle. Each word must be relevant. Each word must be compelling. Each word must be necessary, and make a powerful and direct contribution towards closing the deal.

When you evaluate your own sales message, you must evaluate each individual word and ask yourself, "*Is it absolutely necessary to say this?*" If the answer is *no*, then you must remove it from your message.

Recently, I reevaluated one of my sales scripts for one of my companies. I tend to do this about every nine to twelve months. Whenever I reevaluate a sales script, I have to ask myself several questions:

1. Has anything changed, locally or globally, that has changed my target market's priorities?

2. Has anything changed, locally or globally, that has changed my employees' priorities?

3. Has anything changed, locally or globally, that has created a void in the marketplace, and should we reposition ourselves and our offer, to capitalize on this new void?

4. Has the competition changed their approach to the marketplace, and if so, has this change been effective for them or not?

5. What is the number one, most impactful concept that we should be communicating to our target market, and are we doing it in the most effective way?

6. If we believe that this concept has changed or evolved, is it worth pilot testing, to see if we are right, or should we continue with our proven core message?

7. Is this number one, most impactful concept that we have decided to focus on communicating to our target market being diluted by any nonessential sales talk? If so, we must remove the nonessential sales talk, even if it is good.

You see, the key to mastering your sales and marketing message, as well as effectively communicating your brand, is to strip all nonessential material out of your message. I remember developing a sales script for one of my companies years ago, and I had a problem. It was a good problem to have, but a problem nonetheless. The problem was that we had so many good things to offer our clients, that it became difficult to *not* talk about all of them.

I had to make an executive decision to choose the top five reasons that a client should do business with us, but I had twelve to choose from. Again, the good news was that I had developed twelve really good strategies that would help our clients… but that was also the problem. You never want to sell more than five or six benefits at a time. If you offer more than that, each benefit gets diluted by the other nonessential ones.

Basically, seven of the twelve ended up on the editing room floor. They were all good benefits, but they didn't make the top five. You have to have the wisdom and the discipline to limit the number of benefits you communicate in your sales message to five or six. This is where I see a lot of amateurs ruin their chances at success in sales. They talk too damn much.

I've even experienced this with some of my own employees. They start out memorizing my scripts, and due to the fact that they're brand new in my industry, all they know to talk about is the content in my scripts, verbatim.

As a result, that's all they communicate to the prospective clients, and they do very well because my scripts embody brevity and wit. If they recite them verbatim, relatively speaking, they are as powerful with that prospective client as I would be, because we're communicating the exact same content, in the exact same format, with the exact same style.

But then as time goes on, they become very knowledgeable about my industry, and like clockwork, their success plateaus, and sometimes even decreases.

Why?

The reason is that when they have more knowledge, they feel the need to tell the prospect everything they know, in hopes that the prospect will be impressed with how much they know. On the surface, it's a logical assumption, however nothing could be further from the truth.

They start communicating nonessential material, and that's where the dilution of effectiveness begins. You see, when I engineer a script, it is based on Shakespeare's quote, *"Brevity is the soul of wit."* My scripts communicate *only* the essential content, and nothing else.

If you don't hire me to write your sales scripts (which is a big mistake), you should at least reevaluate your sales and marketing message and convert it into a standardized script.

If you're going to attempt to engineer your own script, you must remember to consider each word in each sentence, and ask yourself, *"Is it absolutely, positively necessary for me to say this?"* If the answer is *no*, then you must remove it. Even if it's really, really, really good stuff, you must remove it if it is not absolutely, positively necessary to say.

A great way to start this self-correction is to listen to voicemail messages you leave on other people's voicemail boxes. If you have the option to listen to the message you're about to permanently leave in someone else's voicemail box, select that option and listen to what you said.

I can almost guarantee that most of your messages consist of 80 percent nonessential babble, and 20 percent core message.

Once you listen to the voicemail you were about to leave, ask yourself, *"What is the core message I really want to communicate, and can I maximize clarity and brevity by cutting out nonessential babble?"* The answer, as you will shockingly and embarrassingly realize, is *yes*.

So in sales, and in effective business communication in general, if it's not necessary to say, it's necessary not to say it.

Chapter Eleven:
How To Effectively Communicate With Clients

"Would you rather be right, or would you rather be rich?"
-Darren Sugiyama

Expectation Management

One of the biggest communication mistakes I've seen people in sales make, is in the area of communicating expected completion dates to a client. So often, people in sales over-promise and under-deliver in an effort to win favor with the client, but the problem is that they're destined to eventually upset the client. What we're talking about here is poor client expectation management.

You should always tell the client that you expect completion of a project to be a minimum of five days after the date you actually expect the project to be completed. If you don't give yourself this cushion, you're setting yourself up for failure. Here's an example of what I'm talking about.

I just recently got a new Porsche. I had a lot of custom work done on it... custom exhaust... custom paint job... custom suspension... custom wheels. It was a pretty intensive job. The guy that sold me the car did a great job in a number of areas, and the entire buying process was incredibly enjoyable. But then came the delivery process. What a nightmare.

When I signed papers with the dealership, he told me the car would be ready the next day. He was expecting my custom wheels to show up the day of the signing, and he said he'd have the car ready the next morning. There was only one problem. The wheels didn't get delivered that day as he expected.

So when I called him the next morning, excited to pick up my car, I was given the bad news. My car wasn't ready. He assured me that the wheels would be coming in that afternoon, and that I should be able to pick up the car that evening.

That evening came and went, and still, no wheels. That was a Friday. The weekend came and went, and still, no wheels.

Monday comes, and I thought for sure my Porsche would be ready. I was anxious and excited to drive my new car. But the wheel company didn't ship my wheels, so there we were, four days past my expectation of driving my new car, and I'm totally pissed off.

Finally, Tuesday comes, and miracle of all miracles, my car is finally ready. The problem was that by this time, my feelings of frustration, due to my perception of poor client service, overrode my feelings of excitement about my new car. The positive buying experience had been totally shattered.

The sad thing is that this could have so easily been avoided if the sales guy had just done a better job of managing my expectations. The key to doing this properly is to give yourself some *cushion* – a few extra days to complete a client project, just in case something goes wrong.

The reality of living on the planet earth is that *crap* happens. From time to time, things happen that you have no control over, and project completion may take longer than expected, to no fault of your own. The problem is, your clients don't care whose fault it is. They will blame you, and you may lose the client eventually.

Here's what you should say to a client regarding the completion date of any project you're working on for them:

> *"The normal turn-around time is typically eight to ten working days, but I'm going to call in some favors and see if I can put a rush on this for you. I can't promise you anything, but I'll do everything I can and see if I can pull some strings for you."*

In this example, you're actual expected completion date is only three days, however you need to tell the client that the typical turn-around time is eight to ten days.

When you do this, if everything gets totally screwed up, whether your vendors make mistakes, or if your own company drops the ball and the completion date takes five to seven days longer than expected, it's no problem. Your client doesn't know you screwed up because you actually delivered according to your client's expectations... expectations that you set.

But if everything goes as planned and you complete the project in three days, and you're able to call your client with the good news that you were able to put a rush on their order, delivering five days ahead of your client's expectations, you'll look like a hero, when in reality, the client just received the standard turn-around time.

It all has to do with managing client expectations. Don't be so eager to impress your client by promising them the world. You're better off under-promising, and over-delivering... as opposed to over-promising and under-delivering.

Create Your Own Deadlines

Another huge mistake I've seen sales people make is telling their clients when the *actual* deadline is. There's one thing I know about clients, prospects, and human beings in general. They all procrastinate to a certain degree.

In most cases, the last day of the month is a stressful day for people in sales. Why? Because they're scrambling, trying to push deals through at the last minute, and usually the thing they're scrambling for has something to do with them needing something from their client, whether it's an application, or a signed document, or a check.

There are several problems that this type of situation creates. The first one is *stress*. Perhaps you can relate to what I'm saying here. In fact, let me ask you a question. Do you often find yourself stressing out, scrambling to push deals through on the last day of the month? It's stressful, isn't it? This stress can easily be avoided if you implement the process I'm about to share with you.

However the problems don't stop here. The second problem it creates is that it threatens your relationship with your client because you're pushing them... rushing them... begging them to do something at the eleventh hour for YOUR benefit, not theirs.

You're trying to jam the deal through at month-end so you get the sales credit this month. Your client is going to feel the pressure you're putting on them, and they're going to figure out that you're pushing them for selfish reasons. This is not good for client relations.

Here's how to fix this problem and set yourself up to be the hero again. If the actual drop-dead deadline is the last day of the month, you need to create your *own deadline*. In this scenario, I recommend making your deadline the fifteenth of the month. Tell your client,

> *"The good news is that we have plenty of time to set this up for you. Today is the seventh, and the deadline isn't until the fifteenth, so we have plenty of time."*

You just told them that they have plenty of time, which makes them feel like you're going to make it easy. At the same time, they're thinking to themselves, *"Holy crap. That's only twelve days away. I'd better get moving on this!"*

As your self-created deadline approaches, who's stressing out about the deadline, you or them? They are. You know you have another fifteen days, but the client doesn't know this, so you're as cool as a popsicle in the freezer, and they're scrambling, trying to jam the deal through.

So let's say it's the fourteenth day of the month, and your self-created deadline is tomorrow. And let's say your client doesn't think they're going to be able to produce the documents needed by tomorrow.

When tomorrow comes, and they don't have the document that's required, you get to display your power by calling in a *favor* for them. Tell them, *"Look, I know you really want to get this in place this month, so let me see if I can call in a favor and get you a one-day extension."*

Then hang up the phone… wait a few minutes… and call them back with the good news. Tell them, *"I've got some good news for you. I called in a favor for you and got you a one-day extension."* Your client now feels like they owe you one, which is exactly what you want.

Let's say the next day comes and goes, and your client still doesn't have their documents together. Tell them, *"Oh, man. You're putting my butt on the line here, but let me see if I can get you another one-day extension."*

Again, wait a few minutes and call them back, saying, *"Oh, man. You're going to owe me for this one. I begged the company to make an exception for you, and I was able to get you another one-day extension."* At this point, your client thinks you walk on water.

But the best part is that you're stress free, because it's only the seventeenth of the month, and you still have another two weeks before your actual deadline.

It's all about how you set up your client expectations. Do this properly, and your clients will never leave you because they feel like they're getting them the V.I.P. treatment.

Expediency vs. Explanation

Obviously, having an expedient turnaround time is great. However, it's not as important as explaining to your client what the process entails as they're waiting for the completion of their project. Contrary to popular belief, clients don't get as upset with longer turn-around times as they do when they feel like no one's working hard on their behalf.

Think about this. Have you ever found yourself, as a customer, complaining about poor service, saying, *"What the hell is taking so long?"* I certainly have. But stop for a second and think about what you were really saying. The basis of your question was centered around wanting to know *the reason* why the completion of the project was taking so long. You wanted to know the reason.

You probably didn't threaten the person, saying, *"Get this thing done immediately or I'm going to kick your ass."* You asked the question, *"What is the reason this is taking longer than I expected?"* Studies show that what makes people feel better about longer-than-expected turnaround times is being communicated to regarding the process.

Here's an example. Have you ever been working on a project on your computer, and gotten that stupid rainbow pinwheel spinning around? It keeps spinning and spinning... and you keep waiting and waiting... as you anxiously stare at your computer screen, saying to yourself, *"What the hell is taking so long?"* If you're using a Mac, it's a rainbow pinwheel... if you're using a PC, it's an hour glass that spins around. It's frustrating, isn't it?

Or have you ever been waiting for a software application to download... or a website to process an order... or for your food to be served in a restaurant... and gotten so pissed off that you wanted to kill somebody? I have.

Common logic would tell you that reducing a client's wait-time would improve client satisfaction. However my research would argue that reducing client wait-time is only part of the solution. Additionally, there are situations where reducing client wait-time is impossible (because sometimes, crap happens). This being the case, due to the fact that we live on the planet earth, my approach to client satisfaction defies conventional wisdom.

You see, when you understand human psychology and human behavioral patterns, you'll begin to understand my unconventional approach to this issue of client satisfaction. It all comes down to effective communication.

As I stated earlier, the common question that most upset clients ask is, *"What the hell is taking so long?"* implying that they actually want to understand the reason, often times more so than they want a faster turn-around time. Clients tend to tolerate longer wait-times when they feel that you're working above the call of duty to get their project completed. They tend to value you and your service more, which is what your sales, marketing, brand and retention strategy should be focused on. You want to make them feel special.

The only way your client is going to feel that you're going above and beyond the normal call of duty for them is if you effectively and strategically communicate what you're doing for them, every step of the way. Studies show that clients who endure longer wait-times who were also given the play-by-play of the progress of the process were actually happier than those clients that were not communicated to, even if their turn-around times were faster.

I recently read about a study that was done at the Harvard Business School where people were observed as participants while they searched for a flight on two different fictitious, simulated airline websites.

On one website, when the participants clicked *search*, the typical, boring progress bar appeared (similar to the spinning rainbow pinwheel on a Mac, or a rotating hour glass on a PC). These participants stared at the progress bar, bored and antsy. I can just imagine them saying to themselves, *"Man, why the hell is this taking so long?"*

On the second website, when a participant clicked *search*, they could see each airline being canvassed, searching for an available flight, airline by airline. This second website that showed the participant the process of the search actually took thirty to sixty seconds longer to process the search and display the results.

Naturally, you would think that the participants preferred the first website, due to its faster turn-around time.

Ironically, the majority of the participants preferred the second website, even though it was slower. Obviously, they didn't consciously say, "*I like the slower one better.*" But subconsciously, due to the fact that they were kept abreast of the process behind the search being done, they didn't notice the slower processing speed. They could *see* that work was being done on their behalf, and it made them feel good.

Now, am I saying that the illusion of work being done on a client's behalf is better than actually delivering superior turn-around time? Of course not. But what I *am* saying, and what this Harvard study proved, was that when people feel that someone is working hard to get the job done for them, and when they're kept abreast of the *process* as well as the *progress* being made, they tend to overlook things like slower turn-around times.

So how does this apply to your business? The key with keeping clients (and prospects) happy is to show them or tell them the behind-the-scenes story of each step along the way. Similar to what I previously said about my car buying experience, when you don't communicate with your client, giving them constant updates regarding the progress being made, they will automatically think you're neglecting them. Whether it's true or not, is not the point. That's their perception, and client perception, though it's not *everything*, is very important.

Expedient turn-around times are great, but never forget to explain to your client what's happening along the way. Always remember that clear client explanations will trump expediency-with-no-explanation every time.

Keeping Your Clients Updated

Have you ever been working on getting an issue resolved for you client, and you had to rely on someone else to handle the actual resolution? What happened? You probably told your client that you'd call them back as soon as the issue is resolved. You probably called whoever handles those issues, delegating the task to that person, and they probably told you that they'd call you back once the issue is resolved.

Well, if you live on the planet earth, you've probably found that sometimes, issues don't get resolved immediately. And so as you're waiting to a call back, you figure there's no reason to call your client until you have some good news. This is a big mistake.

Clients need to feel like you're constantly working on their behalf. You need to proactively call your client giving them the update, even if the update is *no news yet*. If you don't call them, communicating that you're working on it, but that you don't have an answer just yet, your client will think that you don't care or that you're not prioritizing their issue high enough on your priority list.

All you have to do is call them everyday, informing them that you don't have any news yet for them, and that you'll keep giving them the update, whether you have a final resolution or not. This makes them feel good.

So many people in sales are afraid to call their client with *no news*. They'll avoid making the call, and if their client calls them wanting an update, they'll duck their client's call because they don't want to deliver *bad news* or *no news yet*. All this does is piss off the client.

Remember the story I just told you about my Porsche? Not only was I pissed off that it took longer to receive my car than what I expected, but every time I called my sales guy, he never picked up my call, probably because he was afraid to tell me my car wasn't done yet.

But by taking the chicken-shit route, I just assumed that my car wasn't a priority for him.

All he had to do was set my expectation to receive the car later than what he initially expected, and then communicate to me on a daily basis what the status was, and if he ended up over-delivering, I would absolutely love this guy.

Always remember that client perception is of the utmost importance. Set yourself up to be perceived by your clients as the *Miracle Worker* by managing their expectations, and over-delivering.

Dealing With An Upset Client

Have you ever had to deal with an upset client? Sometimes clients have a right to be upset, and sometimes they don't... but it doesn't matter if they're right or wrong. All that matters is your ability to keep them as a client, which can be done by calming them down in the heat of their volatility and eliminating their problem. There is an effective, strategic way to accomplish this. Let's discuss how to do this properly.

You need to take your client's side whenever they're upset. Tell them, *"It sounds like you're not being taken care of the way you're supposed to. Can you tell me a little bit of what happened?"*

Let them vent. Don't interrupt, or apologize, or make excuses. Just let them vent. They're probably going to tell you that *someone* screwed up, or that *something* got screwed up. The key is to identify that it is someone else's fault, and throw them under the bus. Tell them,

> *"You've got to be kidding me! I can't believe they screwed this up! Man, I don't blame you for being pissed. If I were you, I'd be pissed off too. What a bunch of idiots. Let me get on the phone right now and make this go away for you. I'll call you back as soon as I find out what happened."*

It's important to never accept blame when it's not your fault. In personal relationships, it's just the opposite. For example, with my wife, sometimes we'll have a miscommunication and something will get screwed up. In most cases, I'll accept the blame for it, simply to diffuse the tension. In many of these cases, it doesn't really matter whose fault it is, and so in my opinion, it's wise to just accept the blame so we can move on.

But in business, you never want to accept the blame, because subconsciously, your client will lose faith in your ability to deliver. That being said, you need to align yourself with the client and be their advocate. Whether your dealing with a client or a prospect, one of your main goals should be to identify a common enemy. When a common enemy is identified, the two *victims* will bond together.

Take sports fans for example. When two people are rooting for the same team (or more specifically, rooting against the same team), a common bond is formed, and the two fans practically become blood brothers. The same goes with people that are in the same Alcoholics Anonymous class… or a women's liberation group… or an ethnic group that has been racially discriminated against. People tend to bond together in order to rise up against a common enemy.

Using this bonding principle, whenever you have a client that calls you up, ranting and raving, complaining about something, don't argue with them. Take their side. In fact, you need to act like you're even more upset than they are regarding this terrible injustice that has been committed against them. Remember, part of the reason they're throwing a temper tantrum is that they want their feelings to be acknowledged and validated. If you show them that you're even more upset about the injustice than they are, they'll feel like you're fighting their battle for them, which bonds them to you.

In addition, your strategic temper tantrum alliance with them deflects the blame away from you, and redirects it towards your common enemy. The key is to throw the common enemy under the bus, and rant and rave on behalf of your client. One time I had to deal with a very over-emotional, prima donna client, and after I went on my rampage about how outrageous the injustice committed against them was, I semi-sarcastically said,

> *"You know what, I'm not done yet! I'm going to make some calls and get that idiot fired that did this to you. I'll make sure he never works in this industry ever again!"*

Of course, my client knew I was half-kidding, and they started laughing, saying, *"Oh, you don't have to do that!"* My client went from being totally pissed off, to laughing, in a matter of seconds. All he wanted was for someone to acknowledge his frustration, and take his side.

Always remember that people who feel victimized will bond with a fellow victim and rise up against a common enemy. Whenever you have a disgruntled client, identify a common enemy and throw them under the bus, and watch your client bond with you, and together you'll rise up against the common enemy.

Over the last few days, I've had a rather busy travel schedule doing sales coaching seminars across the country. On Tuesday, I was in Dublin, Ohio… on Wednesday, I was in Richmond, Virginia… and today, I'm in Wichita, Kansas.

When I do these trips, I usually have to take connector flights out of Chicago or Dallas. During this week's speaking events, most of my flights connected through Chicago. Unfortunately, Chicago got hit with some challenging weather, including windstorms and a few tornadoes.

When I arrived at the airport in Dublin, Ohio in the early evening, after an all-day speaking event, I was a bit fatigued. I hadn't gotten checked into the hotel the night before until about midnight, and had to wake up at 5:00am EST (which was 2:00am my time), since I had flown in from California the night before.

I boarded the plane as usual, and everything seemed to be just fine. As I sat in the airplane, ready to take off from Dublin to Richmond (connecting through Chicago), the captain informed us that he was waiting for authorization to take off, and that it should be just a few minutes. We waited... and waited... and waited.

No one gave us any updates as to what was taking so long. Over an hour later, the captain announced that due to weather conditions in Chicago, our flight was being cancelled. I tried to get on a different flight to Richmond, possibly connecting through a different city other than Chicago. No luck.

So I spent the night in Dublin, expecting to fly out early the next morning at 5:45am. I woke up at 4:00am EST (1:00am my time), and got to the airport, expecting to just hop on the plane and go. I had informed my client in Richmond that I would be running late due to flight cancellations. They weren't thrilled, but they understood.

Then things got worse.

The weather in Chicago was still bad, so my flight got cancelled again. I was put on a different flight with a different airline, with a connection through Philadelphia. I arrived even later to my speaking engagement in Richmond, but fortunately, my client did a good job of stalling until I arrived.

But then things got even worse. My flight from Richmond to Wichita, Kansas that afternoon got cancelled due to the weather in Chicago not improving, so they transferred me to another airline to connect through Atlanta. Not bad, right? Wrong. I got booted off this flight due to overbooking, and I didn't have my priority status with them because it wasn't my normal airline. So there I was, stuck in Richmond for the evening, which would mean that I'd arrive to my client in Wichita late as well.

I called my client in Wichita, and they were very understanding, and were able to manipulate the event agenda for my late arrival. I was now scheduled to fly out of Richmond at 5:50am EST the next morning, connecting through Atlanta, which meant I had to wake up at 4:00am EST again (1:00am my time).

When I arrived at the airport, I was informed that now my flight to Atlanta/Wichita had also been cancelled. At this point, I wanted to kill somebody. It looked as though I was going to miss my event in Wichita all together, and at the daily rate I charge my clients for these types of events, not showing up is unacceptable, even if it isn't my fault.

So there I was in the airport, exhausted and pissed off, ready to *go postal* on someone. I walked up to the ticket counter at the airline, and the agent said in a chipper voice, *"Good morning sir! How are you doing today?"*

"Shitty," I replied. I was in a bad mood, and at that point, I had lost all patience and social etiquette. I'm not saying my behavior was acceptable. It was not. I don't care how tired or upset you are. It doesn't give you the right to dump your negative energy and frustration on someone else. It wasn't this guy's fault that the weather in Chicago was bad.

But he handled things wonderfully. The first thing he said to me was, *"Wow, it looks like your flights have gotten all screwed up. Let me see what I can do to fix this and get you to Wichita this morning."* He didn't lash back at me, even though I gave him every right to.

Instead, he validated my feelings of frustration, and he took my side. He acknowledged that I had been dealt several lemons, and made me feel like he was going to help me... maybe not turn them into lemonade, but certainly make every humanly possible effort to replace the lemons with some other acceptable fruit.

At first, things looked grim. There were no available seats on any flights to Wichita until Friday morning, which did me absolutely no good. It looked as though I was going to miss my event all together. But then he said seven of the most diffusing words a sales person can say to an upset client.

He said, *"Let me see what I can do."* He got on his computer and voraciously started typing. His brow became more and more furrowed, as it looked like he was practically trying to hack into the CIA's ultra-secured system. He typed faster and faster.

Then he exclaimed, *"Ah-ha! I knew it!"*

"What? What's Up?" I asked.

He explained to me that he found four seats that the system had hidden due to the passenger-weight-to-fuel-ratio. Apparently, on smaller planes, flights will be sold based on this ratio. In other words, if there is a limited amount of fuel, the airline will not book the flight full so that the plane is physically lighter.

He said, *"I'm looking at the amount of fuel this plane has right now, and there's more than enough to accommodate four more seats. Let me call my supervisor."* He immediately got on the phone with his supervisor, fighting for my cause like a defense attorney. I stood there in amazement. I was arguably getting some of the best service I have ever gotten as a customer.

He got upset on my behalf, empathizing with my situation. He said to his supervisor on the phone, *"Look, we've got to get this gentleman to Wichita this morning."*

Do you know how good that made me feel? As I watched this agent plead my case, I actually forgot about how long I had been waiting. I forgot about how many flights had been cancelled. I forgot about how tired I was having woken up at 1:00am PST to get on flights, only to be told they were cancelled. I was entirely focused on how this airline agent took my side.

After pleading my case with this supervisor, he got off the phone and literally pumped his fist in the air and exclaimed, *"Yes! I got you on!"* He was actually excited for me. Now, perhaps that was all an act. Maybe he just did it to make me feel good. But the point is, it didn't matter. He made his customer (me) feel special.

As it turned out, the flight he got me on got me into Wichita ahead of schedule, allowing me to call my client with the good news. The key to making your clients feel special is to understand human emotion and human psychology.

Human beings are much more empathetic than we often give them credit for. If you have an upset client, and you show them empathy, validating their feelings, they will appreciate you more.

They will actually reciprocate empathy towards you, not blaming you, because they see you busting your butt for them. They will shift the blame off of you because they feel like you're on their side, fighting for them, and they'll place the blame on the circumstance instead of you.

The key, however, is that you must communicate with them every step of the way. You need to make sure they understand why the less-than-perfect situation exists, and they need to understand the process you're going through to fix the problem for them, and the only way they're going to understand these things is if you show-and-tell them.

Often times, when you do this well, your client will actually trust and appreciate you more than they would if everything was hunky-dory all the time, because the less-than-perfect situation allows you to play the role of their hero, rescuing them.

Use these situations as opportunities to do so.

The Ohhhhhh Technique

Have you ever talked to a client and realized that you made a false assumption, and said something that you wish you could take back? I certainly have… multiple times in my career.

How do you recover from sticking your foot in your mouth like this? It's really quite simple. Use *The Ohhhhhh Technique*.

If you say something to your client that gets a less-than-favorable response… and you want to take it back… just ask a *clarifying question*, followed by *The Ohhhhhh Technique*. Here's an example…

In the beginning stages of starting my career in the employee benefits arena, I was on a sales appointment, meeting with the business owner and his HR Director. The owner asked me how I would use our proposed benefits package to entice/recruit a six-figure Executive Vice-President to come work for them. I responded by saying,

> "Well, if a prospective Vice-President is going to make a career decision based on benefits, I've got to question if you even want hire them. They should make their decision based on the career opportunity with you, not the benefits."

Man, that was a dumb thing for me to say. My response didn't give him a reason to buy from me, plus he was of the mindset that a strong benefits package would in fact help him recruit a better Vice-President. Who was I to disagree with his business philosophy? I quickly realized the error of my response, so I said,

"Wait a second... So you're trying to figure out how you can use the benefits package to recruit AND retain your high level executives by offering them something that your competitors aren't offering. Is that what you're asking?"

He said, *"Exactly."* So I responded,

"Ohhhhhh! Okay! I understand now. Here's why this program is so perfect for you. You're going to be able to offer a Vice-President a benefits package he won't be able to get from any other employer. My program is going to allow you to differentiate yourself from all of your competitors because no one in your industry is going to offer this benefits package."

Needless to say, he was totally excited. *The Ohhhhhh Technique* makes your client feel like the only reason you uttered such stupid words was that you misunderstood the question. By clarifying the question, you now have a second chance at delivering a strong, compelling reason for your client to trust you. Now you're back in consultative mode. You have re-established yourself as the expert.

The reason this technique is so effective is that when you acknowledge the *words of stupidity* that left your lips, but chalk them up to misunderstanding the question, your intelligence and judgment aren't questioned. Perhaps the client may perceive that you need hearing aids, but they won't perceive you to be an idiot. You're still viewed as the expert. Mission accomplished.

Similar to personal relationships, business relationships can either be solidified with effective communication, or destroyed by poor communication. Use the communication strategies I shared with you in this chapter, and establish the proper client expectations, and watch your clients turn into raving fans.

Chapter Twelve:
Championship Leadership

"No greater love hath a man than he lay down his life for his friends."
-The Bible, John 15:13

7 Essential Qualities Of A Great Leader

How do you define great leadership? It's a difficult thing to evaluate objectively and quantitatively, simply because there has never been a standardized way to measure great leadership. However, as I've studied leadership over the years, I've identified seven key, essential fundamentals that all great leaders practice.

1. Principle-driven, not emotionally driven.
2. Puts the team above self.
3. Leads by example.
4. Consistent in their decision making process.
5. Always over-prepared, and always over-delivers.
6. Never teaches something they haven't done themselves.
7. Accepts the responsibility of living in a glass house 24/7.

Fundamental #1: A great leader is principle-driven.

Human beings are emotional creatures. It's just the way we were built. However in order to be a great leader, you must be principle-driven, not emotionally-driven.

Someone once told me that 90 percent of the emotions we have would lead us to do things that are stupid, irrational, unethical, and sometimes illegal, if we allowed our emotions to dictate our actions. I would have to agree with this statement. What keeps you from doing stupid, self-gratifying, bad things are your *ethics* and your *principles*.

In the world of business, we are constantly being confronted by challenging circumstances, often putting us in predicaments where we need to make important decisions that not only affect ourselves and our companies, but other people's lives as well.

I've seen so many weak people in leadership positions that let their own selfishness and self-preserving emotions override what is ethical, fair and right.

A great leader makes decisions based on principles, regardless of the potential for personal gain or the potential to avoid pain. As a leader, you must realize that in order to truly earn the respect of your people, sometimes you must make decisions that are not popular.

I was on a business trip this past week and shared a taxicab ride to the airport with a Vice-President of billion dollar corporation. As our conversation progressed, we got on the subjects of leadership. He told me about another Vice-President he once knew whose goal was to have everyone *like* him. Basically, he was emotionally-driven by the desire for people to like him.

Well, as your mother probably told you long ago, you can't please 100 percent of the people 100 percent of the time. And if you're a leader, you're going to have to make decisions that some people may not like. Being *liked* is often not synonymous with *being respected*, and often times, as a leader, you won't win today's popularity contest.

But if you're consistently fair in your decisions, and your decisions are based on principles, your people will respect you long-term, even if they disagree with your decisions in the short-term, because they know you have integrity.

I also know of a CEO of a company that was extremely *liked* by his employees. He even partied with some of them, but due to the fact that he never really earned their respect, his company began to fail, and as a result, he was fired. Again, focus on being principle-driven, not emotionally-driven, and your people will respect you at a level that you've never experienced before.

Fundamental #2: A great leader puts the team above self.

I once heard someone say that you can have everything in life you want if you just help enough other people get what they want. I've seen people in leadership positions whose entire agenda is to motivate their people for the sole purpose of accomplishing their own goals. What they fail to understand is that their people can see right through their selfish intentions.

People can tell when you care more about your own goals than theirs, and so when you attempt to give them a pep talk, they know that the only reason you're spending time with them is to get them to be one of your workhorses. Ultimately, they are left feeling used.

To them, it feels like you're taking them to the mountaintop overlooking the universe… putting your arm around them… and telling them, *"If you dedicate yourself, and work really hard, all of this… can be MINE."* Perhaps this sounds ludicrous to you, but I've talked to so many sales reps in my career that have told me that they feel like their sales manager only cared about their own goals, and didn't really care about their sales reps' goals.

I know of a sales manager that constantly talks to his sales producers about his own goals and his own quota for his sales territory. The grave error he's making by doing this is that his people feel unappreciated, used, and devalued. His sales reps have been made to feel like indentured servants to their boss, the sales manager.

Instead, he could win them over, gain their trust, and ultimately double his territory's sales production if he just empowered his people by helping each individual producer hit THEIR goals. You see, if this manager just focused on helping his sales producers hit their own goals, all of his goals would be exceeded.

People can tell when your intentions are pure, genuine and altruistic, and they can also tell when your intentions are self-serving… and when you're selfish, you cannot inspire anyone. I've never met anyone that told me that they've been inspired by a selfish person. People are only inspired by greatness, and greatness is about serving and helping others.

The key to being a great leader is being able to inspire people. All you have to do is find out what's important to each individual person on your team, then help them accomplish their own personal goals, assuming their goals also contribute to the greater good of your company. Find out what their dreams are. Find out what motivates them. Find out what emotionally drives them.

Once you have this inside information about them, base your goal setting meetings with them around what THEY are passionate about. Find ways to make their job easier. Find ways to make them more successful in their job function.

If you're constantly providing them with resources, tools and strategies that enable them to reach greater levels of success, not only will they produce more results, but they'll feel more loyalty towards you because they know that you sincerely care about them and their success. Anything less comes off as disingenuous.

The Biblical scripture, *"No greater love hath a man than he lay down his life for his friends,"* doesn't mean that you have to literally die. It means that you put away your selfish needs and place others needs above your own. This is what Championship Leadership is all about. When your people feel your *love* for them, they'll follow you onto the battlefield. I know this probably sounds kind of touchy-feely to you, but this is a big part of leading an organization. Your people must feel that you have their back.

The Bible also talks about a concept called *Servant Leadership*. What this means is that the leader's job is to serve their people, not make your people feel like they have to serve their leader. The irony is that when done properly, this type of leadership style will make your people want to follow you even more. So if you want to be a great leader, look for ways to better serve your people.

Fundamental #3: A great leader leads by example.

Have you ever heard parents say to their kids, *"Do what I say, not what I do?"* Parents like this have no credibility with their kids. They're hypocrites, and people despise hypocrisy... even kids. Hypocrisy is the antithesis of integrity.

If you want to be a great leader, you've got to win over the respect of your people with your integrity, and nothing validates your integrity and your authenticity more than when you lead by example. People that try to lead from the proverbial *ivory tower* rarely get the respect that *in-the-trench* leaders get. I've never seen a truly great leader ask their people to do something they haven't done themselves.

I once knew a gentleman that was a very smart, and quite talented businessman, however he was missing one key thing. He expected other people to do all of the grunt work... grunt work that he had never personally done himself. In the beginning, his people didn't seem to notice that he had never successfully done what he was teaching them to do. But over time, his people soon realized that he was a fraud.

Sounds harsh, doesn't it? Calling someone a *fraud* is harsh. But what is a *fraud*? I would define a *fraud* as someone that leads you to believe that they are doing something that they aren't actually doing.

This guy would lead people to believe that he was working hard behind the scenes, when in actuality, all he did was get people to do all of his legwork for him. He wasn't willing to do what he expected other people to do for him. It was only a matter of time before his people realized that he was nothing more than a big talker. Great leaders continually earn their people's trust, and they re-earn their trust through leading by example.

Occasionally, I'll get out on the sales floor with my sales producers, and I'll make prospecting calls right next to them. They usually freak out when they see *the boss* jump on the phones with them, but when they realize I'm practicing what I preach, I win over more of their respect.

I remember seeing a documentary about a college basketball team, and one of the coaches participated in all of the strength and conditioning exercises along side all his players. During the pre-season, the team would have excruciatingly painful workouts, and during these workouts, this coach suffered through the process with his players.

When they interviewed the players on the team, they all talked about how much they respected and admired this coach. One of the players even said, *"I feel like he's one of us, and it makes me want to work harder for him."*

When they interviewed this coach, he said that the main reason he puts himself through the same torture he puts his players through during the strength and conditioning process is that he doesn't want to give any player the opportunity to come up with an excuse of why he can't handle the workouts. The coach said, *"If an old, past-his-prime guy like me can do it, then there's no excuse why my players can't do it."* This is the kind of exemplary leadership I'm talking about.

Win over your employees' hearts by showing them through example what to do. Model the proper, expected behavior yourself, and you'll be able to say, *"This is what I do. Do the same."* Whenever I mentor someone in business, this is the process that I go through as I'm teaching them a new skill:

1. Watch me do it.

2. Watch me do it again.

3. Let me explain why it works.

4. Now, you do it as I watch you.

5. Do it again.

6. Let me give you some tips on how to do it better.
7. Do it again as I watch you.
8. Now, you tell me why what you did worked.

This seems like a pretty easy, logical process doesn't it? But trust me, very few so-called leaders do this. They'll tell you stories about what they used to do back in the dark ages, and of course, you roll your eyes at them because you know that they're either out of touch with what's happening in today's market, or they're lying to you about their decorated past. The only way to truly be a great leader is to lead by example.

Fundamental #4: A great leader is consistent in their decision matrix.

When it comes to being a great leader, you won't always please everyone. In fact, often times, being a great leader requires you to make unpopular decisions.

People may disagree with your decisions from time to time, but they will respect you as a leader if they know that you're making your decisions based on a set of pre-determined values and principles.

That being said, you must be consistent with this decision making process for every decision, with every employee. As soon as you change the rules for one employee, the other employees will resent you for it, and they should, because you're being unfair in your inconsistency.

I have a client that I do sales coaching for. She is a very talented and very successful sales executive, and has been for many years. She told me about a case where she had landed a huge account for her company, and although this account that was long sought after by some of her associates, none of them were able to land it prior to her efforts.

Her employer had a company policy that said although each sales executive had a defined sales territory, they could work with clients outside of their territory if they were referred in by a current client. In this case, she was referred in by one of her clients, thus it seemed copacetic that she work with this newly acquired client.

Well, the sales executive who was supposed to be working that territory had tried to land this big client previously, but had failed to do so. When he found out that this other sales executive landed the account, he went ballistic, even though he himself had clients outside of his own territory, as virtually every sales executive in this company had as well.

The sales manager decided to award the account to the complaining sales executive on the basis of the account being in his territory, and stripped the account away from the sales executive who landed it. Not only was this unfair, but it violated company policy. As a result, my client handed in her resignation and left the company.

So not only did this sales manager piss off one of his top sales executives, he ultimately lost all future revenue she would have brought to his sales unit.

In addition, when other employees witnessed the unjust decision to award the account to the other sales executive, three other employees left the company because they felt like they couldn't trust the sales manager to be fair to them on future cases. Inconsistency breeds a lack of trust within an organization.

A great leader knows that everyone is constantly watching and evaluating their decisions, and the consistency and fairness of their decisions will define their integrity as a leader.

Great leaders are usually easy to spot. All you have to do is look behind them and see how many people are enthusiastically following them. This is a pretty simple measuring stick, but it is the most accurate. I know people that strut around, talking about what a great leader they are, but when I look behind them, I don't see an army of loyal followers. That tells me everything I need to know about their leadership abilities.

When you really break it down, the entire point of being a leader in business is to amass an army of loyal followers – raving fans – that look up to you and hang on every word that comes out of your mouth. In order to sustain this type of following, people have to respect you, and their respect for you is contingent on you leading by example.

It probably sounds like I'm beating a dead horse, but I can't emphasize this point enough. Sure, it's possible to intimidate people into following you due to your job title or position within your company, but this isn't a sustainable strategy. Intimidation will only work short-term, if at all.

This is what I call *Positional Leadership*. Due to your position or title, most people will follow you because they know that you're higher up in the power hierarchy than they are, but this doesn't win over their hearts. If you don't win over their hearts, they won't follow you onto the battlefield long-term, and amassing an army of loyal followers that will follow you onto the battlefield long-term is the definition of being a great leader.

Fundamental #5: A great leader is always over-prepared and always over-delivers.

One of the biggest mistakes I've seen so-called leaders make is in the area of preparation. Often times, they'll show up at a meeting, or an event, or an engagement, and they're under-prepared. This sends a message to your people that your personal brand is one of mediocrity. Here's an example.

I can't tell you how many times I've attended seminars or formal group meetings where the event starts, and the audio/visual system doesn't work properly. This absolutely kills the momentum when kicking off the start of an event.

I always show up at least 30 minutes ahead of time and do a sound check, along with an audio/visual check to make sure all of my equipment is in sync with the hotel's equipment. In fact, if you do a lot of public speaking events, here's a little tip. Always do a mic-check prior to the event, and walk around the room while you're doing the mic-check. Here's why.

If you're using a wireless mic, you want to make sure there are no dead spots, interference spots or feedback spots in your room. Talk into your microphone and walk directly under the ceiling speakers to make sure there isn't any feedback. Often times, this cannot be avoided, so it's important to know where those speakers are so that you can avoid walking under them during your talk.

If you're playing videos in your presentation, you want to make sure the volume level is set to the appropriate level. If the volume comes on too loud, people will be distracted and frazzled, and you'll lose the positive build up of anticipation in the crowd as your video starts. If the volume comes on too soft, you'll lose the dramatic impact of kicking off the video with power. The same thing obviously applies to the volume of your microphone. These are simple little things you can do to over-prepare.

Another area that many so-called leaders fall short in is the area of punctuality. There's nothing worse than showing up to an important meeting or event late. It sends a subconscious message to your people that the event isn't that important, and it will create a lazy, sloppy environment, which will eventually lead to a lazy, sloppy culture.

I've heard all kinds of excuses for tardiness, everything from bad traffic… to difficult parking… to getting lost. I always show up to an event or meeting at least twenty minutes prior to my expected arrival time.

Why? Because *stuff* happens sometimes that is completely out of your control. Traffic accidents DO happen. The stupid navigation system in my car has failed me on several occasions. And so it's important to budget in some cushion time, just in case one of these unforeseen things happens.

Another example is when I travel. I travel for business on a regular basis, and I always park my car at the airport in the exact same lot, in practically the exact same spot every time. But one time, for whatever reason, the entire lot was full – which never happens – but it happened on this one occasion. Fortunately, I gave myself a twenty-minute buffer, so even though it took me an additional 15-20 minutes to find an open spot in another lot, it was no problem, and I made my flight.

If you give yourself a 20-30 minute buffer, you'll rarely ever show up late, because when these unexpected occurrences happen, you'll have enough buffer time to allow you to be right on time. Sure, the majority of time, you'll be there twenty minutes early, but so what?

I have my laptop computer with me practically 24/7, so I'll often just do some work or check emails while I'm waiting. It's no big deal. The point is, I'm rarely ever late, and everyone I do business with knows it. This is part of my brand. I always want to be over-prepared, and I always want to over-deliver, above and beyond expectation. Being punctual is such an easy thing to do, and as a leader, you need to set the precedence in this area.

Another characteristic that all great leaders have in this area is the desire to over-deliver. I always want to grossly exceed expectation. It's a difficult thing to sustain, but if you really want to be categorized as a great leader, you must continually over-perform for your people.

I remember hearing a very successful businessman in a seminar I attended years ago talk about the relationship he has with his wife. He said,

> *"Think about what happens when you first get married. You watch TV together, and you're curled up on the couch so close that you can't even tell whose leg is whose. But then what happens over time? You start putting on more weight. You start having hair grow in places you don't want it, and you start losing hair in places that you do want it. You don't have the physical energy you once had when you were younger. You're dinners together aren't quite as romantic as they once were. You're more focused on chauffeuring the kids around from soccer practice, to music lessons, to dance recitals. You barely have any private time to spend together. So how do you stay in love?"*

He said,

> *"I do it by continually winning over the respect of my wife and kids everyday. My goal is to blow their minds by over-delivering to them in every area of my life... as a husband... as a father... and as a leader."*

This really stuck with me over the years, and now that I'm both a husband and a father, I try my best to do the same.

In business, the same rules apply. In order to continually have my people defer to me as their leader, I have to earn it, daily. I have to continually over-deliver. I know of some so-called leaders that think that just because they mentored people once upon a time, that they should get residual leadership benefits that last forever and ever. Wake up guys. The real world doesn't work that way.

Maybe it should. Maybe it shouldn't. But regardless of whether it should or shouldn't, it doesn't. You must accept this fact, because if you don't, you won't be a great leader, by definition.

This is not my opinion. It's a fact. If we agree that the definition of a great leader is contingent upon them having an army of loyal followers, then you've got to understand, accept, and embrace the fact that people need constant reaffirmation that they should be following you... and the only way to create a following that strong and that loyal is to continually over-deliver. Keep them in awe of you, and you'll have their hearts forever.

Fundamental #6: A great leader never teaches something they haven't successfully done themselves.

This goes back to what I said earlier about so-called leaders that attempt to lead from the proverbial *ivory tower*. Generally speaking, people are not willing to follow someone that either:

1. Doesn't have a track record of success, or
2. Doesn't lead by example.

If you really want to create an army of followers, you've got to prove to your people that you're worth following. The easiest way to give them this proof is to show them your track record.

Legitimacy and authenticity are the key factors that I'm talking about here. That's why I don't understand companies that hire *Sales Trainers* that have no track record of success in the sales field. What could you possibly teach someone to do that you've never successfully done yourself?

In my companies, I only allow people with a track record of success to train my new sales people. That's why my new people have so much respect for their sales managers. They know that the person they're learning from started out in the exact same position they're starting out in, so my leaders have credibility.

Even in the interview process, the only ones that I have interviewing sales candidates are either my top sales executives, or myself personally. Why? Because we're the only qualified people in the company to talk about how great our career opportunity is in our sales division. We've all lived it.

I remember interviewing with an insurance company when I first started out my career. The woman that interviewed me was a recruiter. She told me how great the company was, and how great the opportunity was to get into *sales* with this company.

As I listened to her, I thought to myself, *"If the opportunity is so great, why aren't YOU applying for the sales position? Why are you making $35,000 per year as a recruiter, when according to you, you* *could make five times that in sales?"* I thought that was a pretty fair question. She, on the other hand, was offended by my question. Needless to say, I did not pursue a career with that company.

That's why I say that if you're going to be a great leader, you need to lead by example. People come to their conclusions about you based on what they see first hand. They're watching your every move, sizing you up, evaluating your actions.

They want to see if your actions match up with your words. If they don't, you've got no credibility. That's why as a leader, the only advice and training I give is based around this simple concept:

> *"This is what I did. This is what I got by doing it. If you want what I have, do what I did. And by the way, I'll teach you how to do it the exact same way I did it."*

One of the biggest compliments (and endorsements) I've ever gotten was from a *Regional Vice-President of Sales* of a national insurance company. He said,

> *"The thing about most sales trainings is that you have a lot of people who teach, who've never done the job. What's unique about Darren's training is that he does the sales AND sells what he does, showing you how he's become successful."*

To me, this is what sets me apart from so many so-called leaders, so-called sales trainers, and so-called business development coaches. So many of these self-proclaimed success gurus didn't build successful businesses, then turn around and teach people how they did it. Many of these guys' only claim to fame is that they built a successful motivational speaking career by doing motivational speaking. They've never actually built a successful business from scratch.

It's just like so many college professors. Sure, they have their MBA or their Ph.D in business, but they've never actually built a successful company using their marketing philosophies in the real world.

You know what they say about teaching. *"Those that can do, do. Those that can't, teach."* Sadly, in many cases, that is so true. So again, if you want to be a great leader, you must DO what you teach.

Fundamental #7: A great leader accepts the responsibility of living in a glass house 24/7.

So much of what I've been talking about revolves around the fact that as a leader, people are always watching your every move. I recently had dinner with a good friend of mine that owns a very successful company that does a little over a billion dollars in annual sales, and we were talking about marketing and business image.

We probably spent a good hour talking about what kind of cars we should be driving, from an image perspective. I know this sounds obsessive, and I assure you that this was not just two car-obsessed guys chatting about horsepower and leather interior. This discussion entirely revolved around one the most important elements of building an army of loyal followers: *Perception*.

We have slightly different businesses, and slightly different clients, thus our image needs to strategically be slightly different. In the majority of cases, the role I play in my businesses is one of inspiring the troops and laying down the blueprint of how to be successful. In other words, at the expense of sounding narcissistic (not that I have a problem with narcissism) my people want to emulate me, my lifestyle, and my methods. Therefore, showing them my trappings of success is not only a wise thing to do; it's a necessity.

However in my friend's business, being that flamboyant and over-the-top in the luxury department can backfire on him. His employees are mostly administrative people, not sales people. These administrative people are not pulling down the big bucks, nor do they have to potential to in their job capacity, and so he is wise to downplay his wealth.

As he told me about his need to be slightly more conservative than I am in this department, he told me that he had to have a talk with his business partner about this very issue. He told him that he could guarantee that many of the employees have looked up his address on the internet, and have probably driven by his house, just to see where their CEO lived.

This certainly sounds *stalker-ish*, but he is absolutely right. We live in a *stalker-ish* society. Privacy does not exist anymore. With reality shows, online social networking websites, and up-to-the-minute electronic postings of what everyone is doing, our lives are out-there-in-the-open for practically everyone to see. And as a leader, it's even more prevalent.

Leaders, whether you like it or not, live in glass houses, 24/7. That being the case, as a leader, I have realized that there is no distinction between my personal life and my business life. I don't particularly like this, but it is what it is.

This being the case, you're not going to find pictures of me on any social networking site doing anything that isn't in line with my personal brand, which is synonymous with my company brand.

You must accept the fact that you will be judged heavily, and that people are always evaluating you as their leader. You also can't expect to please 100 percent of the people, 100 percent of the time. There will always be people that don't like you, for whatever reason.

There are people out there that hate my personal brand. There are people out there that don't like the way I do business, or the things I teach about business ethics, or the color of my necktie. I've accepted the fact that there will always be a segment of the population that I don't appeal to, for whatever reason. That's fine. As long as I live a life that is consistent with my premeditated, strategically developed personal brand, my status of authenticity is maintained. Again, authenticity and credibility are the two main factors that inspire people to follow you as a leader. It sounds simple, and quite frankly, it is. All you have to do is continually follow these seven key principles:

1. Be principle-driven, not emotionally driven.
2. Put the team above yourself.
3. Lead by example.
4. Be consistent in your decision making process.
5. Always be over-prepared, and always over-deliver.
6. Do before you teach.
7. Accept the responsibility of living in a glass house 24/7.

Be the leader that possesses these qualities, and focus on having the level of integrity that would make you want to follow someone like yourself, and you'll soon have an army of followers, following you onto the battlefield.

Chapter Thirteen: The 5 Fundamental Qualities Of Successful People

"Success isn't necessarily about what you achieve in life...
It's about what you overcome."
-Darren Sugiyama

The 5 Fundamental Qualities

As I've studied successful people over the years, they all had so many unique qualities that have propelled them to succeed at such a high level. However, there are five key fundamental qualities that every single one of them had. These are the very same five qualities I've worked so hard to develop in my own life, and they've served me well.

#1: Motivation.

I've often been labeled as being a *motivational speaker*. I've had countless people come up to me after one of my seminars, sharing with me how much my *motivational talks* have inspired them. I've even had some people come up to me with tears rolling down their faces, telling me that my talk literally changed their lives. I am truly honored by these types of conversations.

However, I think these people are giving me way too much credit. The reason I say this is that I do not believe that I motivated them. I may have *inspired* them, but I certainly did not motivate them. Here's why I say this.

The root word of motivation is *motive*. And the definition of the word motive is *a compelling reason to take action*. When you see a motivated person, what you're seeing is a person with a compelling reason to take action. There is something important to that person – so incredibly important – that they refuse to let anyone or anything stop them from achieving whatever it is that they are motivated to achieve. They have a *compelling reason*.

The reason I say that I cannot motivate someone is that I cannot give them a compelling reason to take action. They have to have their own compelling reason. I, of course, have many of my own compelling reasons to take massive action, which is why I'm such a motivated person. Now, if I share my reasons that are compelling to me, and someone relates to my compelling reasons because they are similar to their own, they can become *inspired*. I think this happens quite often when someone attends one of my seminars. But the point is, I only *inspired* them. I didn't *motivate* them.

So why am I making it a point to distinguish the difference between inspiration and motivation? The reason is that so many people are looking for someone else to motivate them. I have people tell me all the time, *"Darren, I'm so excited to be here at your seminar. I need you to motivate me!"* I almost want to refund their money right there on the spot, because motivation is not an external thing, nor is it an imposed thing. It's an internal thing.

You see, everyone has a different reason that is compelling to them, personally. It's a personal belief that is attached to their individual value system. Anyone that attends one of my seminars or reads one of my books is already motivated. They could have spent their time going to the beach instead of spending the day with me. They could have spent their money on a movie or a ball game than spending it on one of my training DVDs.

You could have spent your money on a few Starbucks coffees, or cocktails, or music downloads from iTunes, but you spent your money on this book that you're reading right now. Why did you do that?

I'll tell you why. Because you're motivated. You have a compelling reason to take action. That's why you started your business in the first place, remember? You could have taken the easy route and accepted the mediocre life of having a cubicle job, but you decided to pursue greatness.

What I'm getting at here is that you had (and still have) a compelling reason to take action. The goal here is to continually remind yourself of what your compelling reason is. It must be so compelling that nothing could take precedence over it. It must be something that you cannot live without. It must be something that you cannot achieve with a regular cubicle job. It must be your *dream*. As we discussed earlier in this book, we all had big dreams when we were kids, but very few of us held on to those dreams into adulthood. Don't give up on your dream.

Sure it takes a huge amount of sacrifice, but you must understand this principle I'm about to share with you. This is perhaps the most important concept in this entire book, and it has to do with *pain*.

You will either suffer the short-term pain of sacrifice and discipline, or you will suffer the long-term pain of regret. When you have a compelling reason to take action, if your reason is compelling enough to you, you'll deal with the immediate pain because you know that it's just temporary. It's short-term.

If your reason is not compelling enough to you, you'll quit. But if you quit, you will suffer the long-term, permanent pain of regret, and there is nothing more painstaking than the feeling of regret. The choice is yours. Pain is inevitable. It's part of life. But you have to ask yourself the question, *"Would I rather suffer the short-term pain of sacrifice, or the long-term pain of regret?"* The first is temporary; the latter is permanent.

The question isn't whether you're motivated or not. I already know you are. But in addition to having a compelling reason to act, you must make wise decisions about what you're going to do in the next 30, 60 and 90 days in terms of action. Don't be fooled by the allure of short-term gratification. It will only lead to long-term, permanent regret. Work hard now so that you'll have no regrets. Again, if you want to be motivated, continually remind yourself of what your compelling reason to act is. These decisions that you need to make right now will be more easily made if you have the second fundamental quality that successful people have; the quality of *courage*.

#2: Courage.

I remember back when I was growing up, I always admired courageous people. Whether it was an athlete that had overcome all odds, or the documentary I saw in high school about the life of Helen Keller, or a character in a movie like *Rocky*, I've always been intrigued by people with great courage. I've always wanted to be like them.

As a type A personality, as well as being an obsessed perfectionist, I've always been very hard on myself. In some cases, being hard on yourself is a good thing, and I would say that all great champions are hard on themselves. It's part of what drives them internally.

But there is a down side. The downside is that there is no such thing as *perfection*. Perfection is an idealistic fantasy that does not exist. So as a self-admitted perfectionist, I always felt that I was letting people down. In the area of courage, I wanted to be like *Rocky Balboa*. That movie really helped define my never-give-up persona in both my business life, as well as my personal life.

The reason I felt like I was always letting people down was that I never felt as though I was courageous. If you were to ask other people that I competed against in sports about whether or not I was courageous, they would tell you just the opposite. In retrospect, I would say that I was extremely courageous, but back then, I never felt like I had the level of courage that I truly wanted to have.

It was only until a few short years ago when I discovered the error in my previous self-concept. I always thought that the definition of *courage* was to have no fear. I looked up to all of these courageous people, and they seemed to have no fear whatsoever. I, on the other hand, was always afraid. I was afraid of failure. I was afraid of what other people thought about me. I was afraid of letting people down. I was afraid of making mistakes. I was just plain *afraid*.

I felt like such a loser because I wanted to have courage, and I thought to myself, *"How am I supposed to have courage if I'm always afraid of failure?"* It really haunted me. This was probably the single most reason why I lacked confidence in my early years. I wanted so badly to be tough, and have courage, but I knew that deep down, I was afraid of failing.

But I had it all wrong back then. You see, *courage* is not the absence of fear. *Courage* is the ability to push yourself forward in spite of the fear. Once I realized this, my entire perspective changed. My entire self-concept changed. I realized that I have always been courageous. Here I was beating myself up all the time because I felt bad about having fear, when all along, I was continually pushing forward in spite of my fear. That, by definition, is courage. I, by definition, was courageous.

Understanding this simple concept changed my entire outlook on life. It empowered me. I no longer felt guilty about being afraid of failure, because I took pride in having the courage to push forward in spite of my fear. I truly believe that this very concept is what most entrepreneurs struggle with, and it holds them back.

Listen, there's nothing wrong with being afraid. Fear is a human emotion that we all have. So instead of feeling bad about yourself because you have fear, you should feel good about yourself that you have the guts to push forward in spite of the fear. That alone is a victory. That alone makes you a champion. And ultimately, that quality – the quality of courage – is something that you've had all along. You wouldn't have started your business if you didn't have courage. If you didn't have courage, you wouldn't have left that dead-end cubicle job in pursuit of financial greatness.

So many people think that once they achieve their financial goals, that somehow they'll feel better about themselves. Perhaps there is some truth to that, however I can tell you from my own personal experience of achieving success in business that the *real* prize is not the money. The *real* prize is the feeling that you have inside; the feeling of accomplishment. But let's dig a little deeper into this feeling of accomplishment that I'm referring to.

When I finally *made it*, yes, I felt empowered. Okay, let's be honest. It felt freaking phenomenal. But when I asked myself why it felt so phenomenal, my answer surprised me. I thought the answer was going to be associated with my material wealth, but it wasn't.

Then I thought the answer was going to be about how I've been able to help other people financially, but it wasn't.

Then I thought it was going to be about the lifestyle I've been able to provide my family with, but it wasn't that either.

Sure these things are important to me, and they were some of the most important factors that drove me to work so hard, but once I was able to do them, none of them ranked as being the #1 reason I felt so great.

To my surprise, the #1 factor of my happiness associated with my hard work was that I knew in my heart that I had courage. I could look at myself in the mirror and say, *"I am courageous. I'm a real man."* I'm telling you, there are few things in life that will bring you more satisfaction than knowing that you have courage.

My main message to you is that you already possess the quality of courage, right now. You're reading this book, trying to figure out if you have what it takes to be successful in business. You have goals of achieving financial greatness, and you know that the odds are statistically against aspiring entrepreneurs. But you told yourself that you're not a regular aspiring entrepreneur. You're one of the special ones that will make more sacrifices and work harder than everyone else. Sure the statistical odds might be against most aspiring entrepreneurs, but the odds are not against *you*. You are not like most entrepreneurs. You have courage.

If you've ever had this conversation with yourself, and you're still pursuing your dream, then by definition, you have courage, and that is something you should be proud of. Few people display acts of courage, and you're one of the few.

So don't feel bad about having fear every once in a while. Having fear provides you the opportunity to display acts of courage. It provides you the opportunity to be courageous.

I know people pray to God, asking God to give them courage. But do you think God is just going to hand over courage to you on a silver platter? Courage is not a *gift*. It's not something that can be given to you. Courage has to be *built*, and the only way to build courage is to be faced with adversity. You must first feel fear in order to display courage. If you weren't afraid, there would be nothing to be courageous about.

God gives us opportunities to be courageous all the time. It's up to us to use that opportunity to build courage. Perhaps you're in a situation right now in your business where things aren't looking so bright, or at least not as bright as you'd prefer. Perhaps this situation is causing you to doubt yourself and second-guess your abilities. This is the perfect opportunity to display acts of courage and push forward in spite of your fear. This is an opportunity for you to be courageous. If you never got knocked down, then you wouldn't know how to get back up, and *getting back up* is what makes a person *great*.

If you ever feel yourself starting to become overwhelmed with fear, just remember what your compelling reason to take action is. You'll find your courage once you find your compelling reason.

#3: Perseverance.

Similar to courage, perseverance is a quality that must be built over time. In America, we live in a microwave society in which people want everything now, including financial success. Most people that have consistently succeeded in business, year after year after year, have generally taken some heavy hits and have had to endure several major setbacks. It happens. This is part of business. But what happened as a result of struggling through tough times? They built the quality of *perseverance*.

The definition of perseverance is *"steady persistence in a course of action, due to a purpose, especially in spite of difficulties, obstacles, or discouragement."* The only thing missing from this definition, in my opinion, is that it doesn't emphasize the element of time. Perseverance is only built over a substantial period of time. These difficulties, obstacles and discouragement must be faced over a long period of time.

A businessman or businesswoman that has built the quality of perseverance has, by definition, been faced with adversities repeatedly, and has felt feelings of discouragement repeatedly. This experience, unless you're one of the overnight success stories, is something that virtually every single successful person has had in the beginning stages of their careers.

Those who know me, know that I'm a huge *Rocky* fan. I love the story of *Rocky Balboa*, but even more than the story portrayed in the movie, I love the real life story of how the movie came to be. In his early years, Sylvester Stallone had a dream of being a movie star. In an interview, Stallone recounted his early years of being a struggling, aspiring actor.

He was married at the time, and he and his wife got into huge fights about his movie star aspirations. They were broke, and he wasn't getting much work as an actor. Stallone's wife pleaded with him to just go out and get a regular job, but he refused. He said that he was afraid that if he took a regular job that he'd get too comfortable and lose his hunger to pursue his dream. The problem was that he wasn't making any money as an actor.

He couldn't afford to pay the gas bill in his apartment, so he and his wife lived with no heat, and if you know anything about the winter months in New York, living with no heat sucks. She was furious. The last straw was when he sold all of her jewelry one month to pay the rent. Shortly thereafter, she left him.

The only friend Stallone had left was his dog. But things got so bad that he couldn't afford to buy dog food to feed his dog, so one day, he went down to the local liquor store with his dog, and tried to sell his dog to someone that could take care of him. Finally, he found a guy that agreed to buy his dog for $25. Stallone said that this was his lowest point, because his dog was his best friend – his *only* friend – and he had to sell his best friend.

His acting career continued to produce dismal results, so Stallone decided to become a screenwriter, but he never gave up on his dream of becoming a movie star. One day, he was watching a boxing match between Muhammad Ali and Chuck Wepner. Wepner was a big, sloppy oaf that was getting his butt kicked by Ali, but the guy just wouldn't give up. He just kept coming back for more. Wepner's perseverance caught Stallone's interest, and watching Wepner inspired him to write the *Rocky* screenplay.

Stallone started shopping his screenplay around, but there wasn't much interest. Finally, he found a producer that was interested in producing the movie. Stallone was offered $125,000 for the screenplay. He accepted the offer, but only on one condition. Stallone required that *he* play the leading role of *Rocky Balboa*. They laughed at him. Apparently, they were planning on giving the role to the actor Ryan O'Neal. Can you imagine that? Pretty-boy Ryan O'Neal playing *Rocky*?

So Stallone declined the offer. Can you imagine being so broke that you can't even afford to feed your dog, and turn down $125,000? Stallone explained that his dream was to be a movie star, and he wasn't going to sell out for $125,000. That takes guts. That takes perseverance.

You see, whenever you have a big dream, and you've suffered over time to achieve it, you'll be faced with several temptations to sell yourself short along the way. Greatness is achieved by having the mindset of never settling for anything less than what you think you deserve. It's not an easy thing to do, giving up the *good life* for the *great life*. But that's what champions do.

So the studio execs counter-offered Stallone with $250,000, contingent on him *not* starring in the movie. He turned it down again. Then the studio countered again with $325,000, as long as Stallone did not star in the movie. He turned them down again. Can you imagine that? Here he was, broke, no other promising opportunities, and he's turning down $325,000. Why? Because his dream was bigger than the temptation of the short-term, easy money.

Eventually, they came to a deal. $35,000 for the screenplay, plus a percentage of the film's profits, and Stallone would play the lead role. As you know, the rest is history. The film cost $1 million to make, and it grossed over $200 million.

Stallone built perseverance in the early stages of his career, and today, he is considered somewhat of an icon. In fact, the Philadelphia

Museum of Art is located at the top of the stairs that Rocky climbed in the movie. When they filmed *Rocky III*, the statue of Rocky at the top of those stairs became a permanent fixture, but the museum eventually moved the statue to the bottom of the stairs because it was attracting more attention from tourists than the museum itself. That, my friends, is iconic status.

But the story gets better. When Stallone signed for the $35,000, he went back to the liquor store, hoping to run into the gentleman that bought his dog, praying that he would have the opportunity to buy his dog back. He went there everyday, day after day, until one day, up walks the man that bought his dog.

Elated, Stallone approached him saying, *"Mr., remember me? I'm the one that sold you your dog, but the only reason I sold him was that I couldn't afford to feed him. He's my best friend. I know you only bought him for $25, but I'll give you $100. Please."*

The man said, *"No way, man. I love this dog."*

Stallone countered saying, *"How about $500?"* The man rejected the offer.

"How about $1,000?" The man rejected the offer again.

Eventually, they came to an agreement. Stallone paid him $15,000 for his dog, plus he gave him a small role in the movie. And remember Butkus, Rocky's dog in the movie? That was Stallone's dog, his best friend.

I love the story of Stallone's rise to success. It may sound cheesy to you, but the Rocky movies changed my life as a kid. They inspired me to dream big and never give up. They inspired me to push myself as an athlete, to take pride in working harder than everyone else, and to believe that big dreams were possible if you sacrificed long enough.

My favorite scene in all of the Rocky movies was in *Rocky III*. Apollo is training Rocky after Mick passed away. Confused, depressed, and full of doubt, we see Rocky for the first time lose his *eye of the tiger*. The scene starts with his wife, Adrian, approaching him after Apollo yells at him for not training hard enough.

Adrian says, *"You've never quit anything since I've known you."*

Rocky finally confesses to Adrian, *"I don't believe in myself anymore, don't you understand? Once a fighter don't believe, that's it, he's finished, he's over, that's it!"*

Adrian yells back, *"That's NOT it. Why don't you tell me the truth? What's the truth damn it?"*

Rocky yells back even louder, *"I'm afraid! Alright? You want to hear me say it? You want to break me down? Alright. I'm afraid. For the first time in my life, I'm afraid!"*

Adrian replies, *"I'm afraid too! There's nothing wrong with being afraid!"*

This scene embodies everything that I was talking about regarding courage. Adrian was right. There's nothing wrong with being afraid. Whenever you are overcome with fear, just remind yourself that God is giving you an opportunity to be courageous. It's an *opportunity*.

It's an opportunity to build perseverance. Always remember, what you are given is never as valuable as what you earn. Take pride in earning the right to say that you have built the quality of perseverance. It will prove to be the cornerstone of your success.

#4: Stand In The Gap

Perhaps you've never heard this phrase before. Standing in the gap embodies these previous three fundamentals we just discussed. It has to do with having a compelling reason to display courage, over and over and over again, while being faced with adversity. It specifically has to do with discouragement from others.

As we discussed earlier in this book, your cubicle-minded friends and family members may not be as supportive of your entrepreneurial endeavors as you might hope the would be. It happens to all of us, believe me. These *dream stealers* are everywhere, and as you may have guessed, the majority of them work in cubicles. The key is to not allow them and their small-mindedness affect your decisions and actions.

I've seen so many people give up on their dreams, simply because they listened to the advice of a so-called friend. I was in a seminar a few weeks ago and heard a great piece of advice from a very successful businessman. He has a network of over 70,000 sales reps spread across several countries. Needless to say, he is very successful financially. He said he's heard just about every nonsensical excuse from people that fall victim to the negative influences of their friends and family.

He said that when people fall victim to this circumstance, they're essentially saying, *"I'd rather take business advice from my broke friends than take advice from a multi-millionaire."* He went on to say that it's like them saying, *"I never make any financial decision without first getting a general consensus from all of my broke friends."* I know this may sound harsh, but isn't it absolutely true? This is exactly what they're saying. Sure, they may use different words, but they're saying the exact same thing.

As I mentioned earlier, when I first started my entrepreneurial efforts in the early stages of my career, I fully expected to be applauded by my friends and family. To my surprise, I was faced with the exact opposite. Some people didn't think I had the ability or the talent to build an empire. Some people thought it was too risky. Some people thought my ambitions were too *pie-in-the sky* and unrealistic. Some people got tired of hearing me talk about my dreams and pointed out my many failures. Some people thought that if success was going to happen, that it would have happened already.

All of these negative opinions and perspectives made me doubt myself. I know that people who've only known me as a successful businessman have a hard time imagining me doubting myself, but I spent many a night crying myself to sleep, thinking to myself, *"Am I ever going to be successful?"* Quite frankly, I felt like giving up several times along the way.

Well, that's where *Standing In The Gap* comes in. What this means is that you're choosing to stand where no one else is willing to stand. You're taking a stand for something you believe in – your dream – when no one else believes in you or your dream. You're standing for something special. What makes your dream so special is that often times, you're the only one that believes in it. Have you ever felt like that? It's hard, isn't it?

Now, that being said, it takes every ounce of strength in your body not to succumb to the nonbelievers. Think of it like this. You wouldn't let someone come along and steal your car, would you? Of course not. You may even chase them down the block, threatening to kick their ass. But what about your dream? Why are you so susceptible to allowing someone to steal your dream? You'll chase a guy halfway down the block for trying to steal your car, but why aren't you as vigilant about not allowing someone to steal your dream?

When I was starting my career out, and someone attempted to steal my dream, talking negatively about my aspirations, I took it very personal. I even physically threatened people that did so, practically chasing them down the block. I'm not saying that physically threatening people is a good thing, and I don't endorse physical violence, but I'm just telling you how I reacted to people that tried to steal my dream. That's how important my dream was to me. That's how personal my dream was to me. That's how intimate my dream was to me.

The unfortunate thing is that these dream stealers are the very same people that you would expect to encourage you and support you. They profess to love you, but discouraging words and negative judgment are not actions of *love*, at least not in my opinion. I think you can tell a lot about a person based on how they react to you sharing your dreams with them. I experienced this with people that I thought would be supportive and encouraging, only to be emotionally devastated when I got the exact opposite response.

I used to get incredibly angry when this used to happen to me. Quite frankly, I was hurt, and my anger was just a self-preservation reaction. But one day, I realized that it had nothing to do with *me*. It had everything to do with them and their limiting beliefs. They live inside the proverbial cubicle. Why would I expect anything greater than their negative response? They're just like the prisoners in *The Allegory Of The Cave*. They didn't have the ability to see what I saw, and thus, their perspective on what was possible was limited.

I think everything in life is a *test*, or rather an *opportunity*. You see, when you're all alone in pursuit of your dream, you are constantly being *tested*. Will you give up, or keep fighting? Will you succumb to laziness, or will you suck it up and work even harder? Will you choose to avoid the short-term pain of sacrifice and be plagued with the pain of regret, or will you be disciplined and keep your eye on the prize?

These are all tests. These are all opportunities to display acts of courage. These are all opportunities to build perseverance and stand in the gap. These are all opportunities to remind yourself about your compelling reason to take action.

Don't look at the hard times as curses. Look at them as blessings. Without tests, you can't build a testimony. This is where greatness is born.

#5: Enjoy The Ride

As I said earlier, when I was a broke, struggling, aspiring entrepreneur, I was always angry. I hated feeling like a failure. It's also very difficult to watch other people succeed while you're struggling without being overcome with envy and negative jealousy. I certainly fell victim to this terrible cycle in the early days of my career.

The irony of this, as I look back, is that the fondest memories I have regarding my career are all about experiences I had in the early years of struggling. I often refer to those times as *The Good Ole Days*.

I remember when I helped one of my top producers get one of his first clients, a small pizza joint in Huntington Beach. We frantically faxed the contract in at the end of the last day of the month, rushing to submit the case in order to get credit for it that month. We were high-fiving each other once we found out the contract got processed. It was a small little deal, only worth about $60 per month in commission, but I was so excited for him because it was one of his first clients. Those were *The Good Ole Days*.

I remember meeting a prospect up in Pasadena at midnight on a Friday night. It was a restaurant owner, and that was the only time he could meet with me. I wrapped the meeting a little after 2:00AM, and I slept in my car that night. As I went to sleep that night at three o'clock in the morning, I said to myself, *"One day, this shit is going to pay off, because no one is willing to work as hard as me."* As it turned out, I didn't convert them into a client, but it didn't matter. What mattered to me was knowing that while my competition is sleeping, or partying or whatever at midnight, I'm working, and that, to me, was what I felt would make me successful. It wasn't intelligence, or talent, or knowledge. It was *heart*. Those were *The Good Ole Days*.

One night, I was driving home from my office at about midnight. I was exhausted, and my business wasn't making any profits yet. I pulled into the drive-thru window at a fast food restaurant, and saw pecan pie on the menu for $1.39. I sat there and stared at that pecan pie for at least five minutes, contemplating whether or not I could afford to treat myself to a piece of pecan pie. Can you imagine that? $1.39. One, I felt like I couldn't afford it, and two, I felt like I didn't deserve it. I ended up not treating myself to the inexpensive desert. I drove home with tears running down my face, because I was so frustrated that I couldn't even afford a damn piece of pie for $1.39. But as angry and frustrating it was back then, I cherish this memory.

You see, those were *The Good Ole Days*. The memories I have of my minor victories in the early stages of my career, and even more so, the struggles I faced, are the very ones that I cherish the most.

So what's my point? My point is that if you're struggling in business right now, what you must realize is that you're living in *The Good Ole Days* right now. In five, ten, twenty years from now, you'll be looking back on these very days of struggle, referring to them as *The Good Ole Days*. I encourage you to cherish today and to focus on enjoying what today offers, knowing that you're creating long-lasting memories, so that when the day comes when you're a massive success in business, you'll refer back to this present time as your *Good Ole Days*. You'll have more memories to cherish.

I've always struggled to *Enjoy The Ride* and *Smell The Roses Along The Way*. As I think back to my early days of struggle, I could have worked just as hard, been just as dedicated, been just as focused, sacrificed just as much, but done it with a heart of joy, as opposed to a heart filled with resentment. It would have been so much more enjoyable, and I would have achieved just as much. I probably would have been a more enjoyable person to be around as well. I should have realized that I was in the process of achieving, as opposed to focusing on the lack of immediate material wealth.

So many people, myself included, achieve to be happy, instead of happily achieving. My wife, Emilia has taught me a lot in this area. She's always so damn happy. It doesn't matter if everything is going perfectly, or if everything is all screwed up. She always finds the time to smile, laugh and enjoy life. She's helped me take the time to smell the roses, without making me feel like I'm losing focus on my goals.

The other night, we were winding our evening down, and we were talking about our lives. We often do this when we take evening walks together. It's our time to catch up with each other to talk about our relationship, our son, parenthood, and life in general. In a world that moves so fast, we're always so busy that I think it's important to slow things down and really communicate with each other on a regular basis. I think every married couple should do this. It's what keeps us on the same page, almost like a relationship check up.

On this particular evening, we were just sitting on our chaise lounge in our bedroom, snuggled up with each other. I asked her, *"Honey, do you think I'm doing a better job of stopping to smell the roses lately, compared to a few years ago?"*

She said, *"Absolutely."*

I asked her, *"Honey, do I seem more engaged with you and Estevan when I walk in the door now? Am I doing a better job at* leaving the stress of business at the office, not bringing it home with me?"

She said, "*Totally.*"

So then I asked her, "*Honey, on a scale of 1-10, how am I doing in this area?*" fully expecting her to rate me at a 9 or a 10.

She responded, "*About a 7.*"

"What! A seven? That's it?" Apparently, I have a little ways to go in this area, which goes to show that we all need to improve a little more in this area, especially us Type-A, obsessively-driven, entrepreneurs. We laughed and laughed about her lower-than-expected rating. This is another area of our relationship that I think makes things work between us. We have the ability to laugh at ourselves.

Emilia has also helped me to stop constantly comparing myself to other people. One of the worst things you can do is constantly compare yourself to other people. There will always be someone that succeeded sooner in life than you. There will always be someone richer than you. There will always be someone that has a bigger business than you. There will always be people that were luckier than you. There will always be someone with a bigger house, a more luxurious car, more expensive jewelry, a nicer watch, and a more lavish lifestyle.

If you constantly compare your success to other people's successes, you'll drive yourself crazy. Truth be told, I'm probably still guilty of doing this, even today.

Several years ago, I got invited to go on a golfing trip with some very successful businessmen. The gentleman that invited me is the CEO of a billion dollar insurance company. Bernie is a dear friend of mine now, but when I accepted the invitation, I was just getting to know him. I had (and still have) great admiration for him, both as a businessman as well as a human being.

Included in our group were two of Bernie's good friends. One gentleman was a very successful businessman in the financial world, and the other had recently retired having sold his hedge fund. Needless to say, these gentlemen were *very* successful. What I didn't realize prior to the trip was that all of them were scratch golfers. I, on the other hand, am the type of golfer that generally shoots in the 90s… and that's just on the front nine holes. I only play about once or twice a year, and I am a horrible golfer.

I got invited on this trip based on the fact that I did a tremendous amount of business with Bernie's company, not because I was a good golfer. Apparently, neither Bernie nor his friends were aware of my poor golfing abilities. We were scheduled to play at two very exclusive private golf clubs.

I arrived to the golf course about an hour before everyone else, just to get some practice strokes in on the driving range. To give you an idea of how nice these golf courses were, one of them costs over $1 million to become a member, and the annual membership dues are well into the six-figures per year. The grass on the driving range was nicer than any fairways I've ever played on, and I've played on some very exclusive courses, including the golf course at *The Grand Hotel* on Mackinac Island, and *The Sanctuary* on Kiawah Island in South Carolina (the Carolina's version of the Hamptons).

As our tee time got closer and closer, I got more and more nervous. By this time, I realized I was in way over my head. I should have known that these guys were excellent golfers, and it was irresponsible on my part for not doing the research to realize that I did not belong on this trip.

To make things worse, even though I was already successful in my own right, these guys were on another level. The most expensive home on this course was worth over $65 million. So not only was I feeling like an idiot because of my lack of golfing skills, I was intimidated by the success level of the guys I was playing golf with.

By the third hole, I had made a complete fool of myself, as it became blatantly obvious that I was not a *golfer*. As I rode in the golf cart with Bernie, he could see me sinking deeper and deeper into my shell. Bernie is a class act of a guy.

He leaned over to me and said, *"Darren, I don't care how you play golf today. Today is about having fun and enjoying some beautiful scenery. The only thing that's going to upset me today is if you curse or throw your clubs. Other than that, we're here to have fun today."*

I can't tell you how relieving that was to hear coming from Bernie. I also, over the course of the day, realized that everyone I was playing with was twenty to thirty years older than me. Of course they were more financially successful than me. Their careers had fully matured, whereas mine was just getting started.

All of these gentlemen were very encouraging and patient with me throughout the day, giving me pointers and tips about my swing. By the end of the day, I had actually connected and blasted one or two powerful drives. It was a great day, but not because my golf game got any better. What made it great was being in the company of other successful businessmen, more successful than I, and hearing their stories about what they went through when they first started building their empires, hearing about their *Good Ole Days*. If anything, they inspired me. I must say, those two days I spent with them in La Quinta made a lasting impression on me.

It's been an important lesson for me not to measure my success based on comparing myself to what other people have accomplished. I now base it on what I've accomplished relative to what I believe I'm capable of accomplishing. Today, I only compete against myself, and I do it with a smile, albeit a *forced smile* (yes I still struggle in this area myself). In all seriousness, it truly *is* a better way to live, and I have my beautiful wife Emilia to thank for teaching me this.

Chapter Fourteen:
Leaving Behind A Legacy

"When a tiger dies, he leaves behind his skin... When a bull dies, he leaves behind his horns... and when a man dies, he leaves behind his name."

-Japanese Proverb

Will People Remember Your Name?

In the movie *Troy*, two armies faced each other in battle. In an effort to save each army's men, the two kings decide to choose a different method of battle. Instead of engaging in a typical blood bath, the kings agreed to have a one-on-one battle between each king's best warrior. One king yells out the name of his warrior, and out comes a huge beast-of-a-man. He is a good two feet taller than all of the other warriors, and is built like Hulk Hogan in his prime. He is indeed intimidating.

The other king yells out for his best warrior, Achilles, played by Brad Pitt. The crowd is silenced, and Achilles is no where to be found. The king, outraged, sends a young boy to go and find the mighty Achilles. When the boy finds him, he informs Achilles that the king has summoned him to fight the other great warrior.

The boy tells Achilles, *"The Thesalonian you're fighting... he's the biggest man I've ever seen. I wouldn't want to fight him."*

Achilles responds, *"That's why no one will remember your name."*

Leaving Behind A Legacy

I used to hear people talk about leaving behind a legacy for their family, and though it intrigued me, I must admit, it never really resonated with me. I don't know what it was about this concept that didn't strike a cord with me back then, but I must say that as a new father, it is perhaps the single most important thing to me in my life.

What we do as adults – as parents – has such a dramatic impact on our kids. It impacts the way they perceive themselves, the way they perceive challenges and victories, the way they perceive gender roles and the role of parents, and quite frankly, the way they perceive the world. Being a parent is a huge responsibility if you break this role down to the core elements. Being a parent, by definition, is about *leadership.*

I know so many parents that will use their kids as an excuse for not pursuing and achieving excellence in their careers. They'll say things like, *"Well I have to spend time with my kids,"* or *"You know how kids spell love? T.I.M.E."* This is pure rhetoric. Just because you're spending large quantities of time with your kids does not mean that you're truly mentoring them. I've seen tons of parents claim to spend a lot of time with their kids, but they spend it watching television. Watching television with someone is not *spending time* with them. Sure, you're in the same room in relatively close proximity to them, but you're not engaging with them nor interacting with them.

The real truth is that kids do not spell *love*, T.I.M.E. They may not consciously spell *love* the way I spell it, but to me, as a parent, I spell *love* M.E.N.T.O.R.S.H.I.P. To be a truly great parent, you've got to be a mentor to your kids. Sometimes you may play the role of the leader, the team captain. Sometimes you play the role of a coach. Sometimes you play the role of a cheerleader. In all of these scenarios, your role requires interaction, unconditional support and encouragement, and guidance.

As discussed in *Chapter Twelve: Championship Leadership*, being a true leader means leading by example. If you want to be a true leader to your kids, you must lead by example. You must show your kids what being a champion is all about through your daily actions. Do you want your kids to build character, perseverance and courage? If you do, then you need to show them how to battle through the tough times like a champion does.

It reminds me of a very successful woman I know in the insurance industry. Elana is a Regional Vice-President with a very well known life insurance company. Last year, I was the keynote speaker at her company's annual kick off meeting in Dallas. The day before my talk, I got a chance to chat with Elana in the lobby of the hotel for a few minutes, and she unexpectedly shared with me how she got into the insurance business.

Twenty years ago, she was a single mother with two baby girls. She told me that she was so broke, she literally couldn't even afford to pay for a postage stamp to mail someone a letter. Elana started off as a straight-commissioned sales rep with no base salary. As with anyone that starts off in a straight-commission position, the beginning of your career is tough because it generally takes a while to start bringing in revenue.

Her baby girls saw her struggle, sacrificing the immediate, in hopes of achieving greatness. Today, Elana is one of the most successful people in her company. But that's not the most impactful part of her story. Sure, her success is something to be acknowledged and celebrated, but the real inspiring part of her story is that her daughter, now in her twenties, has followed in her mother's footsteps, and is a rising star in the company.

Think about how powerful this is. Had Elana not displayed acts of courage, built perseverance, and stood in the gap, perhaps her daughter would not have dreamed it possible for her to become an entrepreneur and succeed. Elana modeled exemplary behavior for her daughter, inspiring her daughter to dream big. This is what I call leaving behind a legacy. You see, legacy building is not about setting up a trust fund for your kids, or merely taking care of them financially. Legacy building is about teaching them the principles and the skills needed for them to succeed on their own merit. This can only be done through mentorship.

Overcoming All Odds

Perhaps you didn't grow up in an affluent family. If you didn't, let's be honest. The deck is stacked against you. Growing up in an affluent family affords you certain resources that make it easier to succeed in life and in business. If you had the luxury of watching your parents succeed, subconsciously, it instilled a belief system in you that succeeding in life was not just possible, but probable.

My wife, Emilia, wasn't so fortunate. She was not groomed for success. She had to make it on her own, finding her own way, with no one to fall back on. Emilia's family immigrated to the United States from Mexico when she was three years old. Her father had come to the states to work on his own, and once he secured a job as a ranch hand in Northern Nevada, he went back to Mexico to bring his family to America. Life in Mexico was hard for them.

Emilia's mother told me of their tough times where at one point, they were homeless and slept under a tree. Sometimes, she would build a fire and burn the mold off the edges of some old moldy tortillas.

That's what they would eat for dinner. Upon hearing these stories, it really made me appreciate the luxuries that I took for granted as a child.

When the family settled in Nevada, things were better, but still tough. Have you ever seen immigrant workers out in the fields, picking strawberries or vegetables? That was Emilia at nine years-old. She was out in the fields with her older brother and her sisters from sun up to sundown, stooped over, picking garlic and onions to help support the family.

She went to a small high school in her small, rural town. She only had six classmates in her graduating class. She had a humble and sheltered upbringing. She told me about a time her family drove down to Los Angeles one summer to visit some family members. Emilia said she vividly remembers the car ride through Downtown Los Angeles, and seeing all of the high-rise office buildings, something she had never seen before. She said that as a kid, she remembers seeing Downtown Los Angeles for the first time and thinking to herself, *"This is where all the money is. I have to move here one day."* That's exactly what she did.

Emilia left home at age seventeen on a small scholarship to the University of Nevada, Reno. But after spending a summer at her uncle's place in Los Angeles, she dropped out of school, permanently moved to L.A., and started working. She started out as a receptionist at a clothing manufacturer in Downtown L.A. Over time, she worked her way up to the position of Office Manager, and before long, she was managing over 70 employees.

During this time, a neighbor in her apartment building sold her some life insurance, but when Emilia found out how much commission he made on the sale, she wanted *in*. She started out selling life insurance on a part-time basis, while still working her full-time job. Emilia has always been a hard worker, going all the way back to her garlic picking days.

And so that's how she initially got into the insurance business. When I met Emilia, we were both thirty-three years old. We were both attending an insurance conference in Las Vegas. I spotted her at a cocktail party that her company was putting on. I saw this beautiful, polished, classy woman and I was instantly drawn to her. She was a successful sales executive, and worked for a large insurance wholesaler. At that time, my firm produced more business for this insurance wholesaler than any other firm in the country, and that was out of 20,000 brokerage firms. Needless to say, I was notorious in both her company, as well as the entire insurance industry. We still laugh about the fact that she didn't know who I was when we first met.

Emilia was standing at a bistro table with some of her counterparts, and she stepped away from her glass of wine to greet other guests. I immediately, walked up to the table where she had left her glass of wine and strategically took ownership of that table. Why? Because I knew she would have to come back to get her glass of wine.

The reason I say it was *strategic* was that she now had to approach me and my table, as opposed to the other way around. This strategy was very similar to what we discussed earlier in this book regarding establishing a different type of relationship with your prospect. You always want *them* to come to *you*, as opposed to *you* chasing *them*.

When she approached the table, I nonchalantly picked up her glass of wine and pretended like I was going to drink out of it. She said, *"Hey, hey! That's my glass!"* I burst into laughter, and that's what broke the ice. From a sales perspective, I broke her emotional state, and put her in an emotional state of receptivity, due to breaking the ice. I told you the dating world and the sales world are very similar in regards to prospecting.

I sparked up a conversation with her, and we instantly hit it off. Some of her counterparts were taking me to dinner that evening, and so I invited her to come along with us. At first, she accepted. But on the way out of the hotel, she changed her mind and backed out. She said she didn't feel it was appropriate because I was the star client of one of her colleagues, and she didn't want him to feel like she was trying to steal me away from him. I said I understood, and I went to dinner without her.

The next evening, I saw her walking through the hotel. I stopped her and said, *"Hey did you get that thing out okay last night?"*

She said, *"What thing?"*

I replied, *"That stick you had up your ass! What's the deal? You should have come to dinner with us. No one turns down dinner with me!"*

I immediately broke out into one of my gregarious laughs. I thought I was hilarious. She, on the other hand, did not seem to think that I was as hilarious as I did. However she later confessed that my cocky comment made her more intrigued with me because she thought to herself, "*Who is this guy, and why is so confident to think he could get away with saying that to me?*"

Later that evening, our respective business parties got together for cocktails, and we ended up talking, and flirting, and talking, and flirting. We talked for hours. But the thing that made our conversation different was that it wasn't based on any normal, shallow conversation topics.

We talked about why each of us was so driven. We talked about our goals, our aspirations and our dreams. We talked about how we grew up and how we got to where we were. She shared with me how her family immigrated to the states and how they struggled to make ends meet. She even shared with me about her garlic picking days.

Emilia told me later that she surprised herself in sharing that information with me having just met me, because it was something that some people might look down upon. But for me, knowing that she came from humble beginnings and worked her way up to being a successful, self-made businesswoman, attracted me to her even more. I thought to myself, "*This girl understands hard work. This girl understands the process of character building.*"

We talked in that hotel bar until 2:00AM, shutting the place down. We got into the elevator to return to our respective rooms, and agreed to have dinner when we got back to Los Angeles. As I got ready for bed that evening, I thought to myself, "*I think I just met my future wife.*" If someone told me that the day before, I would have probably called them an idiot and laughed at them. I've never believed in love at first sight, but with Emilia, it was different. A year and a half later, we were married.

Perhaps you're wondering why I spent so much time talking about Emilia. The reason that her story is so compelling to me is that here you have a girl that came from humble beginnings, from a small town, living a sheltered life with no role models of successful people, and yet she still accomplished greatness all on her own. So what does this have to do with leaving behind a legacy?

Oh, just about *everything*.

Maybe you didn't grow up with any great mentors. Perhaps your parents didn't model exemplary behavior for you to emulate. Hey, it didn't stop Emilia from becoming successful. So what's your excuse? The point is, your destiny, as well as the legacy that you leave behind for your family, is up to you.

It doesn't matter where you come from, or what family you come from. You can start building a new family legacy, starting with you. Sure it would have been easier if you were born into a family that already had a legacy. Sure it would have been easier if you had parents that truly mentored you and groomed you for success in business.

Sure it would be easier if the weather weren't so hot, or so cold. Sure it would be easier if the economy was better, or the stock market was up, or the government didn't charge us so much in taxes, or if Santa Claus and the Easter Bunny existed, but the point is, they don't. Stop spending so much time rationalizing your lack of success, and create a new direction for you and your family.

So many people want to dwell on the past. They become prisoners of their past, and become trapped in their own poor self-image. Some of them will realize the error of their self-pity, and they'll go out and try to *find themselves*. They'll try to get in touch with their true self. Listen, your true self is whatever you decide you want it to be. Life isn't about *finding* yourself. It's about *creating* yourself.

Don't be a prisoner of your own childhood. Make the decision to overcome the limiting beliefs that were instilled in you as a child, and teach your kids to have beliefs without limits. That's what *Championship Parenthood* is all about. Give your kids every advantage to achieve greatness as you can, and it starts with encouragement and mentorship.

Share with them inspiring stories about people that overcame all odds and succeeded in spite of the deck being stacked against them. Show them by example how to win in the face of adversity. You have the opportunity to give your kids something that perhaps you never had. A mentor.

Chapter Fifteen:
The Journey

"The greatest pleasure in life is accomplishing things that other people said you could not do."
-Darren Sugiyama

In The Beginning

My personal belief is that if you're an aspiring entrepreneur, you were born with the entrepreneur gene. What does that mean? It means that you were born with something inside of you that innately drives you to accomplish great things, and this *need* to succeed will push you through the tough times.

Successful entrepreneurs are *relentless*, and I would say that most of the successful entrepreneurs I've met in my lifetime had this quality even during their childhood. Many of them had some sort of *non-job* that generated income from early on. Some of them had lemonade stands, or paper routes, or a neighborhood lawn mowing business.

When I was growing up, I always had some sort of entrepreneurial project I was working on. When I was fourteen, I built skateboard ramps and sold them to my friends. When I was fifteen, I silkscreened Bob Marley and Jimi Hendrix t-shirts and sold them to my skateboarding friends. When I was sixteen, I had a car stereo installation business.

When I was in college, I had small business giving batting lessons to Little League players, and I installed boom boxes and car stereo systems in college students' cars.

Notice that none of these sources of income came from traditional *jobs*. They were all independent, small businesses. I always hated the idea of having a *boss* in the traditional sense of the word. *I wanted to be the boss.*

Have you ever heard the phrase, *"Working your way up the corporate ladder?"* There was never anything appealing to me about that concept. I could never be passionate about working my way up someone else's ladder, especially when it generally requires sucking up to someone that I don't aspire to be like. That's what having a corporate cubicle job is all about. Politicking, schmoozing, and convincing your boss to like you… that's how you climb the corporate ladder.

I never liked that idea for several reasons. One, I refuse to kiss anyone's butt. Two, I hate disingenuous schmoozing. And three, I enjoy succeeding on my own merit, based on my performance. You can't deny performance, and in business, similar to sports, it's all about production numbers. In baseball, if I routinely hit 40 homeruns per year and bat over .300, I'm an All-Star. And in business, if I'm routinely making sales, closing deals, and building a successful sales force, I'm an All-Star. No one can hold me down.

Paid The Cost To Be The Boss

As James Brown, *The Godfather of Soul*, said in one of his songs, "*I paid the cost to be the boss.*" I've started my own companies, which by definition, makes me the boss. But you don't necessarily have to be the President and founder of a multi-million dollar company to be *The Boss*. If you're in a position where no one can restrict the amount of income you can earn, then to a certain degree, you're a boss. If you're a commission-driven sales rep, to a certain degree, you're your own *boss*. You may have a manager to report to, but he can't keep you from closing more business and making more money.

If you're an independent insurance agent, or a commission-based sales rep, or an owner of a fast food franchise, or a multi-level marketing distributor, by my definition, you are a boss; *your own boss*. The reason I say that you paid the cost to be the boss is that your success is up to you, and you can create your own destiny. Your income is a direct reflection of how hard you push yourself. This takes guts, and you should be proud of yourself for having the guts to take on this challenge. Virtually anyone can just show up at a job, sit in a cubicle, and collect a paycheck. But you want more out of life. I can relate. I was the same way when I first started.

As I discussed earlier in this book, I've always been an entrepreneur at heart. I always wanted to be the *boss*. A lot of people look at me today as a polished, successful businessman, but I assure you, I did not start out this way, and my image was drastically different in the beginning.

Thug Life

When I was in Junior High School, school districts, in an effort to promote integration of different races and students from different socio-economic backgrounds, placed students from different neighborhoods in the same school together. This was called *busing* at the time. As a result, even though I grew up as the son of a successful orthodontist in a big house with the proverbial white picket fence, the friends I made at school lived in the ghetto.

When I got to high school, my parents yanked me out of the Long Beach Unified School District and sent me to Los Alamitos High School in Orange County. They used my dad's office address on the transfer papers, which was located in Los Alamitos. Half of my friends in Long Beach were drug dealers, and several of them carried guns. The friends I made at Los Alamitos High School came from drastically different backgrounds.

Los Al was a predominantly *white* school in an upper-middle class community. My Long Beach friends, however, went to Long Beach Poly High School. In fact, they were all classmates with Snoop Dogg (the rapper). Poly was filled with gangsters and drug dealers, but also had rich white kids that got *bused* into the same school. In fact, Cameron Diaz, whom I went to Junior High School with, lived just a few blocks away from my parents' house where I grew up, and she went to Long Beach Poly High School.

I think the *Poly experience* was unique because you had the likes of Snoop Dogg sitting in the same classroom as Cameron Diaz. Talk about extremes. So as a result of socializing with friends that grew up with these drastically different elements, I experienced both sides of the tracks, so to speak.

When I went to college, I quickly gained the reputation of being the *tough guy* from Long Beach. I went to Loyola Marymount University in Los Angeles, California on a small baseball scholarship.

At the beginning of my sophomore year at LMU, I was driving a couple of my baseball teammates home from a party one night. A car pulled up next to us, staring us down. In those days, if someone even looked at me wrong, I'd challenge them to a fight.

It seems silly and immature to me now, but that's how I was in my younger years. I sped up and cut in front of them, slamming on the breaks, just to piss them off. I figured we'd get out of the car, and I'd kick all of their asses. Another routine night of so-called *fun*.

I was driving about five miles per hour on a forty mile per hour street, waiting for them to pass me. They just kept trailing me at five miles per hour. I boasted to my teammates that these guys were afraid to pull up next to me, so I pulled over into the left lane, anticipating them pulling up next to me in the right lane.

As I saw them slowly approach us, before I could look them in the eye, I heard this incredibly loud *BOOM!* It was like a bomb went off in my car. As I saw the car take off, the barrel of a shotgun was hanging out of their window, and at that point, I realized what had happened. We had just gotten shot in a drive-by shooting.

My ears were ringing, and the back of my head felt like someone had taken a blowtorch to it. I quickly pulled the car over, and fortunately, there was a gas station about half a block up the street. My friend Todd Gates (whom we called *Gator*) was sitting in the front seat. He didn't even get a scratch, so he ran into the gas station to call 911.

My other friend Tim Williams (whom we called *T-Dub*) was sitting in the back seat. He got shot in the eye, and was screaming, "*Yo D, I can't see, man! I can't see!*" Everything started moving in slow motion. I reached my hand back to touch the back of my head because it felt like it was on fire. I looked at my hand, and it was covered in blood. I had no idea how bad it was, but I had basically been shot in the head in a drive-by shooting with a shotgun.

I was driving a Chevy Blazer, and the blast came through the passenger side back window, so both the buckshot from the shotgun blast and the shattered glass from my window came spraying into the car. Most of it went into the back of my driver's seat, but some of it went into the back of my head.

I was kind of groggy, but I was conscious throughout the entire time. I ripped my T-shirt off and plugged the back of my head to try to stop the bleeding, but less than five minutes later, my T-shirt was soaked in blood. My shirt was so soaked in blood, you could almost wring the blood out. My mouth got extremely dry, and I got light headed. A few minutes later, I heard Gator running up to my car yelling, "*Sugi! Sugi!*" Apparently, I had momentarily passed out, and I was slumped over the steering wheel, covered in blood. Gator thought I had died.

If you've ever seen someone get shot in the movies, I can assure you, it is nothing like that. It is incredibly painful. As I sat there, slumped over my steering wheel, waiting for the ambulance to come and rush us off to the emergency room, my whole life flashed in front of me. I thought about all the things I hadn't done yet. I thought about all the people I had hurt in the past. I thought about all the mistakes I had made. I thought about my friend T-Dub in the back seat, and how I had put him in danger as a result of my stupid, immature actions. I thought I was about to die.

I've heard people say that you're not supposed to negotiate with God, but I did it anyway. At that time, I was an atheist. Imagine that, an atheist attempting to make a deal with God. I told God that I knew I had screwed up bad, but I begged Him for a second chance. I promised to change my ways and that if He let me live, that I would dedicate my life to helping other people. At that time, as a nineteen year-old college kid, I didn't know exactly how I was going to do it, but I made that promise anyway.

Finally, the ambulance came, and rushed us off to the emergency room at Daniel Freeman Memorial Hospital in Marina Del Rey. As I lay on the operating table, T-Dub laid on a table next to me, with a hanging sheet separating us. About every one or two minutes, T-Dub would say, "*Yo, Sug. Are you still there?*"

"*Yeah, Dub. I'm still here,*" I'd reply.

We both went into surgery that night. The surgeon had to remove the lens of T-Dub's right eye because it had been destroyed by the shotgun blast. For me, the surgeon removed as many buckshots and shattered glass from the back of my head as possible, however about twenty-four were embedded in my skull, and still exist today. I have the x-ray framed on the wall in my office to remind me everyday how fortunate I am to be alive.

But the main reason I have that x-ray on display is to remind me that my actions not only affect my own life, but they also affect those around me. You see, T-Dub didn't grow up around this kind of violence, whereas I did.

When I got shot in the drive-by shooting, it wasn't outside the norm of what I was used to seeing. But for Gator and T-Dub, it was a foreign thing. Today, every time I look at that x-ray of my head, I think about how selfish it was to put my two friends in that situation. I provoked it, and it was entirely my fault.

T-Dub was an incredibly talented baseball player. He could run. He could hit with power. He had a great throwing arm. He had all the key ingredients to become a big league ball player. But when the scouts found out he had a damaged right eye, they became less interested in him. T-Dub was a left-handed hitter, and as a lefty, your dominant hitting eye is your right eye. Despite him having a banner junior year as an All-Conference left fielder, T-Dub didn't get drafted by a professional team. And after having another great senior year, the professional teams passed on him again.

I cannot express the amount of guilt I had, knowing that T-Dub's career had been cut short because of my irresponsible, stupid actions. It made me rethink my entire life. That was the second deal I made with God. I guess it was more of a *commitment* than a *deal*. I swore that I would somehow repent and repay the world for the damage I had caused. A year later, I converted from being an atheist into a Christian. I started going to church, and before long, I was sharing my story with people about how God had given me a second chance at life.

I started working for a gang prevention program in Downtown Long Beach, California, and later went on to work with incarcerated youths at The Honolulu Detention Home as well as at Halawa Prison in Hawaii. It had been years since the shooting, and I had never really talked with T-Dub about the incident. As I started to change my life and my values, I thought about T-Dub, and knew that I had to formally apologize, something that I had never done before.

A mutual friend of ours that we played ball with at Loyola told me that T-Dub was living in Arizona, and that he had just spoken with him on the phone. He said, "*Sugi man, you should call Dub. I'm sure he'd like to catch up with you.*"

I thought to myself, "*Dub's not going to want to catch up with me. I totally screwed up his dream of becoming a Major League Baseball Player. It's all my fault. He probably resents me, and I wouldn't blame him if he did.*"

But I knew I owed him a long overdue apology. At the very least, I owed him that. So I dialed his number. My fingers were shaking. I had no idea how this conversation was going to go. It had been years since we had spoken.

He answered the phone, and I said, "*Hey Dub. It's Sugi.*"

Without hesitation, he replied, "*Sugi! What's up man? How you been?*"

It was like nothing had ever happened, and no time had passed. We spent a few minutes catching each other up on where our lives had taken us, you know, just small chit-chat. We reminisced about the *Good Ole Days* of playing ball, chasing college girls, and clowning around with the fellas. But then I got serious.

I said, *"Dub, I've got to talk to you about something that's been weighing heavy on my heart for years."*

I confessed to him that I had carried so much guilt with me because of the situation I put him in. I told him that I knew it was all my fault, and that I knew I had screwed up his future as a pro ball player. I started crying as I begged for his forgiveness. I had no idea how he was going to respond.

Again, without hesitation, T-Dub said, *"Sugi, man. I never blamed you for any of this. What happened to us was unfortunate, but it wasn't your fault that they whipped out a damn shotgun and shot us. Sometimes bad shit happens to you in life, but if it wasn't for that, and I went on to play pro ball, I wouldn't have my two daughters today. Things worked out okay for me."*

It's hard for me to describe the feeling, but it was if someone had removed a 500-pound backpack off my shoulders. They say that the real gift of forgiveness is for the forgiver, but in this case, the gift of forgiveness was definitely for me, the forgiven. I knew in my heart that it was still my fault, but just knowing that T-Dub didn't resent me or blame me gave me an overwhelming sense of relief.

I guess we both learned valuable life lessons as a result of going through the horrific experience of getting shot in a drive-by shooting. I still keep in touch with both Gator and T-Dub. That experience has formed a bond between the three of us that will last a lifetime.

Personal Growth

There are several reasons I felt compelled to share that story about getting shot in a drive-by shooting with you. The first one is pretty obvious, which is to never take anything in your life for granted. The mere fact that you're alive is a miracle.

The second lesson to be learned here is that your actions not only affect your own life, but also those around you.

But the third lesson to be learned here is, in my opinion, the most important. The biggest lesson I want you to take away from this story is that you can reinvent yourself. It doesn't matter what you've done in the past, how many mistakes you've made, or how little success you've had in your life up until this point. You can hit the reset button right now and start over.

Again, I don't measure success by how much money I make, or how big of a house I live in compared to other people. I measure success by comparing what I've accomplished relative to what I know I'm capable of. It's about fulfilling your potential that matters.

In my own life, I was heading down a road that wasn't where I wanted to end up, so I hit *cancel* on my proverbial navigation system, and input a new destination. Anyone can do this at any time, as long as you do it before you die, which means that if you're reading this book, you can do it right now. So what are you waiting for? Do it now.

Don't wait until the economy gets better. It might not improve. Don't wait until the government changes. They might not. Don't wait until people get more ambitious. They probably won't. I've met so many people with every excuse in the world.

Right now, the common excuse is the *economy*. Everyone is blaming the economy for their lack of success. Hey, last year, 2010, was one of the worst global economic years we've seen in a long time, but I personally made more money in 2010 than I've ever made in my entire career, and 2011 is looking even better for me. You see, external factors may present challenges in business, but it is these very challenges that can turn into opportunities.

There will always be external factors and external challenges that you'll face in business. It comes with the territory. The key is to view these challenges as *small things*. I'm not trying to take away the significance of these challenges. They're real, no doubt about it.

However, relative to your goals and your vision, you must see them as being *small*, comparatively. *Big people* aren't bothered by the *small things*, but ironically, *small people* aren't bothered by the *big things*, which is why they're small people.

Small People

Now, when I say *small*, I am not referring to the physical stature of the person. I'm talking about them being *small minded*. Small people are always bothered by the small things. They perceive every challenge to be a major, devastating problem. They are experts in making mountains out of mole hills.

Every time something isn't perfect, they throw a tissy-fit. Every time things don't come easy, or don't come in a convenient, pretty little package, they give up. They have excuses for everything, which is why they're not successful.

Sure the economy is in recession right now, and sure, consumerism is down, but with challenges come opportunities. I was driving by the *Apple Store* the day they released the new iPad. There was a line going out into the parking lot.

Do you think Steve Jobs said, *"Well, the economy is down, so we better not release the iPad until the economy turns around."* Of course not. He developed a hot product that people want and has found a way to market it in such a way that people want it, despite the economic recession.

When I was a kid, I used to love playing soccer in the rain. The reason I loved it was that the other team would be complaining about how slippery it was, whining and making excuses. Hey, it was just as slippery for me too, and yes, it *is* harder to play in the rain. But because I knew the other team would be focused on the problem and making excuses, I felt like I had the upper hand. I was focused on *winning*, whereas they were focused on *not losing*. There is a distinct difference between the two mindsets. They were small. I was big.

Another interesting thing about *small people* is that even though they freak out about the small things, they don't seem to be bothered by the big things. They don't seem to react when I talk about leaving a legacy behind for their family. They don't seem to think there's anything wrong with watching hours of mindless television with the kids. They don't seem to be bothered by the idea of the *pain of regret*.

To me, these are all *big* things. These are the things I focus on, and it always boggles my mind that more people don't place as high a priority on these things. But that's why they're small people. Their incomes are small. Their homes are small. Their mindsets are small. And most of all, their dreams are small.

Big People

When I say *big*, again, I'm not referring to the physical size of the person. I'm referring to their mindset. People that think *big* aren't intimidated by the small obstacles and challenges they face in business. Things that bother *small people* do not bother *big people*. Big people don't sweat the small stuff.

Sure, I get *frustrated* from time to time with things that happen to me in business, but I rarely ever *worry* about them. As discussed earlier in this book, the only reason someone worries is that they do not foresee a solution. They lack that type of vision to see past the short-term, temporary setbacks.

Remember, *frustration* is an emotional response to a short-term problem that is perceived as being short-term and temporary. These temporary nuisances are bothersome, but they can be dealt with and squashed. *Worry* is an emotional response to a long-term and potentially permanent problem that does not appear to be fixable.

Big people get *frustrated*, and will often use this frustration to drive them to find a solution, but they seldom *worry*. In order to be successful, you've got to be *solution-centric* instead of *problem-centric*. Most people get overwhelmed by their problems because instead of spending their energy focusing on finding a solution, they wallow in the misery of their problems.

As I discussed earlier in this book, you've got to ask yourself the right questions. Instead of asking, *"Why am I not making more money?"* ask yourself, *"What can I do to make more money?"* Your subconscious brain will work to answer both questions.

The first question prompts answers related to everything you're doing wrong. The second question prompts answers related to things you can do to change your current circumstance. It focuses on finding a solution.

The concept of *Thinking Big* extends far beyond having grand financial aspirations. It really has more to do with having a constructive, optimistic perspective on current circumstances.

Helping Yourself So That You Can Help Others

I learned a valuable lesson early on in my career. As I mentioned earlier in this book, back when I was a broke high school teacher, I had several other concurrent part-time jobs in addition to teaching. One of them was a straight-commission based sales job with a vitamin company.

I would go to as many sales seminars as I could in an effort to become more skilled at sales. One day at the end of a seminar I attended, I got the chance to chat with the speaker of the seminar. He asked me what I was doing being a high school teacher if I really wanted to succeed in sales.

I told him about my background and how I wanted to help young people make better life decisions. His response radically changed the direction of my life.

He said, *"Do you think you'd have a greater impact on kids doing what you're doing now as a teacher, or spending just one hour per week talking to kids about whatever you wanted to, completely uncensored?"*

I quickly responded, *"I'd take the one hour per week."*

So he said, *"Well, what the hell are you doing being a teacher? Become a successful businessman and get rich, then go back and donate your time talking to kids about whatever you want."*

It took me about two years to actually quit my teaching job, though I emotionally quit teaching right there on the spot.

Whenever you look at non-profit organizations, or church groups, or charitable organizations, you must understand that they're all funded by someone that has an abundance of money. Lots of people say that money isn't the most important thing in life, which I would agree with, however money is incredibly important, especially when it comes to helping other people.

So what does this encounter with the seminar speaker have to do with being successful? This five-minute conversation changed my life. It fundamentally changed the way I viewed my own ability to impact the world.

It's very similar to what the flight attendant tells you just before your plane takes off. As they're explaining how to buckle your seatbelt (as if you couldn't figure it out on your own), they also instruct you on what to do in the event of a plane crash.

What do they tell you to do when the oxygen masks drop down from the ceiling? They tell you to put on your own mask first, then assist your child. Now, as a parent, I know that my first inclination would be to help my son first, then worry about my own oxygen mask. However, that's the worst thing you could do.

The reason they tell you to put on your own mask first is that you can't help someone else unless you can breathe with ease yourself. This concept is very analogous to the issue we're talking about right now. I realized that I could better help others and impact the world if I wasn't worried about my own finances, and so my entire focus at the beginning of my career was on building my financial empire.

Sure it took several short-term sacrifices, and sure, a lot of people viewed me as being selfish during that time, but a leader (and a visionary) must have the emotional discipline to forgo the immediate temptation of short-term gratification, even if that short-term gratification is feeling good about helping people.

Even today, I will have people that want to argue with me about this, but ironically, most of these people have never accomplished anything great in their lives. Sure, they're nice people, but they've never achieved greatness. And as a result, they don't have the resources, financially or experientially, to make a major impact on the world.

Jay-Z, the infamous rapper and entrepreneur, says in one of his songs, *"I can't help the poor if I'm one of them / So I got rich and gave back to me, that's the win-win."* Whether you're a fan of Jay-Z or not is not the point. The point is that being able to truly make a positive impact on the world in great magnitude, takes a tremendous amount of resources.

As I said, these resources are not just financial resources. Some of the most valuable resources I share with young people today are *experiential*. When I talk about the importance of working hard, dedication, sacrifice, persistence, and courage, I'm talking about things that I've personally developed through my own experiences.

In my opinion, you can't empower people with mere philosophy. Religion, in and of itself, doesn't get the job done either. There's a lack of authenticity when a teacher hasn't *lived* what they're teaching. These textbook teachers don't have the credibility that teachers have that actually *lived* what they're teaching.

When I give empowering talks to high school students and college students, I talk about adversities I've faced in my life and in business, and what I've learned in the process of overcoming them. I talk about what I had to do to achieve what I've achieved. I talk about the dedication it takes to continue to persevere when things get tough. Unless you've *lived* through this process, you can't legitimately teach these principles.

One of my life missions is to empower and inspire young people to think big, to rekindle those dreams they had when they were kids. Back when everything seemed possible, that was when their minds were open to exploring, experimenting, and enjoying the process, regardless of the outcome. My goal is to get people, young and old, to regain that mindset – to think big again.

Thinking Big

My first big success in business was building an employee benefits consulting firm. Last year, we did over $37 million in annual sales. I started this company in 2003, with very little initial capital, simply because I was broke at the time.

I couldn't afford a real office, so I used the lobby of *The Four Seasons Hotel* in Newport Beach because it was *free*. The bellhops and the people at the front desk probably thought I was a guest of the hotel, in town on a business trip. Little did they know I had to park my car across the street because I couldn't afford the valet parking.

I recruited my entire sales force out of hotel lobbies. Some of them were in Orange County, and some were in Los Angeles. I looked for people that caught my vision of what I was in the process of building. I didn't have any experience in the insurance industry, and I didn't have any money. All I had was a dream. That's it.

Initially, I recruited six sales reps. All we had were cell phones and hotel lobbies to work out of. Gary was a guy that previously sold software; Owen was an ex-business consultant; Diane had a background in selling credit card processing services; Ron previously sold commercial internet services; Janet used to work for *Yahoo*; and Glenn worked at *Circuit City*.

Within three months, all of them had quit. So I chang recruiting model. I started targeting recent college graduates out how to attract these young guns that wanted to drive and were willing to be semi-workaholics in order to do had any insurance experience. None of them h experience. None of them had any sales experienc guts.

I told them that I was going to build the firm our industry had ever seen, and that we w that no one else had ever done it. They bou started blazing the phones like stock broker

Everyone was on straight-commi to kill me for talking them into a caree was their alternative? A cubicle job? our universities) brainwash young commission careers aren't desir believing the myth of *job securi* with a guaranteed paycheck, wi don't tell you is that you're practically guaranteed to get laid off at some point. You've got no control of your destiny whatsoever.

My intent was to show these *kids* another type of career. People always ask me how I was able to build a company predominantly comprised of straight-commissioned sales reps.

The answer is that I did it by inspiring them to dream big. The only way to do this is to *live* the dream. I took them to Mercedes dealerships and Range Rover dealerships, and test drove luxury cars with them. I even let them drive my BMW and my Mercedes. I exemplified the very same lifestyle they wanted. I showed them the *great* life.

At that time, I was living in a cruddy one-bedroom apartment, but I was always talking about the dream. I was always talking about my vision of what we were going to build. All they saw was a flashy BMW, luxury hotel lobbies, and me wearing suits and ties. All they heard was me talking about how we were going to dominate our industry and make our competition look stupid.

My Personal Brand

I built my entire firm around my personal brand. I was brash, cocky, and unapologetically blunt. I believed that we were the best at what we did, and I inspired my team to take pride in that. I've found that people want to follow a leader that exudes ultimate confidence.

They look to their leader to embody the level of confidence that they do not have themselves, and they're looking to put their confidence in you. They're depending and relying on your confidence to carry them through. It's a heavy burden for a leader to carry, but it comes with the territory.

For whatever reason, people have an easier time believing in someone else than they do in luck, karma, themselves, and even God. Everyone is looking to put their faith in a hero. Right or wrong, it is

people need to feel like there is someone they can count on to lead them to the *Promised Land*. That's why most people choose a job to a cubicle. Though it's a false sense of security, they believe a corporation will take care of them better than they could themselves.

For some people, perhaps they're better off working a cubicle job. Perhaps their fear is warranted, and they are not talented or driven enough to venture out on their own like you are. They're *followers*, and there's really nothing wrong with being a follower, unless you're bowing out of a leadership role simply because of fear.

If it really is a personal preference to not be an entrepreneur, I'm not in a position to judge that person. However if you really do want to be an entrepreneur, but you're afraid of the unknown, then join the rest of us entrepreneurs.

Every successful entrepreneur had a certain level of fear when they first started out, myself included. But that's what makes people that have achieved greatness *great*. If you're reading this book, you were not destined to be a follower. You were destined for greatness. You wouldn't have decided to read this book if you weren't.

That being said, understand that when you're an entrepreneur, the majority of your career will be spent winning people over, whether it be your employees, joint-venture partners, vendors, or clients.

That's why your personal brand is so important. It communicates to all of these associates why they should do business with you. They're looking for you to *lead* them, and as we discussed earlier in this book, the only effective way to lead is to lead by example.

As an entrepreneur, everything you do is put under the microscope by the people you do business with. People will constantly be sizing you up based on what they see, what they hear come out of your mouth, and what they experience during the time they spend with you.

That's why I always buy the most expensive car I can afford. I always buy the most expensive suits I can afford. I always lease the most expensive office I can afford. And often times when I made these decisions in the past, I could *barely* afford them.

My CPA might even argue that I *couldn't* afford them back then, but I looked at these decisions as marketing expenses. These were all tools I used to create a certain image that I wanted for my companies.

Always remember that as an entrepreneur, your personal brand *is* your business brand. People choose to do business with you because of *you*, not because of a product.

If you can win over their confidence, generally speaking, the deal will get done.

Your Brand Must Be Targeted

Again, my brand has always been flashy and unapologetically brash. In my particular businesses, it has always worked to my advantage. Whether your personal brand is flashy or more subtle, it's always important that you maintain brand consistency. There's nothing worse than hopping from brand image to brand image.

Obviously, brands can evolve over time, but this evolution must be well thought out. Brands that aimlessly evolve organically often lose their core following.

I remember several years ago, I second-guessed my own brand. I heard rumblings of some of my employees and ex-employees, commenting on my life of luxury, and I felt that perhaps my flashy brand was breeding internal negative jealousy and contempt.

What began as a brand that was intended to inspire people, appeared to be having an adverse affect on some of my employees. In the beginning, my people aspired to be like me, but as my success grew and grew, I began to worry that my new level of success was being viewed as being unattainable to my people.

So what did I do? I made the mistake that so many people do. I second-guessed my brand. I started thinking that perhaps it was wise to tone my flashiness down a few notches.

In theory, there was *some* sound logic that led me to make this decision. My thought process was that at that stage in my career, everyone already knew I was successful, and that a more understated brand was better. Brands do evolve, and I thought that perhaps it was time for my brand to evolve into something more understated.

Man, that was a dumb move on my part. Why? Because I am not understated whatsoever. My brand is brash and unapologetic, and here I was, dumbing myself down, apologizing for being so successful. This new understated brand was in direct conflict with my core brand.

Sure, I won over some people that would have been intimidated, even offended, at my flashy brand, but I also lost my core followers. You see, my core followers decided to follow me in the first place *because* of my flashy brand. The mistake I made in this process of losing my brand identity was that I forgot who my core audience was.

Whenever you're establishing and promoting a brand, it is absolutely imperative that you understand who your target demographic is. When I first started my insurance consulting firm, my brand was *very* flashy. Everything was over-the-top... from the car I drove... to the penthouse I lived in… to the diamond rings and cufflinks. So guess what demographic I attracted in terms of recruits. I attracted driven people that wanted the finer things in life, and they were willing to work for it. My over-the-top lifestyle appealed to them. It inspired them to work harder.

In retrospect, the rumblings of jealousy and contempt from some of my ex-employees were routed in their excuses of not working harder. Here I was, trying to appeal to a demographic that, quite frankly, I didn't want as employees in the first place.

The brash, unapologetic, flashy brand – *my brand* – was the key to my rise to success in the first place. Those people that were offended or intimidated by my brand would have never made it in a straight-commission environment in the first place. They were weak and full of excuses. They weren't driven people.

Today, as I continue to recruit sales producers, I'm looking for the type of person that abhors the idea of working in a cubicle on a fixed salary. I'm looking for mini-entrepreneurs that want to be mentored by a mogul. I'm looking for people that are willing to work hard and sacrifice in the beginning, in hopes of achieving the *Great Life*. And guess what.

Most people that fit this profile not only like the flashy stuff, but it also inspires them to want to achieve more.

I'm sure some people think I'm materialistic because I talk so much about cars, custom suits, jewelry and exotic real estate.

First of all, I would emphatically disagree with that label. I'm not materialistic at all. Do I like nice things? Of course. Who doesn't?

Anyone that says they'd rather live in a modest house instead of a luxury estate is lying to you.

Anyone that says they'd rather drive an economy car instead of a luxury car is lying to themselves. We all want the finer things in life.

The difference is that I realize that these things are just *things*. Family, health, values and quality of life are much more important than *things*. No doubt about it. But here's what I've found.

Almost everyone that has ever called me *materialistic* has been broke. Isn't it interesting that successful people, as well as people that are driven to be successful, are *intrigued* by people that talk about success, and broke people are *offended* by people that talk about success?

I remember I posted a question on a social networking site once, regarding a car I was thinking of getting. My post said, "If you saw a guy driving a Bentley, would you say to yourself, *"Wow, I wonder what he does,"* or would you say, *"What a rich prick?"*

Like clockwork, all the driven people responded with, *"Wow, I wonder what he does."* All the cubicle-minded people responded with, *"What a rich prick."* You see, when a person aspires to achieve greatness, they're inspired and intrigued by another man's success. When a person has accepted mediocrity in their lives, they take personal offense when someone else has not settled for mediocrity with them. Misery loves company, and so does failure.

Whenever I meet someone that has achieved greater financial success in business than I have, I'm intrigued to learn how they did it. That's what separates entrepreneurs from cubicle-minded people. I'm always fascinated with other people's success because I'm eager to learn and grow as an entrepreneur.

In several of my businesses, part of my role is to recruit sales producers and groom them to achieve greatness. The key to successfully building sales teams is to inspire those people that are predisposed to being mini-entrepreneurs.

My goal is NOT to attempt to motivate a lazy person. My goal is not to convince a cubicle-minded person to be an entrepreneur. My goal is to simply identify those driven, aspiring entrepreneurs, and teach them how to be successful.

That's why my personal brand is so important. When I made that stupid mistake of dumbing down my brand, making it less flashy, and more understated, I temporarily lost my core audience. I was trying to appeal to a demographic that my core brand did not appeal to, and as I said, this less-driven demographic was the *wrong* demographic to recruit from and build with.

In developing and promoting your brand, you must make sure you do three essential things:

1. Identify the specific target demographic you are attempting to capture and construct your brand to ONLY appeal to this target.

2. Accept the fact that you will never appeal to 100% of the population, nor do you want to.

3. Never apologize for your brand and what you stand for.

Getting Back On Track

Once I *reinstated* my original personal brand, I began to promote myself shamelessly again. Within the first week, my original core group got fired up again. They said things like, "*D is back!*"

They needed their leader to embody that which they aspired to be like. They needed their role model back. They originally came to work for me because they knew that I had the blueprint for mega-success, and they wanted to follow that formula.

I went back to my unapologetic, brash, flashy brand. Now, understand that when I say *flashy*, I'm not talking about being all *flash* and no substance. If you're going to be flashy, you'd better have the substance to back it up, which I certainly do, and always have had.

My core brand is about delivering unparalleled value to my clients, as well as to my employees… and for that level of performance that I deliver, I make no apologies for my success. Once I got back to this mode of operation, all of my businesses took multiple, consecutive quantum leaps.

I built a second marketing consulting firm that outperformed my $37 million insurance consulting firm that took me a little over six years to build, and I did it in less than eighteen months. I also have three other major businesses that I'm currently in the process of launching, and they should all be big winners. That's the magic of believing in your personal brand. Anything is possible when you have a strong brand. People know that you hold your convictions strongly, and no one wants to follow someone that isn't passionately convicted about their beliefs.

All great leaders are obsessive about what they do, and I must say, I'm certainly obsessive about what I do.

The Power of Faith

Faith is defined as believing in the unseen. Faith alone is worthless, however faith combined with the right action plan, and the ability to execute with precision, is one of the most powerful things in this world. It's almost *magical*.

At the same time, having faith – believing in something that you cannot see – is very difficult for most people. Most people say they have to *see something to believe it*, and that is why most people never achieve greatness.

I heard a story about Walt Disney and the vision he had as a creator. Mike Vance, former dean of Disney University, tells this story of Walt Disney's vision even in his final hours in 1966.

> "At Disney studios in Burbank, California, Mike could gaze out of his office window across Buena Vista Street to St. Joseph's Hospital, where Walt Disney died. Mike was talking on the telephone when he saw the flag being lowered over the hospital around 8:20 a.m. His death was preceded by an amazing incident that reportedly took place the night before in Walt's hospital room."

> "A journalist, knowing Walt was seriously ill, persisted in getting an interview with Walt and was frustrated on numerous occasions by the hospital staff. When he finally managed to get into the room, Walt couldn't sit up in bed or talk above a whisper. Walt instructed the reporter to lie down on the bed, next to him, so he could whisper in the reporter's ear. For the next 30 minutes, Walt and the journalist lay side by side as Walt referred to an imaginary map of Walt Disney World on the ceiling above the bed."

> "Walt pointed out where he planned to place various attractions and buildings. He talked about transportation, hotels, restaurants, and many other parts of his vision for a property that wouldn't open to the public for another six years."

> "We told this reporter's moving experience, relayed through a nurse, to our organizational development groups... the story of how a man who lay dying in the hospital whispered in the reporter's ear for 30 minutes, describing his vision for the future and the role he would play in it for generations to come."

> "This is the way to live – believing so much in your

vision that even when you're dying, you whisper it into another person's ear."

Soon after the completion of The Magic Kingdom at Walt Disney World, someone said, *"Isn't it too bad Walt Disney didn't live to see this?"* Vance replied, *"He did see it. That's why it's here."*

I Didn't Always *Know*, But I Always *Believed*

People ask me all the time if I knew that I would be successful when I first started out. I always reply, *"Are kidding me? I was scared out of my mind!"* I never let anyone know that at the time, but I was always afraid of the possibility that I wouldn't ever *make it*.

But you see, that's where faith comes in. I didn't always *know* I would be successful, but I always *believed*. There's a fundamental difference between *knowing* and *believing*. *Belief* and *faith* are really one and the same thing. Both are triggered by a *decision*. You *choose* to have faith. You *choose* to believe.

Now, I'm not likening myself to Mr. Disney, but I do understand the concept of having such tremendous belief in your vision that when you see it in your mind, the level of clarity is such that the line between *creative fantasy* and *reality* becomes so blurred that you cannot decipher which is which. That's when you know your dream is *real*.

When people ask me if I *knew* that I'd be successful, as I said earlier, no, I did not *know* that I'd be successful. But that didn't stop me from *believing* that I'd be successful. Again, *believing* is a choice to put your faith in something that you can't see. If you could *see* it, then you'd *know*. But when you can't see it, and your success hasn't materialized yet, it is imperative to *believe* in spite of the absence of physical proof.

I spent many nights crying myself to sleep in the beginning of my career. I wanted so badly for other people to have the same belief in my vision that I had, but to my disappointment, practically everyone in my life doubted my ability to manifest the level of success that I aspired to achieve.

Have you ever felt like this? Do you have people in your life that you would have hoped would be more enthusiastic about your dream, only to find out that they didn't believe in you? It hurts, doesn't it? But as I've said throughout this book, if you're going to be an entrepreneur, you'd better get used to it.

Remember, *you're* the one that has escaped the cubicle-minded life, just like the ex-prisoner that escaped captivity from the cave in Plato's *The Allegory Of The Cave*. You must accept the fact and expect that most people will not understand nor support your entrepreneurial endeavors until you make it big. Most people will say, *"I have to see it to believe it,"* whereas you have to say, *"I believe it in spite of you not seeing it."*

The reason most people get excited when I start a new business venture today is that I have a strong track record of success, and that track record gives me credibility. You know, I used to wish that these same people could have been excited about my endeavors back when I was first starting out, which they were not. That's when I really needed their support the most.

But in retrospect, apparently I didn't *need* their support, because I succeeded anyway. And so you can't use that as an excuse anymore. You can't blame your lack of success on other people that aren't supportive. You must succeed on your own, in spite of the doubters. In reality, that lack of support in the beginning has made my victories that much sweeter for me, because I can now appreciate just how much emotional strength it took to persevere.

What you must understand is that the best part about your future success is being able to tell people about your war stories and how you got knocked down, but still got back up. It is these testimonies that will encourage other people once you make it big.

In my opinion, one of the greatest (and most powerful) elements of your future success is being able to share your journey with others that aspire to achieve greatness, just like you did. That's one of the biggest reasons why I wrote this book. As you continue your journey as an entrepreneur, never forget that you're writing your own history right now – your own book – of how you overcame all odds.

Let not your struggles discourage you. Let them empower you, knowing that no great *testimony* has ever been built without being greatly *tested*. These tests are opportunities to develop greatness, which you were born to achieve. Now is your time. Today is the day to take charge of you life and to go out and accomplish your dreams. This is your time.

Chapter Sixteen:
A Message To My Son

"This closing chapter is a letter I wrote to my son that he will read when he is old enough to understand the importance of being a real man."

-Darren Sugiyama

March 7, 2011

Dear Estevan,

As I think about all of the success principles I've learned over the years as an entrepreneur, they really apply to everything in life, not just business.

In life, you're going to experience a lot of ups and downs. You're going to have peaks and valleys, both financially and emotionally, both in your career and your personal life.

The key is to apply all of these principles and lessons I've shared with you throughout this book. Some of them will help you alter your perspective on these things, and some of them will actually help you change your situation entirely.

The main reason I wrote this book was to take all of the success principles I've discovered and implemented in my own life over the years, and consolidate them into one manuscript to share with you when you're old enough to understand them.

Son, you were just one-year old when I started writing this book, and you were about two-years old when I finished this last chapter. I thought it was important for me to be able to pass on to you the many principles that have made me successful in business, as well as in my personal life.

If you're reading this for the first time, this is a special moment in your life, because this is the beginning of your transition from boyhood into manhood.

I recently had a young man interview me about my success in business, and he asked two very important questions. The first question he asked me was, *"What do you need to BE in order to be successful?"* I thought this was a great question. Simple, but great nonetheless.

I replied, *"You either have to be exceptional, or you have to be lucky."* When you think about business, as well as your overall life, being lucky is great. It's just that you can't control luck, and so I've never relied on good luck. Strategically planning and creating a successful life comes from developing yourself as a person. You must become exceptional.

You must be exceptionally motivated. You must have an exceptional level of perseverance. You must have an exceptional amount of courage. You must become an exceptional communicator. You must become an exceptional leader. You must become an exceptional visionary. You must develop exceptional character.

The second question the young man asked me really made me think about my own life, and how I've gotten to this point in both my business life, as well as my personal life.

They asked me, *"Which one are you? Exceptional or lucky?"*

I really had to stop and think about how to answer this question. Up until about two years ago, I would have answered this question without hesitation. I would have immediately said, *"Exceptional. I am exceptional."* I've never viewed my success in life as having anything to do with me having good luck. In fact, I've had to overcome so many adversities and great challenges that if anything, I'd say I've had to overcome bad luck for the majority of my life.

But when you were born, my entire perspective on life changed. During your mother's pregnancy, I was so worried about you. I was worried that something might go wrong with your health or your mother's health. I prayed that God would make you a healthy baby, and that your mother would have a healthy pregnancy and delivery.

Son, I was right there by your mother's side when you came into this world. I saw you take your first breath. They immediately ran several health tests on you, and when they confirmed that you were a strong, healthy baby, I literally started crying.

I was so thankful to God. With so many things that can go wrong with the health of a baby, everything went *right* with your birth. You were the most beautiful baby I had ever seen.

At that moment, I felt so incredibly *lucky*. It was the first time I felt like I had been given something that I had done absolutely nothing to deserve, and for that, I felt lucky. But this feeling also made me reevaluate my life. I've always viewed all of the challenges and adversities I've been faced with in life as *bad luck*, but when you were born, my perspective completely changed.

You see, every challenge that was placed in my life was an opportunity to develop character and perseverance. These challenges created *opportunities*, and being granted opportunities is a form of luck.

I was also fortunate enough to be born *driven*. I believe that a person is either born with the desire to achieve, or they are born to accept mediocrity. I was lucky enough to be born with an exceptional amount of drive, and so I was lucky in this regard too.

I was lucky to meet your mother. When you think of everything that had to happen in order for us to meet at the right time, at the right place, in the right way, it would have been very easy for us to have never met. And so I was lucky in that regard as well.

And so to answer that young man's question about whether I was exceptional or lucky, I told him, "*I am both... and person cannot be successful without being both.*"

You can attain wealth through good luck alone, but you have zero control over making this happen. Plus, when it comes to becoming truly successful (on your own merit) you must become exceptional.

In addition, you must be lucky enough to be afforded opportunities in order for you be able to capitalize on being exceptional.

I have learned to never take anything for granted in this lifetime. I have cherished each day that God has granted me to spend with you as my son. Not a day goes by that I don't stop for a moment and thank God for blessing me with you as my son. You are the best thing that has ever happened to me. Watching you grow up has been a privilege.

As I think about what I can contribute to your life as a father, I know that you will be confronted with many adversities in your life, as all of us are. You'll experience failures, heartache, and encounter adversities throughout your lifetime.

However, equipped with the success principles in this book, which are really *life* principles, I have faith that you'll become a strong and confident leader. You'll be able to handle whatever life throws at you, because you're strong inside. Having unshakable confidence will allow you to prevail, regardless of any adversity you may face.

When your mother and I began choosing names for you before you were born, we had several criteria. We wanted your name to be original. Before you were even born, I felt as though God was telling me that you would be extraordinarily special, and that you would somehow make a significant impact on this world. Even before you were born, I knew you would be special, and so your name would have to be special. Estevan Kane Sugiyama.

We didn't want you to have a name that people could shorten with a nickname. You were not to be common or diluted, and thus, your name could not be a common name or one that could be shortened. Because you were to have a Japanese last name (Sugiyama), I wanted to honor your mother's heritage and give you a Latin first name.

We felt that *Estevan* was a *strong* name... an *unique* name... a *regal* name. We had commissioned an artist to paint an original piece to commemorate your birth, which is the large, blue piece of art that hung on the wall of your first bedroom. The artist told us that he began working on your painting, and that he envisioned a crown floating in the clouds, and so he began working on it. Your mother wanted it to be completed and hanging on your wall when we brought you home for the first time.

A few days later, the artist called us and asked us what your name would be, and we told him we had decided on *Estevan Kane Sugiyama*. And so the artist researched the name *Estevan*, and immediately called us back, and told us that *Estevan* means *crown*, which neither us nor the artist knew prior to him beginning your *crown-in-the-clouds* painting. Call it destiny.

Your middle name, *Kane*, has many meanings. In Gaelic, it means *battler*. A battler never gives up. A battler is tough. A battler will fight to the end, and shine, especially when things get tough. I have raised you to never give up on anything in life that is important to you.

I will be proud of you, regardless of what becomes of your life because of your effort, not your results. As long as you don't ever give up on your dreams, under my definition of success, you will always be *successful* in my eyes.

Society has a way of only focusing on a person's results, but what will always make me proud of you is your effort and your courage displayed in pursuing your dreams. Son, you are a *battler*.

In Hawaiian, *Kane* (pronounced *Kah-nay*) means *man*. Manhood is something that a lot of people get confused about. Being a *man* isn't about being *macho*, or being *Mr. Tough Guy*, or getting the most girls. Being a *man* is about being a true *leader*. Now, when I say *leader*, this can apply to being the leader of your family, your company, your community, and even your friends. Being a leader means that you make your *own* decisions, based on *your* value system and belief system, not somebody else's.

Son, you will have many people in your life that try to make decisions for you, but always remember that *you* are the one that will have to live with the consequences of these decisions. There's nothing wrong with making decisions that don't pan out perfectly, as long as you learn from them. The key is to own up to the consequences of these decisions and take responsibility for your results. That's what being a leader is all about.

You'll be blamed from time to time for making decisions that result in imperfect outcomes, and sometimes even when you make brilliant decisions that result in great outcomes, you'll often times not get the credit you deserve. But in your heart, you'll know that you made these decisions as a true *man*, and that as a leader, you had the guts to stand up and take charge.

That, son, is what being a *man* is all about. Being a *man* is about being a *leader*, and being a leader is about having *courage*, especially when you're afraid. This is what you were born to be. A *real man*.

In Japanese, *Kane* (also pronounced *Kah-nay*), means *money*. Son, when I was young, I was very idealistic, and I thought money didn't matter. The reality is that in this world, money *does* matter.

Money is a tool that can be used to help your family and those that you love. Money can open doors that were once shut. Money gives you access to resources that you otherwise wouldn't have access to. The key is to not fall in love with money or material things.

Things are just *things*... and *things* can be replaced. People and relationships however, cannot be replaced, and neither can time. I believe that making money is important, as it can be used to contribute more towards relationships, giving people special experiences that they otherwise would have never experienced.

For example, when your mother and I got married, I sent her and your Grandpa and Grandma Pineda to stay at our place in Hawaii. Your mother told me that every morning, as your Grandpa Pineda walked down to the beach, he had tears in his eyes, saying, *"Never in my life did I ever think I would see Hawaii."*

Had I not worked hard, sacrificed, and built the foundation of my business when I was young and single, your mother and I would not have been able to give them that kind of experience.

Life is so short, and it goes by faster than you think. When you look at your life, you basically have an undisclosed number of days on this earth to do something special, both for yourself and for other people. Each day is truly a gift, because tomorrow is never promised. Make the most out of each day, maximizing your experiences and maximizing your opportunities.

Money allows you to maximize both in a greater capacity. Work hard so that money is never a limiting factor in your life to be able to do what you really want to do. You want to be able to make decisions based on your core values, not based on what's available in your bank account.

Another significant meaning of your middle name, *money*, refers to your abilities in whatever you do. By the time you're an adult, I'm sure American slang will have changed, as it always does. The younger generation always comes up with new slang words and phraseology that fits the pop culture of that time.

When you were born, there was a slang phrase that was used when describing someone that was extremely talented and at the top of their game. We would say, *"You are so MONEY right now."* This meant, *"You are so at the top of your game right now."* When you were born, I knew that one of my jobs in life was to be your mentor and to train you to be at the top of your game as often as possible.

Sure, you're going to have *on days* and *off days*, good days and less-than-perfect days, but if you apply the principles in this book, you'll minimize your *off days*. Just remember that although I have high expectations for you, I will never expect you to be perfect. It's okay to make mistakes along the way. It's part of the learning process.

You can always come to me and tell me that you made a mistake, and I will always support you in coming up with a solution to your mistakes. That's my job as your father. You will never let me down because of a lack of results. What will make me proud of you is to see you exemplify courage and to always put forth your very best effort.

Son, choosing to always give your best effort, and to never give up on your dreams, is never easy. You'll have times in your life where you may question your dreams, and even doubt your abilities to make your dreams come true. There's nothing wrong with being afraid from time to time.

When I was starting my career, I was always afraid of failing. I just promised myself to never give up on my dream. The key is to not let other people's opinions about you and your current results negatively influence your vision. Keep pressing forward, always, in spite of any fear you may have.

You were born, as my son, to be a *battler*. To be a *leader*. To be a *man*. Always know that no matter what happens in life, I will always love you unconditionally, even when you make mistakes.

You can always come to me with anything, even if you know I'll be disappointed in your actions, because my temporary disappointment will never outweigh my everlasting, unconditional love for you. I will always do my best to mentor you, lead you, and help you make your dreams come true.

Lastly, you must always honor your mother. From the very beginning, even when you were a baby, your mother was an amazing mother to you. Much of the confidence that you have was instilled in you by your mother, from a very young age.

Even back when you were a child, she worked hard to make sure you developed confidence. She knew how to make you feel safe and confident. She knew how to encourage you and make you feel comfortable with other people. Any deficiencies that I ever had as a father were brilliantly compensated for by your mother.

Son, I plan on living a long, healthy life and being part of your life for a very long time, but in the unexpected event that my time on this earth is cut short, I wanted to be able to teach you these life lessons from the grave, in my physical absence.

If things go as I hope they will, I will be part of your life for many years to come, well into your adulthood, continuing to mentor you and assist you in accomplishing all of your dreams.

But there will be a day when I am no longer physically here, and I will be with God in heaven. Just know that in my physical absence, my spirit will always be with you, guiding you and cheering you on.

I wrote this book for you, son. I wrote this book to make sure that you would always have me as your teacher, no matter what happens to me. I wanted to make sure that I could pass on to you everything that I have learned about living a successful life... not only about how to be financially successful in business, but also how to be emotionally successful, spiritually successful, and successful in your relationships. Estevan, use this book as your playbook for success, and always know that I loved you before you were even born.

It is important to me for you to know that my entire life's work has been based on three main motives:

1. To build an amazing life with you and your mother.

2. To pass on my knowledge to you, developing you as a real man.

3. To contribute to other people's lives that dared to dream the impossible.

Son, whatever path you decide to take in life, let it be one that you're passionate about, and live it to the fullest. My number one goal for you in this world is to believe in yourself, regardless of what external factors you're confronted with.

Of course I want you to be happy and healthy above and beyond all things, but I've learned one key thing about happiness. When you look in the mirror, and you're proud of the man you see… if you believe in yourself… only then will you truly be happy.

If you've developed character, and you live with integrity and honor… which can only be done if you believe in yourself… then I will feel that my primary job as a father has been successful.

I thank God everyday that he has allowed me to be your *papa*. It has been the greatest blessing I have ever experienced in my life. Son, I will always love you no matter what, and I will always be with you, and I hope that you will carry me in your heart as I have carried you in mine.

Love,

Your Papa

About The Author

Darren Sugiyama was born in Long Beach, California and attended Loyola Marymount University where he earned his Bachelor's Degree in Sociology. Darren was the team captain of the varsity baseball team at LMU and was selected as an All-Conference player in the 1991-1992 season.

Upon graduation, Darren returned to his home town of Long Beach, working with at-risk youths as Director of the LBCGP Gang Prevention Program. He went on to further his philanthropic work counseling inmates at Halawa Prison and incarcerated youths at the Honolulu Detention Home in Hawaii. During his counseling work in Hawaii, he continued his education at the University of Hawaii at Manoa and earned a Master's Degree in Multicultural Education.

After his time working with youths, Darren spent several years in the fashion industry, primarily as a runway model in Los Angeles; Milan, Italy; and Honolulu, Hawaii; working with top designers including Georgio Armani, Hermes, Christian Dior, Donna Karan and Nordstrom.

He later expanded into the entertainment industry, appearing in television commercials for AT&T, Polaroid, Sprite, and several international companies. Darren went on to co-host *Kiana's Flex Appeal*, a fitness show on ESPN. *Flex Appeal* is still heralded as the #1 fitness show in the history of the ESPN network.

Darren eventually returned to his love for business, and became the Western Regional Sales Director for the $200 million denim company, Mudd Jeans, acquiring clients such as *Forever 21* and several boutiques across the country.

Eventually, his entrepreneurial spirit led him to launch several small marketing firms in various industries. Some of these companies had moderate success, and some failed miserably.

Darren admits, "*I've figured out every way to fail in business. But without the failures, I wouldn't have been able to develop many of the business processes and strategies that have made me successful today. Everything can be converted into a learning process that makes you smarter, stronger and tougher.*"

In 2003, Darren founded Apex Outsourcing Insurance Services. Literally starting Apex out of a hotel lobby with nothing more than two suits, a cell phone, and a ton of ambition, Darren built and led Apex to being the most notorious employee benefits consulting firm in Southern California. By 2009, only seven years in the insurance industry, he led Apex to produce over $37 million in annual sales.

Darren currently sits on Kaiser Permanente's esteemed Broker Advisory Board and has been invited to speak at exclusive roundtable planning meetings by Aetna, Blue Cross and Blue Shield. He has consulted multi-billion dollar corporations, developing business development strategies for them, as well as revolutionizing their marketing, branding, and sales approaches. Today, his success has expanded outside of the insurance industry.

In addition to serving as the President of Apex, Darren also founded Ontogeny Group, a business development consulting firm. His consulting services range from corporate motivational/keynote speaking engagements, to sales coaching, to brand development, to streamlining operations.

With an All-Star client list that spans over multiple industries including the Employee Benefits industry, the Financial Planning industry, the Software Industry, the Commercial Real Estate Brokerage industry, and many more, Darren is one of the most sought after business development consultants in the country, due to his unique and often counter-intuitive business strategies.

Darren also hosts business development and sales coaching *Boot Camps* where entrepreneurs and sales executives from all over the country fly into Orange County, California and learn from Darren himself, often times personally hosted in his office.

Despite Darren's busy schedule, he still finds time to give back to the community, talking with and encouraging young people to think about their life choices and their future careers. He has done several speaking engagements at various universities, high schools and middle schools.

For more information about Darren Sugiyama and his consulting services, visit his website at www.DarrenSugiyama.com.

CPSIA information can be obtained at www.ICGtesting.com
Printed in the USA
LVOW120044221211

260591LV00001B/2/P